GW00644941

A TOUCH FROM GOD

It's Only Rock and Roll

Del Newman

Foreword by Gordon Giltrap

APEX PUBLISHING LTD

Hardback first published in 2010 by

Apex Publishing Ltd
PO Box 7086, Clacton on Sea, Essex, CO15 5WN, England
www.apexpublishing.co.uk

British Library Cataloguing-in-Publication Data
A catalogue record for this book
is available from the British Library

ISBN HARDBACK: 1-906358-79-6   978-1-906358-79-2

Typeset in 11pt Baskerville Win95BT
Production Manager: Chris Cowlin
Cover Design: Siobhan Smith

Printed in Great Britain by the
MPG Books Group, Bodmin and King's Lynn

*To Richard Dodd, a friend and colleague,
and a wonderful recording engineer.*

FOREWORD

I first met Del Newman in 1970. My then manager Miles Copeland had just secured a recording contract with MCA records. The producer of that record Derek Lawrence had hired Del to arrange the music for the material I was going to record. At that time I was very much cast in the mould of the singer songwriter. Later on in my career I dropped the vocals to concentrate on instrumental music, but that is another story.

I remember that first meeting so well. It was in a basement flat in Earls Court. Del and I were sat at his piano, me with guitar in hand, slowly going through the pieces we were working on. It was the first time I had ever worked with an arranger and found the whole process utterly fascinating. From the word go this man was full of encouragement,patience and enthusiasm for the material I was presenting.

Since those far off days of the early 70's Del and I have worked on three recording projects. The MCA of 1970, one in 1973 and in 1997 my Troubadour album which Del arranged and produced. To this day I regard this as my finest work, and I take great pride in the fact that Del came out of retirement to work with me.

To watch Del Newman at work is to watch a man at the height of his powers. The way he communicates with an orchestra is a joy to behold. One knows instinctively that the musicians before him have the highest regard and respect for his gifts as arranger and conductor.

There is always mutual respect here. To hear Del Newman weave his special magic on something one has written can be a very moving experience.

In my opinion there is a very thin line between arrangement and composition and I have always felt that some of his superbly crafted arrangements could be stand alone pieces. Such is their beauty.

The many and varied artists that Del has worked with reads like a virtual Who's Who of legendary music icons from Cat Stevens(Yusuf Islam) through to Sir Paul McCartney with Paul Simon, Charles Aznavour, Elton John and many more in between. The list goes on!

Although Del to all intents and purposes has retired from the music business he hasn't for one minute sat on his laurels, basking in past glories. This book is testament to that fact. Retirement, if that indeed is the correct terminology, has given him the freedom to pursue the things he has been yearning to do for years. These days he spends much of his time composing. For a man who has spent most of his professional career writing for others, I say 'about time sir'.Oh, and I forgot to mention that he also teaches piano to a small number of students in his village. Mr Newman is without doubt busier than ever.

I feel very privileged to have been asked to write the foreword to this amazing and entertaining book and indeed to have been a small part of his long and distinguished career. I am indeed proud to call him my friend.

Best wishes
Gordon Giltrap

CONTENTS

PROLOGUE

The title of this book was inspired by the wonderful painting on the ceiling of the Sistine Chapel in Vatican City, Rome. Michelangelo's work, 'The Creation of Adam', is a message telling us that all creation is divine. I choose my words carefully because we live in a world where destruction is the order of the day to a large extent. The real gift that we have been given is the ability to exercise our imagination; Einstein said, "Imagination is more important than knowledge," and I believe that it is the element in us that allows us to express our greatest achievements. When observing the music industry, it appears to be the truest statement ever uttered.

This is the age of the celebrity. Whether it is the television presenter reading a card under a camera and wearing an audio earpiece, showing how clever they are, or an interview host contributing to Andy Warhol's 'fifteen minutes of fame' theory, the celebrity is now famous for being famous. Talent seems to have very little to do with fame these days, and the size of the ego seems to be inversely proportionate to ability. It wasn't always so, for I remember a time when talent was the only priority needed for a successful career in the entertainment business in general, and in the music industry in particular.

The advent of independent television and the need for high viewing ratings by the sponsors brought about a huge change in the way that programmes were structured. What we now know as 'mass media' decided that the visual aspect of television was more important than content. When we consider that millions of people could be reached in their homes in an instant, it is easy to see why the power of the advertisers was wielded like an avenging sword. The nature of the administration of audio companies also changed. The management, who were often interested in the music that their clients produced, gave their artists time to mature. The present policy seems to indicate that the immediate sales number is the only relevant factor. Lawyers and accountants have tended to infiltrate the management structure and the element of nurture has disappeared. Immediate results are required or the artist will soon be dropped from the company's list of clients, and the only people making money are those who make programmes about the potential talent of the masses.

The introduction of the Internet has had a great effect on the music industry too. The enormous profits that were made by record, CD and publishing companies were gravely affected because young people could copy commercial products without necessarily having to pay for them. Technology has allowed a 'do-it-yourself' society to blossom, which means that a great deal of revenue has been lost. Not even the film industry has been spared, and enormous promotions have been displayed regarding copyright laws. It appears that the fear of losing tremendous profits has made the various companies pronounce that the law will deal heavily with anyone who is caught copying their merchandise.

I have worked with more than 60 artists, and this book is a personal view of 35 years' experience as a back-room boy, writing orchestral arrangements and conducting orchestras at live concerts and recording studio sessions. Like all people, the artists were a mixture ranging from saints to sinners. Most of them were fine, hardworking people, but some were a nightmare. We were all carrying the baggage of our own experience, but I believed that the manner in which we controlled that baggage was the important element. The relationship that we had with our colleagues was paramount in achieving good results, but this wasn't a perfect world, so everything in the Garden of Eden wasn't always what I'd hoped for.

The closeness of our relationships depended on a simple ingredient: a sense of humour. It is said that a person's essential nature is formed by the age of seven and, although experience after that age contributes to our development, the early childhood experiences determine our degree of insecurity. I'm not certain that these theories are true, but I do know that the people I worked with had different degrees of insecurity. It was hard to believe that a person with tremendous wealth and adulation from fans could feel so insecure that he or she behaved like a spoilt child. This happened several times during my career, and all I could do was to walk away from our association. Occasionally I met an artist who believed everything they read about themselves in the papers or magazines, and their ego manifested itself in treating everyone who worked for them as if they were a piece of garbage. Everyone deserved respect unless they did something that was disrespectful, and when these occasions happened I decided that I would never work with those people again. The beauty of being a freelance musician was that I could choose with whom I worked, so it wasn't necessary for me to work with someone a second time if previously they had been rude or impossible egomaniacs.

Writing this book has been a trip down memory lane for me, and if I have omitted anyone that I knew I apologise. The memory is a strange creature and seems to lead a separate life, but everything in this book actually happened and isn't the product of a Chinese whisper. Always remember that my comments are observations and not criticisms, for there, but for the grace of God, go I.

www.apexpublishing.co.uk

CHAPTER 1

Meeting Cat Stevens was an unexpected occasion. I had acquired an accountant in 1970 named Norris Masters, who was shrewd enough to buy The Dance Studio in Soho and later open shares to the public and make a million pounds. He was a tall, fair-haired man in his forties and a workaholic, who often spent 16 hours a day in his office. He always wore suits and ties, and I could see his mind clicking like a cash register. He had a young wife and two small children, and he always gave me the same advice. Never spend your own money, he said, always borrow it. Buy a bigger car, buy a larger house, take a cruise around the world, but never use your own capital. It never seemed to occur to him that I would have to work all the hours in the day, as he did, to pay for such a lifestyle. I learnt later that he died of a heart attack in his early fifties.

Soon after engaging him he telephoned me and said he had a client who was looking for someone to write orchestrations for his new album. He told me his name was Cat Stevens. He remarked that he was 23 years old and asked whether I would be interested in meeting him. I had not heard any of the hit singles of his earlier work, but a meeting was arranged. Everything went well and we seemed to have similar ideas. The theory of 'less is more' appealed to both of us and we agreed to work together. I wasn't to know that it would give me an international shop window for my work that I had never thought possible. It was a perfect example of being in the right place at the right time, being lucky, or perhaps just coincidence, but individual moments can play a tremendous part in shaping our lives.

Steve, as he was called by people who knew him, was a complicated individual. There were things going on in his mind that created secrets none was destined to fathom. He was very intelligent and hypersensitive, which sometimes made it difficult to get close to him. His father was Greek and his mother was Swedish, and he had a brother that I never met. His parents owned a restaurant in Holborn, and I was invited for lunch to meet them. It was an ordinary place without frills, where hundreds of city workers would go for meals to get good value, quickly.

They were charming and generous, and I could see that they were the reason for Steve's good looks. His father seemed to have a strict, decisive way about him, which I believe was a Greek trait, but his mother had a serene quality that I found not uncommon in Scandinavian women. It was not difficult to see that she must have been quite beautiful in earlier years. Later, I realised from some of his lyrics that Steve had had a difficult childhood. The words of such songs as 'Father and Son' reflect a period in Steve's life when growing up as a young boy must have been almost intolerable. It may well have sown the seeds for some of Steve's attitudes and his general mistrust of adults.

He was a very attractive young man. He had thick, long, black curly hair, a slim physique, and an infectious smile. Like Joni Mitchell, he was also a talented artist who created his own record sleeves. He was quiet and had a boyish enthusiasm for everything. He often looked as if he needed mothering and at times seemed to be quite vulnerable. Perhaps this quality gained him many female fans, for I noticed that the audiences at his performances usually had a greater proportion of women.

Steve was meticulous about the sound he wanted on every track. He and Paul Samwell-Smith, Steve's producer, spent more time than most creating the perfect atmosphere for Steve's songs. Steve had a special relationship with Paul. They had spent thousands of hours together, over many years, planning how to present Steve's songs. They were ideally suited and they made each other very wealthy. Paul had played bass guitar in bands before he worked with Steve. He was a gentle, public school type, with a generous spirit, and I knew that Steve trusted him completely.

When I listened to the tracks with an orchestral background, I found that the level of the orchestra never interfered with Steve's voice, or any member of the band. Paul would spend a great deal of time listening to the tracks, and he and Steve would discuss what to do next. On some records that I have arranged for other producers, the mixes (sound levels and quality of different instruments) have been so bad that it was a waste of time writing the arrangement. But in terms of what Steve wanted, and the relationship between the band and the orchestra, Paul always got the production right.

My first arrangements for Steve were on the Mona Bone Jakon album, which he recorded for Island Records, situated in Basing Street, Notting Hill. The company was owned by Chris Blackwell, and I was told that Chris was a member of the second half of the family firm Cross and Blackwell, who produced tinned food. Chris had an aristocratic air about him. He spoke softly and showed a gentle nature. I remember not only was he wealthy, he also looked wealthy. His family were in the West Indies, and Chris began selling records in the Portabello Road from a small van in his early days.

He was very instinctive about his choice of artists for his company and always listened to every prospective client for his label. This was not usual, as company minions were often given the task of filtering out new talent, and sometimes many future household names were allowed to pass through the company net. He had the ability to recognise talent and, what is more important, potential talent that needed nurturing, and he immediately saw that Steve was destined for great things.

I was told, by people who had known Steve for some years, that through neglect and bad management he had contracted tuberculosis and was close to death's door. They said the songs of the first album were written whilst Steve was recuperating. If this is true, it is not difficult to understand the words in such songs as 'I Think I See the Light' and 'Trouble'. In fact when I heard the title track the last section made me feel that Steve was crying out for salvation. Steve was one of the few successful artists whose lyrics were autobiographical. Most successes came from songs that had lyrics that were perceived from a third-person perspective; great examples being the Beatles' 'She's Leaving Home', and nearly everything they wrote, and Elton John's 'Candle in the

Wind'.

The single was 'Lady D'Arbanville', referring to Patti D'Arbanville, and I heard that she was the only lady that Steve had ever loved. I know that rumours spread like a wild fire, but if an artist wrote a song about someone who happened to be an attractive lady, it would be reasonable to assume there was a great deal of emotion involved. I thought that fame and financial success entering a young person's life could be very destructive where the opposite sex were concerned. It was a question of identity. In Steve's case I got the feeling that he wasn't sure whether a lady was interested in Steve the person or in Cat Stevens the pop image. This must have been a dilemma for many in the same situation. But in the years that I worked with Steve I saw some very attractive women come and go.

It was certain that Steve had a unique way of expressing himself. I found it interesting that many performers, who were quiet to the point of being shy, showed great energy in their public performances, as if they were another person. Elton John was another good example of showing an external image that was the antithesis of his essential self. Steve managed to draw his public to him like moths to a flame. Whenever he gave a live performance the expression on the faces of the audience gave testimony to that fact. It was certainly an innate gift that wasn't bestowed upon every performer I knew.

In the summer of 1972, Steve asked me if I would like to go on his world tour. By this time 'Tea for the Tillerman' and 'Teaser and the Firecat' had been released and Steve was an international star. He suggested that each country might supply its own orchestra, which would allow the complete arrangements to be enjoyed by the fans. I happily agreed because the tour meant that we would be visiting all the major cities in Australia, Japan, the USA, Toronto in Canada, and ending in Oxford, in Britain.

The band consisted of Jean Roussel (keyboards), Alan James (bass), Gerry Conway (drums) and Alun Davies (guitars). It was a dream realised because I had never travelled with a band. Jean was enormous, with lots of curly hair, and he ate everything he could get his hands on. Alan

James had a sculptured face, which reminded me of the stone figures on Easter Island. He was the quiet one, and generally he only spoke when answering another person's remarks. Gerry was the fun person. He was wide open to any experience that might come along and he was always smiling, imparting his energy to everyone he met. Alun Davies was stoic and seemed to have everything in his life under control. There were domestic complications for me, though, for I had just married my second wife, Hilary, two weeks before the tour began, and leaving for three months wasn't exactly the best thing I could have done.

We flew from London to Sidney and refuelled at Bangkok. We were allowed to leave the plane for half an hour but could not leave the airport. I remember that opening the door of the plane at seven in the morning was like walking into an oven. I wondered what it would be like for the workers on the runway at two in the afternoon, but they must have been used to such a scorching heat. The band hated the heat, and a few tempers displayed themselves during the refuelling, but Alun Davies was able to cool things down. Many of the group didn't sleep very well, so this was probably the reason for their sensitive behaviour. We all managed to get a quick coffee before taking off again for Hong Kong, where we had our only one-night stopover. Stranger things were about to happen.

When we arrived at Hong Kong airport we were greeted at reception by army personnel carrying machine guns. It was very intimidating, and I think being threatened by people carrying firearms was a first time for all of us. I can remember the scene as if it happened yesterday. Not only did every member of the band have shoulder-length hair, wear 'flower power' clothes and have an unshaven and generally unkempt appearance, but also all the road crew looked exactly the same. For some reason Hong Kong didn't want people who looked undesirable entering their city. There was a great deal of drug trafficking at the time and it was possible that powerful people in the USA had told them to clean up their act. Every member of the group except the road manager and I had their passports taken from them. We two had short hair and were soberly dressed, although I didn't know what that had to do with 'clean' living. The band and crew were told that they had better turn up for the flight the next morning or that would be the last time they saw their passports.

We set off the next morning for Sidney, and as we flew over Sidney harbour we saw a half-finished building that looked like a sailing ship, which I was told had already cost nearly three times the original estimate. It was the famous Opera House, which is probably one of the most recognisable structures in the world. The harbour area of Sidney was beautiful, with its bridge and boats galore, and it wasn't unlike some of the expensive Mediterranean ports we have in Europe. The bay had a grandeur that was a delight to see.

We had the usual press conference, as we had in most of the cities in which we played, which included groupies from magazines as well as the national press. One of the musicians was seduced by a groupie and was given herpes as a result of a one-night liaison. Luckily, he was treated in the USA and was cured before we returned to Britain. Long periods away from home often made it difficult for some of the guys to control their urges. I believe that most transient relationships occurred in order to relieve them of utter loneliness. Roadies (who moved the equipment and built the stages) were often away from home most of the year, for they would go from one tour to another, and it was the only way they could support their families.

Steve did some radio interviews, but I don't think he liked them very much. He loved young children and teenagers but was very suspicious of adults. I don't think he trusted them, and perhaps that made him feel uneasy. I remember that on one occasion he said the wrong thing at a radio interview and the national press wrote a scathing article, telling him that if he didn't like being in Australia he knew what he could do. The one sure thing you could count on with regard to Australians was that they were not backward in telling you what they thought.

Steve felt he wanted to give his concerts an intimate atmosphere, and he didn't enjoy playing to thousands and thousands of people. He decided that, whatever the capacity of the venue, he would have it transformed to a size that made him feel he could communicate in an intimate fashion. Many of the enormous venues on the tour were cut down to between 3,000 and 5,000 seats. This is quite small when you consider that some of the American venues held between 30,000 and 60,000 people. Curtains, scaffolding and anything available were used to create a feeling of intimacy, and it gave every ticket holder a chance to see and hear Steve from a relatively close position.

In Adelaide the band had its first taste of relaxation. Steve would join us and we would sit around the pool and get to know each other. Various stories were told about our past musical experiences, and the ones we loved to relate were about situations that made us laugh so much it brought tears to our eyes. My tale told them of the time I went to visit a flautist to discuss her part in an orchestral arrangement I had written. I arrived a little early and she obviously hadn't expected me so soon. The door to her apartment was slightly open, so I walked slowly into her living room to find her studying some music in her bra and panties. I started to withdraw when she beckoned me to stay. She didn't bother to dress, and she offered me tea and crumpets as if we were in some coffee house. We chatted about the arrangement without one blush appearing on her round, beautiful face - the only one blushing was me. After an hour or so I left her apartment and couldn't quite believe what had happened. Needless to say, none of the band believed me and we all laughed, but I still had my memories.

Alan James told a story about a dog that upset all the music stands during an open-air rehearsal, probably because it didn't like the sound the players were making. Jean told of an evening in a restaurant when he was unable to sit comfortably on the seat they gave him, but they wouldn't change it and it eventually collapsed into pieces. The members of the band were typical musicians, for they had a sense of humour that I only experienced with musicians. I would even say that the type of instrument people played often defined the parameters of their humour.

Adelaide was a beautiful city and was surrounded by mountains. Steve invited us to go horse riding. I didn't know about the other members of the band, but I hadn't been on a horse since I was 14. We all rode for two or three hours, and when we returned and finally got off our horses our thighs and calves were really aching. Steve seemed fine, so I assumed he often rode, and possibly wanted to see how we would react after such a long ride. We were exhausted. Luckily for the horses, Jean decided not to ride. I think most of us went to bed for a few hours, but nobody complained, and after the evening concert we all laughed about the ridiculous situation of being on horses in the first place.

In Brisbane, which I thought was the prettiest of all the places we visited in Australia, our concert took place in the gymnasium of a small school. There were climbing bars along the walls, and, apart from long benches close to the sides of the room, everyone sat on the floor. There was a makeshift stage for the band and a small string orchestra of eight. The leader was the school music teacher and the rest were young teenage girls whom I assumed were her pupils. I remember that they made a grand sound and I was terribly proud of them. From an orchestral point of view, Brisbane was the exception. Each country we visited supplied a large, professional group of players, but the size of the hall in the Brisbane school required something different. As it turned out, I was pleased with the change, for youth brings a freshness to things that made the evening quite charming.

Needless to say, 80 per cent of the audience were female. At the beginning of the concert the front row of the audience, who were sitting on the floor, were some 30 feet from the stage. However, as the evening progressed and emotions grew in the fans, the distance between the front row and the stage got smaller and smaller. I became really worried because the stage, which was made of wood and was put together by some DIY person, began to shake and make noises. Towards the end of the show the front row was only two or three feet from the stage.

I envisaged the stage collapsing and hundreds of young fans stampeding towards us as we fell in a heap due to the enormous weight on the rickety platform. I'm pleased to say that we were saved by the bell. Another ten minutes and my thoughts would have been realised. At the end of the concert the audience queued up in an orderly fashion to get Steve's autograph, and all was well. All the musicians laughed as they packed up their instruments, and many of the audience laughed with them. The night was a great success, and the intimacy of the occasion made the event one that I will never forget.

The greatest surprise came when we reached Perth, as we had been informed that Perth had the best climate in Australia. Well, the four days we were there were the wettest days of the whole tour. I don't think there was a moment, day or night, when the sky wasn't full of clouds or rain. At that time the suburbs we drove through were full of quaint wooden houses decorated in individual colours, but great changes since then have transformed it into a large metropolis that I wouldn't recognise today. The weather made most of the group feel depressed and nobody said much to anyone. During our free time we either read newspapers at the hotel or went to see a movie. There wasn't a great deal we could do in the rain and their spring weather brought many showers to the region.

I had always perceived Steve to be self-contained. He was never unfriendly, but in all the time I worked with him, and that was on four or five albums, we hardly ever had a conversation that was to do with something other than the music at hand. Once he invited me to his home in Fulham. It was a small, old cottage off the market street, and he had gutted the inside and made a mezzanine to sleep on. It was very cosy and very him, I thought, and he showed me some of his artwork. We went around the corner to a small restaurant for dinner, but we only stayed there 15 minutes because he was asked for autographs all the time. For me, the price of fame was too much, as I could see that Steve wasn't allowed much peace when he ventured outside his home.

I suppose Steve was making an effort to socialise, but I felt he was holding back, as if he thought I might criticise something. It was possible he was naturally shy or he felt insecure with me, or perhaps he just didn't like me. It was possible that I was projecting my insecurities onto him, as relationships at the best of times are not easy and we're all carrying baggage. I've never fathomed it out, and maybe that's the way things are sometimes when you meet someone who impresses you but there appears to be a wall that you just can't scale. I only know that I never got close to him and I would like to have been a good friend.

I also thought it was interesting that other members of the band found their own company. Gerry Conway seemed to pair up with Alan James and on the tour they would often go on outings together. Jean Roussel kept to himself a great deal, eating large amounts of food at every opportunity. He sometimes ordered two dinners from the hotel's room service to devour alone. He got so big that he wore a kaftan, but many years later I saw him on television at least five stones lighter, and I had to look twice in order to recognise him. Alun Davies had known Steve for years and I believe they were quite close. I always felt that he was a serious person, who kept in touch with his family at every opportunity. I didn't see much of him off stage, but he was an excellent musician. He was quiet and very professional, but kept to himself a great deal.

Japan was something else altogether. I must admit I had no idea what to expect because I had never travelled further east than Greece. It was a strange experience because the Japanese showed their respect by being silent during the shows. They neither showed emotion, nor did they clap at the end of a song. It seemed that Eastern people had different concepts and expectations to Western people. The Japanese did not shake hands or touch a stranger in any way. They kept a respectable distance from everyone. They bowed their heads to show respect and were the politest people I had ever met. I was told that their conception of physical freedom was different to that of people in the West. To be imprisoned was of no real consequence to them because they believed the mind was the most important aspect of a person's being. I must say I will never forget how their notion of respect towards others affected me, and still does to this day.

CBS Records were our hosts in Japan and they were very hospitable to Steve and to his entourage. They arranged for the band to visit one of the most expensive bathhouses in Tokyo. I was told that there were thousands of bathhouses in the city, and the price depended on the quality of the service as well as the sumptuousness of the establishment. They are amazing places. It seemed that the women's role in life was solely to satisfy men. I didn't subscribe to this philosophy, but in order not to offend our hosts it was a case of 'when in Rome, do as the Romans do'!

We entered a splendid building that reminded me of a Victorian hotel. We were greeted by a very beautiful and cultured woman, whom I can only describe as the 'madam' of the house. Each of us was led away in turn to a small room. The atmosphere was like a Turkish bath, and in the centre of each room was a circular bath about ten feet across. I was greeted by a charming young girl of about 18 years of age, and she showed me to a cubicle and told me to undress and put on a small linen coat. I came out of the cubicle and she led me down some steps into the bath. She then took my coat off, took off a similar one she was wearing, and proceeded to bathe me with sweet-smelling soaps and lotions. It was the most erotic sensation I had ever known. In fact that particular feeling has never been recaptured.

She told me her name, which she said meant lotus flower in English. She said her father had died and she was the breadwinner of her family. She had three brothers and a sister, and at that time they were dependent on the money she brought home to her house. Most of the money she got was from the tips that customers gave her. She said that all the girls had regular clients and that we were an exception. Her clients would come twice a week to see her, and I deduced that they must have been very rich to frequent the place that often. CBS gave each of us the equivalent of £30 to give to our respective girl as a tip. This was a great deal of money over 30 years ago, but the industrial world was booming and Japan had developed the microchip, which had produced many prosperous businessmen. The interesting thing was that none of the band ever spoke of the event when we returned to the hotel, and throughout the whole tour it was as if it had never happened.

Tokyo was like an Eastern New York: tall skyscrapers, hundreds of billboards, thousands of camera shops and streets congested with noisy traffic. Kyoto (the same letters in a different order), on the other hand, was a city of temples, water gardens, space and a feeling of spirituality. It had been Japan's first capital and had an atmosphere of calm, where the pace of life was slow. It was more like a large country village than a city. Everyone in the band said that they got more enjoyment from being in Kyoto than in Tokyo. The subject started many discussions about the pros and cons of technological environments as opposed to spiritual ones. Often they became quite heated, and it was obvious that the members of the band had different views about their spiritual beliefs that were quite strong.

America, or should I say the USA, was quite a unique experience. The band's first landing in the USA was in Hawaii, where we had to have our bags checked. We were not allowed to leave the airport, so I didn't experience those wonderful beaches one sees in films. The weather was great and, being September, I expected California to be the same. We landed in Los Angeles, where the temperature was in the high seventies, and that was good enough for me. Steve was very generous and gave the band a week free from concerts. He allowed our wives to come and visit us, and he paid their airfares and hotel expenses. It was a sign of his generosity and it boosted everyone's morale. We all went to Disneyland, but most of the time we just hung out at the hotel because touring was hard going and a week's rest was exactly what we needed. We would be performing in 26 cities before finishing our tour of the continent in Toronto.

I have already mentioned that each country supplied its own orchestra for the tour. I would spend at least three or four hours on the first full day rehearsing the arrangements so that the first night would go smoothly. After that the orchestra and I would be free until the next concert. Steve and the band, however, had to have sound checks every afternoon that there was a concert, so they had a much tougher schedule to keep. All touring band musicians expect sound checks every working day as part of their obligation to their contract. Orchestral players only rehearse the music once because when their parts are known they only have to play at each evening concert, and the sound engineers do the balancing between the band and the orchestra.

The orchestra in the USA was picked from New York

musicians. Because New York was to be our last gig in the States this made great sense, as it meant that they didn't have to travel home by plane after the last night. I will never forget one of the cellists in the orchestra called Rachel, who told me that every time she sat in a plane that was taking off she had an orgasm. I can say I often sat next to her on those occasions, and I believed everything she told me. At the point of leaving the ground, when the engines were roaring at full blast, she would squeeze my hand and cover her mouth with her other hand to muffle the scream she always made. It was very sensual, and I assumed that her apartment walls were covered with egg boxes to make it soundproof.

She was a lovely person with a generous spirit, and I was very fond of her. However, there was an occasion when she nearly got three of us killed. She, a violinist whom I believe was sweet on her, and I decided we wanted to see the Grand Canyon, so we hired a car for a day. En route we almost left the edge of the road, which plunged into a ravine. Luckily for us we hit one of the posts and that halted our momentum. I could have forgiven her anything, for it gave me such pleasure to watch her reaction every time our plane took off from the airport. It was also lucky that Alan James and Gerry, who had decided to accompany us in their own car, weren't too close behind.

All of the concerts were a great success. The hotel rooms were all very similar and it was difficult to tell the difference between one flight and another, but a wonderful aspect of the tour was the personal things that happened between people who worked together over a long period of time. We began to see each other's strengths and weaknesses, and I think this brought us closer together. I think most of us got a little homesick after weeks of travelling. Even the orchestra, who were New Yorkers, began to show photos of family and home, which was a sure sign that they were ready to be back in the bosom of their loved ones.

By the time we got to Boston we were near the end of the tour and things were running smoothly. After each concert Steve would allow a few young fans to come backstage and have some food and wine with the band. It was on such an occasion, in Boston, that I realised what power really was. We were in a large hotel room and were quite high up. The room was crowded and Steve was standing in the middle of the room talking to three or four young girls. I was sat in a large chair in the corner of the room observing everyone. I noticed that two of the girls were physically shaking and were trying desperately to hide the fact. Although they had never met Steve before, their fantasy of the Cat Steven's image made it impossible for them to contain themselves. I remember thinking at the time, if Steve had asked them to jump out of the window they would have jumped. I wondered how many famous artists were aware of the power they hold over their fans.

Another incident in Boston will always remain in my mind. After the concert two of the band said they were going out to a club to have a couple of drinks and asked me if I would like to join them. We got a cab to a bar that they had been told was very well known. The place was packed with people and the atmosphere was dark and smoky. It had a long bar down the centre of the room; in fact I think the place was called 'The Long Bar'. Ten minutes and one drink later, a voluptuous young lady appeared from behind a curtain and began to dance along the top of the bar. All the clientele immediately seated themselves along each side of the bar and began cheering the dancer. She was topless, and I then understood why the place was so popular. I told my two colleagues that I was tired and was going to return to the hotel, so reluctantly I left.

A couple of hours later I was watching a late-night movie on television when the door of my room burst open. In walked the two members of the band with ladies on their arms. I recognised one of them as the dancer at the club and assumed the other lady was also a dancer. The reason I remember the occasion so well is because the familiar lady took off her coat to reveal that she was wearing a white string vest, and nothing else. She had a curvaceous form that left nothing to the imagination, and her coming back to the hotel with the boys was a good example of how people that are assumed to be famous appear very attractive. The ladies were very pleasant and we all sat around talking for at least an hour. They wanted to know about Britain and we wanted to know about Boston. We were polite enough not to ask them how or why they were in their particular profession. Needless to say, they went off to their respective rooms and I never saw the ladies again.

The last city in the USA was New York. As the plane was landing, the on-board radio announced that there had been 27 murders that week in Manhattan. This really made me feel nervous, but the leader of the orchestra assured me not to worry. He said he had lived in New York for more than 60 years and nothing had ever happened to him. He also told us that if we went out we should only carry 20 dollars or so, but that it was important to have some money on us as muggers would quite likely kill us for wasting their time if they found nothing on us. None of this conversation filled me with confidence, but I understood his meaning. He was a white-haired, white-bearded Jewish gentleman, who obviously knew New York like the back of his hand. He had a twinkle in his eye, so we felt that he was streetwise and was somebody we could trust. We were soon to experience New York in the raw.

In Britain we have a saying: "If you want to know something because you are lost, ask a policeman." Gerry, Alan James and I decided we wanted to walk down Broadway. As soon as we booked into the hotel, which was at the southern tip of Central Park, we set off on our journey. We knew nothing about 'jaywalking', and on our way we got lost. We saw a policeman standing in the middle of a crossroad junction and we thought this would be the perfect chance to ask his advice. Now this man was exactly what you would expect an American policeman to look like. He was portly, wearing sunglasses, and kitted out with a baton, handcuffs and a revolver. We stepped off the pavement, walked three feet and then stopped in our tracks. He immediately put his hand on his gun and half drew it. He said in a low, slow voice, "Move on!" I'm certain he thought we were New Yorkers and about to do him harm. That was quite enough for me. I really felt threatened for the first time in my life. I could feel my heart pumping. I told Gerry and Alan I was going back to the hotel, but they were determined to fulfil their desire, so they hurried away with great expectations to see the land of the Broadway theatres.

I was not surprised that there was a great deal of violence in New York. The very next day the band were taken to Maxwell's Plum, a very expensive restaurant. The ceiling was decorated with designs in copper and there was a glass conservatory surrounding the circular dining room. As we were eating our fabulous meal I noticed some children playing on the opposite side of the street. They had no shoes on and their clothes were torn. Behind them was an alley full of fire escapes, and washing lines stretched across the alley as far as the eye could see. In Britain we have the wealthy and the poor also, but the living areas are defined in such a way that most people in one income group rarely see how the other income groups live. The system of wealthy blocks being close to poorer blocks in some American cities allows the poor to experience inequality daily, and perhaps causes dissatisfaction to be more widespread.

On leaving New York we flew to Toronto. One of the most amazing things about the North American continent was its size and the fact that, after hours of traveling, people still spoke English. We played in Massey Hall and the audience went wild. The band seemed to be more relaxed in Toronto, and I believe this was because at the end of a long journey, and a great deal of stress in trying to get things right, they could feel they were going home. I believe every married tour member missed his family and his home, and he was ready for a rest.

The next day everyone but Steve went to lunch together to celebrate an enjoyable tour and to say thanks to each other for their contribution to the success of the project. Canada seemed more European than the USA. There were French and British influences there which reminded us a little of home, and the pace of life was considerably slower. People spoke softly and there was less concrete around, so Mother Nature felt accessible. I even went to see some friends who had emigrated to Toronto a few years earlier. I asked the boys to join me, but I think they had a bathhouse in mind as a last rebellious act.

We left Toronto for London, and it was certainly a delight to be back in Britain again, surrounded by a familiar culture that we identified with because that was where we grew up. Steve gave the last concert in Oxford. It was memorable for two reasons: it was the last concert, and it was a conductor's nightmare. During the song 'Sad Lisa', which had difficult rhythms, the orchestra and Steve's piano playing drifted apart for about 10 seconds. After 35 concerts I couldn't believe my ears. At the end of the song, Steve announced to the audience that it was my fault and gave an apology. If there had been a hole around, I would have jumped in it gladly. Whatever the cause of the problem I had learnt that, like a boy scout, you have to be prepared for anything that might happen. I thought I wouldn't see Steve again, but in the coach back to London we talked normally. I was certainly angry; it was a pride thing. I didn't think it was handled well and felt that a display of humour would have included the audience. On our way home I was so affected by the incident that I told Steve I never wanted to work with him again. He never said anything, but he got the point.

The relationships between people in the music industry were no different to those in other areas of work. We were used to different levels of power in the same way that someone working in an office or shop was used to having a manager or a boss. The people that we socialised with usually depended on our particular function within the organisation. In music, orchestral players would do things together (especially sections: woodwind, brass, strings and percussion). In bands, rhythm sections would socialise and the roadies (the hardest workers and least noticed of all) would eat and drink together after a hard day of manual labour. The beauty of being a freelance musician was that you were never tied to one group of people and you could choose with whom you worked, or socialised, and for how long.

I did work for Steve again on the Catch Bull at Four and the Buddha and the Chocolate Box albums. Paul rang me and asked if I would do some arrangements. It was interesting that Steve didn't ring. He probably thought I'd say I was unavailable. Steve was the first artist I worked with who gave me international recognition in the music industry. I have always appreciated his importance in my professional life, and time heals all wounds.

I do remember one occasion when a concert had finished and an American girl came up to me and said, "Are you Del Newman? I always thought, when listening to your arrangements, that you were a blue-eyed blond." Since I was African-Irish, I wasn't quite certain whether she was complimenting me or not! If it was meant as a put-down, there wasn't even a sign of a scar. I do hope that Steve found the peace and happiness he always wanted, and that Alun Davies, who was always a sensitive guitar player, has had as happy a life as I have had. As for Gerry Conway, Jean Roussel and Alan James, stay cool. They were halcyon days indeed. They gave me fond memories that will never be forgotten.

The relationships between people in the entertainment industry could be fragile. There were many egos floating about and much insecurity. It was probably no different to any other field of endeavour. The persona that people projected was the most important element in their career. It was necessary to be positive and enthusiastic, open to suggestion, and willing at all times to compromise if necessary and not take oneself too seriously. The old saying, "Laugh and the world laughs with you, cry and you cry alone," I believe to be as true as anything ever uttered. Don't forget, a day without laughter is a day wasted, and our days go so quickly.

* * *

A tough schoolboy was asked to make an outline.

"Where's the body?" he replied.

CHAPTER 2

All that can be said about Rod Stewart is that he was larger than life. He was a star in every sense of the word. He reminded me of one of those famous film stars of the '20s and '30s, whose lifestyle and behaviour were more like a fantasy than real life. He would have been perfect in any of those movies about Los Angeles, such as Chinatown, for even the cars in front of his Beverly Hills house were modern replicas of the splendid vehicles of the 1920s. He was striking to look at and wore the most expensive clothes with great taste. He lived in a wonderful house surrounded by similar houses owned by various film actors, and when I first visited it I realised the meaning of the phrase 'how the other half live'. He had another great house on the beach in Malibu, where the living room was a sunken, circular room, as well as a house in England and, last but not least, he also had a beautiful wife, Alana, to keep him company. What more could a man ask for?!

Rod Stewart's manager at that time was Billy Gaff, who always telephoned me when Rod wanted some orchestration for any of his songs. There was a London office for Rod's company, in the New King's Road, called Riva Records. I only went there once, but I'll tell you the story of that incident a little later on. In the USA Warner Communications took care of Rod's business, and everything in Rod's material garden always seemed to be successful.

There was a period, some years ago, when there were certain differences of opinion between Rod and his record label about the retail price of his records. Rod believed that the price of his records in some territories was too high and affected the sales in those areas. I'm sure he had a valid point to make because in Britain the product always cost the same number of pounds as dollars in the USA. This also applied to CDs. Rod thought that it affected his earnings because many people couldn't afford his products, and he was right. I don't know why our Monopolies Commission thought that this was fair trading, but when questioned they decided not to intervene. I'll leave the reason for their decision to your own intelligence.

The first record I was asked to work on was 'Foot Loose & Fancy Free' (1977). Billy Gaff said that Rod wished me to fly to Los Angeles to arrange two titles for his next album. When I arrived I was given an apartment with everything you could wish for. There were two king-size beds in the bedroom and it had its own kitchen for those who wished to stay home and eat. It was situated close to Rodeo Drive, the most expensive shopping area of Beverly Hills. A car was waiting for me in the communal garage, and the only thing I had to pay for was any alcohol. As I didn't drink that wasn't a problem. I was told by one of Rod's band there had been some enormous drinking parties in the past, so Rod was adamant that he wouldn't pay for any more liquor. Knowing how much alcohol a band could devour, I completely understood his decision. I found him to be a most generous artist, and an easy person to work with.

Rod invited me to his home to talk about the songs and meet the rest of the band. Jim Cregan and Gary Grainger (both British) were the group's guitarists, Carmine Appice played the drums and Phil Chen was the bass player. Everyone was friendly, and it was comforting to hear those British voices around me. Jim was married to Linda Lewis, who had a hit with a song I worked on called 'Crocodile Rock'. I remember she was a lovely lady, but I think Jim's presence in America for long periods did harm their relationship. The entertainment industry was a very difficult area to work in if you were married. There was always a great deal of travelling to do, and many temptations were often placed in the way of a musician who was on the road.

I believed that Rod missed Britain a great deal, and that was part of the reason for having three English musicians permanently by his side. They joked and bantered most of the time, and even in the studio the atmosphere was more like a party than work. Because of Rod's generous attitude to the band they would have done anything for him. He had a mesmerising effect on people, which was evident wherever he went. But under that easy-going exterior there was a very acute awareness of the need for exactitude in the musical solutions of the moment. Rod's attractiveness sprung from his open, natural personality. There were no airs and graces in his behaviour. I certainly got the feeling that he would not have stood those attributes in others. He had been a success, and very wealthy, for many years, and I felt he knew who he was and was quite content with what he knew.

One day I walked into the kitchen to get a glass of water and noticed that on the table there was a glass fruit bowl full of white powder. I thought it was sherbet, and as the boys were passing in and out of the kitchen they dipped their fingers into the bowl and took a slurp. When they told me it was cocaine I felt such a naive fool. I had no idea how much that amount would cost, but it was very fashionable in the States at that time for people to indulge themselves in that way. I believe people who could afford it had their own psychiatrists too! It seemed that to belong to a kindred group was just as important to wealthy celebrities as it was for tramps living rough. Our insecurities allowed the fashion industries to thrive, whether it was on the catwalk, in our minds, or in a sleeping bag under a bridge in subculture land. Needless to say, music was my high, and I never felt the need for stimulants other than coffee and the occasional cigarette.

Carmine was an Italian-American who was very well known in the States in his own right. I got the feeling he was a little jealous of an outsider coming in to help Rod, as his attitude towards me was rather cool. I remember on one occasion Rod asked three of us to sing a backup line on one of the songs. Carmine had a little tantrum and told Rod I was singing out of tune. I couldn't believe my ears. I may not have the best voice in the world, but I can certainly sing in tune. Just before that, Rod had said that he wanted to do something with me, implying that perhaps some joint writing or a joint production might be on the cards. I felt that this was too much for Carmine to handle and he just couldn't contain himself any longer. It is sad, but in all things relationships can be difficult if there are hidden agendas, and the music world is no exception when it comes to egos.

Months later Rod told me that he was having trouble with Carmine, and it looked as if the drummer's days were numbered. As they say, "what goes around, comes around," and in my experience it was a very true saying indeed.

Rod's producer was Tom Dowd, a very able and experienced man. He was like a father figure and had worked with many of the great American names in the business. I had a great respect for him. He was a quiet man in his fifties, and he knew how to get the best results when recording the boys. He never raised his voice or lost control of the situation, and that was a rare gift indeed. He gently told the band his ideas for achieving what Rod wanted, and his wealth of experience was obvious to everyone. The final mixes of the tracks were always just right. The bass and drums were always strong behind Rod's voice, and the remaining instruments were subtle, well to the front but not intrusive. Tom was like a guru to the band, who would calm things down if there were any tense moments due to frustration when something wasn't going too well. On one occasion Carmine was having a tantrum, due to a rhythmical problem, and Tom became so diplomatic that Carmine's rage gradually subsided, which allowed the band to get back to the music at hand.

I was invited to go to Rod's home, and as I walked up to the house, which was very large and set in spacious grounds, I saw a new replica of a 1920s open roadster. It was magnificent, gleaming in the sun like a knight's charger, and I thought to myself that this was one of Rod's typical gestures. It was only a car, but it wasn't only beautiful, it was also unique. I thought Rod had great taste. The image of his being a 'Jack the lad' was fine on stage and for the media, but in his private life I sensed that there was a natural awareness of beauty that wasn't always present in some people who acquired great wealth.

I was introduced to Rod's wife, Alana, who was charming. I had been told earlier that she had previously been married to actor George Hamilton. She had the typical look of a model, as did all Rod's partners, with the kinds of features that millions of women spent thousands of pounds trying to acquire. She was softly spoken and, like the best wives, she was an excellent listener. They led me into an enormous living room with a high ceiling. On the walls hung large oil paintings, and somehow it didn't surprise me that Rod would relate to such grandiose works of art. On a later occasion I was taken to their Malibu home, which was situated overlooking the Pacific Ocean. The view was stunning, with waves crashing down only a few hundred yards from the house.

Many famous actors and musicians lived along the beaches of the Pacific coast, for it was not only beautiful, it was also a statement about status. I thought the house was more to my taste than the one in Beverly Hills, and beach living seemed to me to be the healthiest choice one could make. But with all these assets Rod was never showy. He took everything in his stride, as if he'd never known anything else, and I knew he wasn't born into wealth. His sense of humour seemed to encompass all classes of people in all walks of life, and I believe that's why he was so well respected.

Alana said very little, and since we didn't know each other it was only natural that she sat and listened to Rod and I talk. Rod wanted to know what was going on in Britain and how the football league was shaping up. He was very easy to talk to, and it was obvious why the band stayed with him for such a long period of time. His generosity knew no bounds, for he proportioned much of the writing to different members of the band so that they received royalty money. I believed that this was rare among artists. It should be remembered that when a band worked for an artist the relationship was based on the premise that they were not only good musicians, but also that they wished to please their employer in every respect. The closeness of their relationship was generally measured by the length of time they had been together. There were cases when money was the only reason for interaction, and some bands reunited after terrible differences of opinion because they felt the pinch of losing their grandiose lifestyle.

Usually I was asked to do orchestral arrangements on the slow or medium tempo ballads. I preferred the way Rod sang ballads to his rendition of the faster numbers. I think it was because of the gritty quality in his voice and the way he could effortlessly phrase a sentence so that it reached the very heart of the music. He once told me, many years ago, that he always wanted to make an album of ballads, the way Barry White did, but his public expected him to perform rock and roll and he thought they might be disappointed if he did release such an album. How wrong he was! Years later he did just that, and his fans showed how much they enjoyed the 'new' Rod by making his offerings a tremendous success. It was a case of being typecast, as many film stars were, and it was never easy to reinvent yourself successfully, although David Bowie was the past master of that art.

The band did a great deal of socialising together and they were the best of friends. Time in the studio was always pleasant because the atmosphere was so relaxed. They had their private relationships in their lives, but these didn't seem to affect the band's professional purpose. Business and pleasure were never mixed, and I didn't detect any hidden agendas lurking in dark places. The temperature was always in the high seventies in Southern California and the outdoor life prevailed. There were many beach parties and moonlight liaisons going on, and I could see that there were great advantages in living in such a fine climate. But the lads always wanted to talk about Britain; as enchanting as California was, there was no place like home, and home to them was where they grew up when they were at an impressionable age.

The heat was so intense at times that I hired a Mercedes 450 SL with an open top. I forgot the temperature and left the top of the car down. Three hours later, after the session with the orchestra was finished, I came out to a car upon which you could fry an egg. The studio engineer said that he would move the car into the shade and told me to come back in an hour. I didn't ask him how he did it, for I was just grateful for his help, and I bought him a drink for his trouble. Only when I was returning to London did I discover that a car had been waiting for me in the garage, so I needn't have hired the Mercedes. The kind of help the engineer gave me was typical of the degree of generosity that was shown by the studio staff. Every studio we used had staff that were diligent, courteous and extremely helpful. They, too, didn't suffer fools gladly, and any relationship problems would soon have been nipped in the bud and the musicians would have been shown the door.

It was a time when studios were being updated with digital recording machines, and I saw my first machine at Cherokee studios in Los Angeles. Andy Johns was the engineer, and he said that these machines were the future. Many musicians and technical staff didn't particularly want the change or believe that it would happen on a global scale. The devil you knew was always more comfortable to deal with than new procedures. But analogue machines were on their way out. How right Andy was. Who would have thought that the digital revolution was on its way and that its development would change the world in which we live. Television, cameras, a myriad of machines, and much of the technology we mere mortals knew nothing about, became digitalised.

Misunderstandings happened on occasion, as they can in any relationship, and I found Rod to be very strict about punctuality. There is a sad tale to tell about what happened during the last album I worked on, Foolish Behaviour. I was at Rod's Beverly Hills home and he said he wanted to record a song called 'My Girl'. He suggested that we should do it together and asked me to come to the piano and play to the words he had written. After ten minutes things were going well and he asked me to be at the studio the next day at 1.30 p.m. in order to record the song. However, I'm afraid that 'Fate' took a hand.

I was busy working on the arrangements of two other songs for the album and realised I needed some more manuscript paper. The nearest music shop was 20 minutes' drive from the studio. I managed to get there at 12.35 p.m. only to find that the shop shut for lunch at 12.30 p.m. for an hour. I decided to wait because I needed the paper that evening and knew that after we had finished the recording the shop would be closed for the day. So I waited and left the shop at 1.40 p.m. I arrived at the studio half an hour late and the band were already halfway through the song. The pianist had obviously supplied a chord sequence and that was that. Rod looked at me with some disdain and I was invisible to him for at least two hours. But he never asked me why I was late, and I didn't tell him. Situations like that happened often and we had no control over their outcome. Had the shop been open I would have gained thousands of pounds as the joint writer of the song. It would appear that the 'Touch', like the Muse, is not always available, and we just have to wait in line for its next appearance.

There was still a worse storm on the horizon. When Billy Gaff, Rod's manager, had called me to come and work with Rod on this album, I had told him that I couldn't as I was working on two other projects. He had told me to cancel the work and come to California. I explained that the production advance and the arrangement fees for the current work came to £10,000 and that, as much as I liked working for Rod, I would have to reject his offer. Billy was very persuasive on the phone, and told me that Rod really wanted me to come and that I should forget about the money because he would make certain that I got that amount. Surprise, surprise, he didn't tell Rod a thing about the phone call. I soon realised that talking to people on the telephone without the artist's knowledge was very dangerous for my material wealth and my career.

I didn't know that Rod's manager was about to be fired due to financial discrepancies and that I was going to be left high and dry, with every member of Rod's organisation believing that I was trying to take advantage of Rod's generosity. It was an excellent example of not knowing other people's agendas and being the innocent victim of another person's actions. Without speaking to someone face to face, it was always possible for intentions to be misunderstood. It was also true that many artists felt insecure in their dealings with colleagues where money was concerned. I understood the situation, but it affected the working relationship between Rod and me, and the future possibilities.

When I arrived home I sent my invoice to Riva Records and all hell broke loose. Someone in the office phoned me to ask me what the invoice was all about, and I tried to explain what had happened. All I got from the gentleman was that Rod was furious. I held out and I did get the money, but at the expense of not working for Rod again. To add insult to injury, in order to get me on a quick flight from Heathrow the company had sent a limousine to my cottage in Gloucestershire so that I wouldn't be tired on the journey, and as soon as they got my invoice they sent me a bill for £296 for its hire. The lack of opportunity to discuss the issue was the real crux of the matter. Too many cooks spoil the broth, and the Chinese whisper does a great deal of harm. But history repeats itself, and another whisper happened when working with Paul McCartney.

I was well aware that Rod had a very generous nature, but it was never my intention to take advantage of his generosity. Billy Gaff, who had all the facts at his disposal, decided not to divulge them to Rod. I could only deduce that he, in some way, benefited from his silence, and so he left me to fend for myself. Situations like this were not uncommon in the entertainment world. Many managers had been known to cook the books and take advantage of their artists. It always seemed to me to be a really stupid thing to do, because it was biting the hand that fed them. I knew that temptation was a strong aphrodisiac, but managers of successful artists were already wealthy because of the percentage they received from their clients, and so greed and a desire for more wealth than they deserved could have been the only motives for disloyalty.

I really did enjoy the work that Rod gave me, but sometimes things happen that are beyond our control. By this time it was 1980. A couple of years later, at Christmas, I received a phone call from a drunken band of musicians who were calling from Los Angeles. Yes, it was Rod and the boys, but the language was so slurred because of alcohol, that I could only laugh at the idea. I have often thought of them, and wish them well. But I must admit I was not very pleased with Billy Gaff, and wherever he is I hope he can sleep well at night.

* * *

Q: What do you call a guitar player who has broken up with his girlfriend?
A: 'Homeless'.

CHAPTER 3

The first time I met Elton John was at a music publisher's recording session for promotional purposes. An American named Joe Boyd, who was a well-known producer in Britain in the late sixties, called me and asked me to arrange the rhythm sections for 11 demonstration songs for Warlock Music. He chose a small demo studio in New Bond Street, which I believe was owned by Chappells, a large piano, sheet music and publishing house. The rhythm section consisted of piano, guitar, bass and drums, and Elton was the pianist and also sang seven of the songs. The other four songs were sung by a young girl named Linda Peters, whom I had known as a regular visitor to the Troubadour restaurant. She later married Richard Thompson, the well-known guitarist, and sang duets with Richard on his albums. The Troubadour had a basement where music of all kinds was played on a regular weekly basis. Bob Dylan and Paul Simon performed there when they were young.

Elton had paid his dues with a band called Bluesology, and had spent five years playing in clubs like the Marquee, the Whisky-A-Gogo and the Flamingo, which were all found in London's Soho district. Long John Baldry was a great influence on Elton, for Long John and Alexis Corner were exponents of the blues sound in London, and Bluesology became the backing group for Long John's singing. Elton's name was derived from two members of the band. Elton was the name of the saxophone player in the band, and John was taken from Long John, his great influence. In the middle sixties Elton and his lyricist, Bernie Taupin, signed a contract with Dick James, a very successful Soho publisher. They wrote many songs that became single records, but they had little success. However, things were about to change for the writers, and the popular music scene would witness a phenomenon that was quite unique.

It was 1969 and Elton's first album, Empty Sky, had been

released but had not made a great impact. It only sold 5,000 records, which was nothing compared to the millions that were yet to come. Elton's second album, Elton John, changed his life completely, as it became hugely successful. The songs, with arrangements by Paul Buckmaster, went straight to the hearts of the people and Elton the superstar was born. When I listen to the Bond Street demo today, I wonder how many people have ever heard it. Probably only a handful of music industry people ever knew it existed. I, along with half a dozen other people, was given a copy of the disc a couple of weeks after the session, and it's possibly the only copy in existence today.

I arrived at the studio with a bundle of music under my arm and Joe suggested I give the parts out to the musicians. I had been involved with popular music for only two years, and most of that time had been spent working for Derek Lawrence at EMI studios. I wasn't conversant with the names of any of the musicians because I was being trained in the 'classical' tradition as a student during the sixties. I walked up to the drummer, who happened to be Jim Capaldi of the band Traffic, and gave him his parts for the session. He looked at me in amazement and said he didn't read music. "Don't worry, it will be all right," he said quietly, and he gave me a big smile. Joe had heard the conversation through the speakers and called me back to the control room. "Do you know who that is?" he spluttered. I told him that I had no idea, but he was very sympathetic. I always found the musicians calm, helpful and talented. They had the patience of Job and took everything in their stride.

The session got under way and it was easy to tell that the quartet was of the highest standard. Simon Nicol and Pat Donaldson completed the band. To complete 11 songs in one evening was quite a feat. The instruments were recorded first, with a guide vocal to help the musicians. After this the master vocals were recorded. This was common practice when making a record or disc. Singers could make as many attempts as they wished to get the vocal that pleased them, and this did not disturb the instrumental track at all because it was already pre-recorded. I have known some artists spend six hours on one song to get the vocal satisfactory. Another time, when the artists have felt on good form, they could be happy with the first effort. I have even known the guide vocal to be the definitive one because none of the latter attempts were as relaxed as the very first rendition.

Elton's vocal style was already formed by the end of the sixties, and he had the same quality at the demo session as he did when he recorded his later work. He was very quiet and polite, and he just got on with the task as all professionals do. Both of the singers had done their homework because they knew the songs without referring to the music. Linda was a little nervous, giving me the impression that the session was her first professional engagement. Elton sailed through the work. It was obvious that he had been playing and singing for many years. I didn't know he went to the Royal Academy of Music in London, but he had a command of the material that was a delight to witness, and the calm way he approached the session told me that he had a great future ahead of him.

The album I orchestrated was Goodbye Yellow Brick Road. I got a call from Gus Dudgeon, who had produced Elton's albums up to that time. He was an absolute gentleman. He reminded me of an overgrown public schoolboy and he always called me 'squire'. He worked quietly and was very professional in the way he approached the challenges that were presented to him. Elton would not have had a producer who was anything less than excellent. Gus told me that Paul Buckmaster, Elton's orchestral arranger, was indisposed and asked if I would be kind enough to help out on this particular album. Of course I agreed, as I was curious to meet the talented musician I had worked with in Bond Street a year earlier.

I went to France, where the band were recording the rhythm tracks. Elton had chosen a well-known recording studio called The Chateau. It was a country mansion where you could eat well and work quietly without interruptions. The engineer was Dave Hentschel, who was a fine musician, and the assistant engineer was Andy Scott. The band lay around discussing various approaches to the songs. It felt like a co-operative effort rather than a dictatorship, and when things were done they were done quickly. The band had been together for many years, so everyone was comfortable with one another. When the album was completed it was mixed at Trident Studios, which was a very popular venue in Soho. One of the directors of Elton's own record company, Rocket Records, was responsible for co-coordinating the project. His name was Steve Brown, and to show you how generous Elton could be when he appreciated the work someone had done for him, I'll relate to you an incident that happened after the album was made.

Steve and his wife were staying with me and my long-term partner, Denise, over the weekend at my cottage near Cirencester. They were a quiet, intelligent couple with deep religious beliefs. They obviously belonged to that rare species, the functional family, and throughout the weekend they supported each other in everything they did and said. We began to rise around noon, and everyone was hungry and volunteered to help. While we were cooking breakfast there was a knock on the door, and when I opened it I found a large man in a grey uniform standing on the doorstep holding a large bouquet of flowers. He asked me if Mr Brown was in the house. I asked Steve to come to the door and receive the gift the man was carrying. He took the flowers, thinking they were a gift from me to his wife. Attached to the bouquet was a bunch of keys. The man asked Steve to go down to the gate and then quickly disappeared.

We all went to the gate, and standing in the lane outside the house was a red Mercedes 450 SL open-top car. It had a white ribbon tied around it and an enormous card on the windscreen. Steve and his wife got into the car and pulled it into our driveway. They hugged each other and explained that this was a normal occurrence when you knew Elton. I could agree with that statement, as the house I was living in was mine only because Elton approved a loan to me. I was given a year to pay back the loan and John Reid, Elton's manager, made sure that I complied with the terms of the contract. There was something really cold about John. He was a closed book, and I imagined that he probably counted pound notes jumping over the fence rather than sheep in order to get to sleep at night. Later I believe that Elton had a financial problem because of John's bookkeeping skills, ending in a settlement in court. I was given the loan through Rocket Records and I am eternally grateful for it.

The tracks I orchestrated were 'Goodbye Yellow Brick Road', 'Sweet Painted Lady', 'I've Seen That Movie Too', 'Roy Rogers', 'The Ballad of Danny Bailey' and 'Harmony'. It was general practice for the artists to allow me to do what I thought would enhance the emotional quality of the songs, and it seemed to work very well. Elton was just as trusting as many other artists. I guess it was a matter of leaving things alone and wanting to be surprised. An artist would listen to your work and decide whether the arrangements were sympathetic or not. Some artists were more protective of their songs than others. In fact, in some cases I was surprised that the artists contacted me at all, for they seemed to resent needing someone to supplement their work.

I remember being on holiday in Tunisia when I met Hal Shaper at my hotel. He was in the industry and he invited me to his London home for dinner. His wife was charming and had cooked a delicious meal. After dinner he took me into another room where a young man was sitting at a piano. The young man rose, shook my hand and introduced himself as Harry, the son of Bing Crosby. He said he was studying Art in London and was keen for me to hear a song that he and Hal had written. He sat down at the piano and began to play and sing. Both Harry and the host kept incessantly telling me, line by line, what the arrangement should be. I wondered why they needed me, as really all they required was a music copyist to write down their ideas. It never occurred to them to ask me whether I wished to do the arrangement. Perhaps I was taken for granted because the young man had a famous father. Perhaps he was rude by nature. I will never know because I stopped them in their tracks and told them they had the wrong man. I thanked the host and his wife for a lovely meal and quickly left the house.

The next day I got a call from the host wanting to know why I hadn't taken the job. He was surprised that anybody should want to turn down the possibility of an offer of work. I suppose he will never know why. The fact that I was taken for granted never entered his mind. I met many people who, because of their fame, thought they were doing me a favour by employing my services. It never occurred to them that I might be financially secure and that not only did I not need their patronage, but also I was in fact doing them a favour. Acquiring wealth could be achieved by means other than the music industry, but some people believed that their world was the only world in the universe. How wrong they were.

Elton, on the other hand, was completely different. He was a quiet, intelligent, considerate person. When you consider the outfits that he wore on stage, it was almost a Jekyll and Hyde situation. I couldn't believe the transformation the first time I saw Elton on stage. The exhibitionism and the talent certainly worked well because the audiences took him to their hearts. The response to his talent was overwhelming at live concerts, and I'm certain the fans wondered how far he would go with regard to his on-stage apparel. The strange thing was that it was the antithesis of his natural self. I found Elton to be a shy person and not an extrovert by any means. I was certain that he meant the whole visual charade as a joke. I'm sure the audiences knew that too, and they went along with the game quite happily. Elton knew who he was, and he knew his music, and that was enough for him.

Soon after the album was finished Elton gave a party at one of the London clubs. Everybody who was anybody attended the occasion. Musicians, artists, disc jockeys and record company people were there, and the water had been turned into wine. It was another example of his generosity. He seemed to have a compulsive streak in his nature, and all or nothing seemed to please him more than moderation. On the night of the party I was sitting at the bar when halfway through the evening Elton came up to me. He gave me an enormous kiss on the mouth and floated away to the other side of the club. Everyone around me smiled and waited to see my reaction. I just smiled back at them and thought it was fine. A little more kissing and a little less killing wouldn't be a bad thing.

Elton's generosity encompassed a great deal of charity activity. That, too, was an example of the compassionate nature within him. I met many artists who, with all their wealth, would never have considered helping anyone less fortunate than themselves. Some were so wrapped up in their own importance that they weren't conscious of the needs of others. This related, once again, to the essential self that I mentioned earlier. I found that truly generous spirits were uncommon in the music industry. Perhaps this was true of the entertainment industry as a whole. The need to succeed in the many areas of that world created all kinds of individual agendas. The desire and need for survival were so strong that often any means to the end prevailed. Jealousy, envy and spite were all there in glorious Technicolour, but they were the silent variety, and it was hard to detect their sources until a great deal of damage had been done.

The last work I did for Elton and Gus was to orchestrate 'Don't Let the Sun Go Down on Me'. Their relationship was very solid. They had worked together for such a long time that they didn't need to talk much. I think there was a great deal of telepathy going on, as they had learnt each other's likes, dislikes and habits. I noticed this with many artists and producers who had worked together for long periods of time. I suppose it's common in every walk of life, but it's still amazing nonetheless. It was interesting how later versions of the same song could be so different. The George Michael version that was released years later was fantastic, and showed that a great song could carry any treatment and be just as satisfying and successful.

The song entered the charts in 1974, a year after the album was released. I thought it was one of Elton's best efforts, and other artists who have covered the song must have felt so too. It had a grandiose dimension to it, although its roots came from the southern states of America. The brass gave it weight, and this helped to build the momentum, coming in late in the song and adding to the glorious finale. The use of voices in the track, and indeed throughout the whole album, gave the work a dimension that would diminish it if they were not present. It reminded me of the wonderful part singing that The Eagles were so famous for. I take my hat off to Gus Dudgeon, for it was one of the best productions to come out of the seventies. Unfortunately, Gus and his wife were killed in a car crash while driving home late one night. I miss his wry sense of humour and his eloquence. I wonder if his spirit is listening to the music of today; if I know Gus, he is analysing every note. I'm pretty certain that Elton misses him, as they were like brothers. It seems like only yesterday....

Ringo Starr was right: 'time' is our master, and we have to make the most of every minute of our existence. As a badge that I sometimes wear states, "Enjoy Life, it is not a Rehearsal".

* * *

The grass may be greener on the other side, but you still have to mow it.

CHAPTER 4

When the Beatles were mentioned in conversation there was an immediate positive response in reverence to a rock and roll phenomenon. Each generation was attracted to their music like a magnet attracted iron filings. They seemed to be timeless, which was a manifestation of their excellence. It was sometimes difficult to remember just how important they were to the changing social patterns of the sixties. They were four young boys from Liverpool who grew their hair long, wore denim clothes and could afford to buy most of the London hotels that, before their success, would not have allowed them through their doors.

The decade was a time of change for many things, and not only in the various fashions of the clothes industry. Wealthy families had always existed, but suddenly for the first time young people from ordinary backgrounds had money to spend. The youth of the day were to be catered for, and not only were they to be seen, but also they were to be heard as never before. The music industry played a major part in the social 'revolution', which created subcultures and allowed an enormous expansion of consumerism by young people that was unheard of a decade earlier.

Whenever Paul McCartney needed my services, Alan Crowther from MPL, Paul's company, would call me and I would do whatever was required. I always found it rather strange that many artists wouldn't contact anyone directly and instead would get a minion to give you a message. Perhaps they were frightened that you were going to refuse their request, and if that were the case it showed a certain degree of insecurity. Many artists that I worked with showed insecure tendencies. I knew that the very nature of creating a body of work involved a degree of self-doubt, but some artists were hypersensitive and permanently on the defensive, and any criticism, even of a constructive nature, was dangerous for the perpetrator.

Paul wrote the title music for the James Bond movie, Live and Let Die, and he booked a large orchestra for the Abbey Road EMI studios in London. He asked me to conduct the orchestra, and I was required to wear an evening dress suit with tails for a photo session after the performance. We used Studio Two, Paul's favourite, and, as the film had already been released and there wasn't a vocalist present, I assumed that the recording was for his own personal library. Paul was always calm when he was working, and I never saw him raise his voice one decibel. He mingled with the orchestral players during the coffee break, joking and bantering as if it were a picnic on the lawn. The picture that was taken, which included Paul, my second wife Hillary and myself, still adorns my living room wall and it reminds me of halcyon times.

One summer afternoon I was invited to Paul's home in St John's Wood, London, for lunch. When I entered the gates to the front garden I was surprised to see how overgrown it was. It reminded me of Miss Haversham's garden in the film of Dickens' Great Expectations. In front of the house was a green Rolls-Royce Corniche, which looked as if had never been cleaned at all. I liked the idea of having so much money that the simple pleasures in life, such as owning one of the most expensive cars in existence, were of no consequence. The large, spacious house looked Georgian and was situated in millionaires' row. I was particularly interested in meeting Linda, as I'd heard so many positive things about the way she perceived life.

On entering the house I was pleasantly surprised to find a cosy, comfortable home, in spite of its size. I thought it felt more like a country cottage than a London mansion. It was their home, and that's the way they were. They had a couple of large dogs wandering about, and you could see the back garden through the open French windows of the large kitchen. Linda was kind, gentle and completely open; she could have been the girl who lived next door in any place in the world. She was an Eastman, a very wealthy family that partnered the Kodak family in making film for millions of consumers.

We sat in the kitchen while Linda prepared lunch, which was another surprise. It was 1973 and she was not known at that time for her healthy eating literature. She was dressed in old, comfortable clothes and spoke with a soft voice that made me want to listen to every word she said. Linda showed the kind of hospitality and ease that was common to people who came from a life of wealth and awareness. It reminded me, once again, that it was generally people with new money that tended to be ostentatious. She only wished to talk about my activities and never once mentioned anything that alluded to herself. I found her to be a very warm and attractive person who cared about world affairs, especially the plight of the underdeveloped countries.

After the meal, which was absolutely delicious, Paul took me into another room where a grand piano stood. He sat down and told me that he had been working on a new song and wanted my opinion. He hadn't written any words to the tune at that time, but he asked me what I thought about the feel of the music. He began to play and hummed the tune as he played the accompaniment. It was a ballad, and as I sat next to him I knew that I was listening to something special. I had no idea what the song would eventually turn out to be, but Paul needn't have worried about whether it would be a success or not. It finished as 'The Long and Winding Road', and there weren't too many musical creations that were better received than that incredibly beautiful song.

An amusing thing happened later in the afternoon that gave me an insight into the couple's perception of parenthood. Their two daughters arrived home from school and came into the kitchen. The youngest one was about six and the eldest girl, who was Linda's by a previous marriage, was some years older. Linda asked them how their day had gone and the little one almost burst into tears. She said that one of her friends, named Jimmy, was really nasty to her about her dad in the playground. She said there had been an argument about money and it had upset her. She believed that Jimmy's father was much wealthier than Paul because Jimmy had told her he was an accountant. All the adults burst out laughing because we couldn't contain ourselves. Linda and Paul had raised their children to be unaware of the amount of wealth the family had acquired. Linda explained that it didn't matter how much money people had and that the problem was that some people didn't have enough money to live properly.

When the children had disappeared Linda talked about the terrible things that were happening in the underdeveloped countries. I could see that she felt deeply about the subject and was acutely aware that the developed nations wanted no changes, as their prosperity depended on the poverty of other countries. She said that slavery had always existed, and today it took the guise of cheap, or no, labour. The shareholders must be kept happy at any cost, and that cost was inestimable. I thought that Paul was very lucky to have found someone like her to share his life with, and her premature death was a great loss to us all.

I found that my experience with them made me think of other wealthy artists I had worked with and of the difference in their perceptions and behaviour. There is a notion that acquiring a great deal of wealth changes people. I don't subscribe to that belief. I found that a person's essential character, probably developed in their formative years, always shone through the glitter. Where a person's wealth and power were abused, it was only the monster being allowed to break out of its cage. Shakespeare said, "A monkey in silk is still a monkey," and I believe that all the wealth in the world will not change that statement one little bit.

Later, I had to work with George Harrison for his Dark Horse Records label, which was under the Warner Brothers umbrella. It was 1979 and the members of The Beatles had been going their own way for a long time. George and I had had no previous discussion about the work to be done, and at the studio he thought that one of the three pieces I had written was inappropriate. It was an arrangement for a string orchestra, and George expected to hear a Mexican outdoor mariachi band with fiddles, trumpets and guitars. Although he said he liked the arrangement, there was a strong tone of sarcasm in his voice. I didn't possess psychic powers and, in view of the absence of any earlier collaboration, I didn't feel his sarcasm was justified. I soon found out that complete freedom was not always the best solution to a problem.

A few weeks later I went to his home in Henley-on-Thames so that a flute player could add some melodies to a track that was recorded in George's own studio. His home was sumptuous, with sunken gardens and complete privacy. I arrived early and heard some argumentative voices coming from a distant room. I had a feeling that it wasn't going to be the best day of my life, and I was right. When the musician that was to play arrived, he was accompanied by his young son. The flautist said he was terribly sorry about bringing his son with him, but his wife had needed to visit a sick relative. I told him that I was certain that George wouldn't mind, and we waited for his arrival.

George greeted us in a really foul mood, and I knew that I should have been somewhere other than Henley. I introduced the musician to George and asked if it would be all right for the boy to stay, assuring him that he would be quiet and wouldn't cause any disturbance. George got very angry and began shouting and ranting as though the world were coming to an end. He bellowed, "What do you think this is, a circus?" Well, I was so embarrassed for the boy and his father that I didn't know what to say. There was a pregnant pause, and then George said that the boy could stay. The three-hour session that followed was the worst time I spent during my whole career.

I couldn't understand George's attitude. Nobody meant any harm, and in such opulent surroundings I felt that his reaction was trite and insensitive. Whatever personal traumas might have been happening, it wasn't very professional to lay it on innocent bystanders. I thought as we left the house, having spent three hours in an atmosphere that you could cut with a knife, that I never wanted to see that gentleman again. I apologised to the musician and his son for what had happened, and thanked the flautist for enduring the insult without walking away - something I would have done. There are only two things that make my blood boil: being taken for granted and rudeness.

It was always a mystery to me how people with a great deal of wealth could be so insecure. I have always believed that people are defined by their actions and not by what they say. Someone could say, "I love you," and at the same moment stab you in the back. When I did an arrangement for Peggy Lee, a famous jazz singer and the composer of the music for the film Lady and the Tramp for Walt Disney, the name of every arranger involved was on the album except for mine. My efforts weren't mentioned because of a very significant factor: Paul was someone who found it very hard to share any kind of glory. It could well have been because a series of incidents in his childhood made that kind of generosity impossible for him to show. Where money was concerned I found him very generous, but glory was another matter. I felt he needed to be the only flower in the garden. I felt sorry for him, and still do.

The last time I received a call from Paul's office, Alan, the go-between, said that Linda wanted to have some piano lessons. She was going to join Wings and tour with the band. I was really naive. I thought she wanted to learn the piano properly and have regular lessons on a weekly basis. I was living in Gloucestershire at the time, which was a two-and-a-half-hour drive to London, and the office knew this. I thought I could help them most by giving them the name of a London-based friend of mine, who could give Linda regular lessons very easily. Paul got a message from Alan that made him think that I didn't want to work with him anymore. I believed it was a Chinese whisper. I never heard from the office again.

This was another example of how sensitive you had to be when dealing with artists' egos. The slightest expression could be taken the wrong way and change the nature of a relationship. When talking to someone face to face there was room to express reasons for your actions, but negotiating through a third person allowed for statements to be misunderstood. I knew this kind of thing often happened in a situation where there was no choice, but it was hard to accept that a good deed could be taken as aggressive behaviour. Pride reared its ugly head in many guises and, whether it was fate, bad luck or the moon, we could never fathom the reasons for the directions that life laid open to us. Perhaps these mysteries make life more exciting, for it would be a daunting prospect to know your future before it actually happened.

I only met Ringo Starr once. I was sitting in the foyer of Nova Sound Studio while Richard Dodd, my engineer, was

41

editing some rhythm tracks. It was a very small foyer, with only two chairs facing each other. After a few minutes Ringo appeared from another recording room and sat in the opposite chair. He smiled at me, but said nothing. I wanted to send my regards to Paul, but I didn't want to intrude on his silence. We sat for a good ten minutes saying nothing, but he kept chuckling to himself as if he were remembering something that had recently happened. Finally he smiled again and quipped, "The time we spend wasting time takes time, doesn't it?" He then rose from his seat and went back to his recording room. I was completely frozen. He seemed like a person who was really worth knowing. Later, I wished I had said something to him to break the silence, for that's how potential relationships begin, and who knows where it may have led us?

* * *

A friend was looking for a foreign car for his next vehicle. I suggested a Japanese car because I'd heard they were excellent value for money. I thought I'd better use a spellchecker because I wasn't familiar with the language. To my surprise it seemed to double as a career adviser. Every time it stopped on the word 'Mazda', it suggested that I change it to 'Mercedes'.

CHAPTER 5

I first met Charles Aznavour in 1974. Barclay Records in Paris asked me if I would consider working with him. His reputation preceded him, because I had read about his early life with Edith Piaf. I had also seen the Truffaut film Shoot the Pianist, in which he starred. He was about to begin an album called Tapestry of Dreams and he had heard some of my work prior to our meeting. Knowing Charles as I do now, he would never have taken a chance on an unknown quantity. We liked each other at once and he played me some of the songs he wanted on the new project. He joked with me, and when playing the songs he said, "I play everything in the key of C, so it is like writing different lyrics to the same piece of music." He suggested that we do a co-production, which really meant that I would do the production and he would get the glory. What he and I didn't know was that Barclay Records had arranged for Lord Snowdon (Princess Margaret's husband from 1960 to 1978) to photograph the recording sessions for the album.

After a few days in the studio we were told to expect Lord Snowdon the next morning to take some pictures of us in action. I must say that we were a little nervous, as it was the first time any of us had been in the position of meeting a member of the royal family. Lord Snowdon arrived while I was deep in conversation with Charles regarding some rhythmical point. We immediately stood up to meet him and he was absolutely charming, without a hint of his royal status. He was casually dressed and very unassuming, and he took great interest in the activities going on around him. He asked many questions about recording techniques as he was photographing us, and the results he achieved were amazing. I asked him about cameras and lenses and he was very obliging.

It was soon lunchtime and one of the musicians suggested that we go to the nearest pub and get some bangers and mash. To our great surprise Lord Snowdon asked if he could join us. There was an old inn close by with a restaurant on the upper floor. He sat next to me and I wasn't sure how to address him, so I said, "Excuse me, but what shall I call you?" He gave a large grin and replied, "Just call me Tony," which laid all my anxieties to rest. I thought that he was unique, for I couldn't imagine any other member of the royal family being so informal or showing such generosity with their time. Lord Snowdon offered to pay for the meal, but the boys gently refused. He impressed me a great deal. We talked about photography and music, for these were areas we knew something about, and it was an interesting and relaxed conversation. When I saw the inside of the album sleeve I realised how good the quality of his work was. The picture of my head was the best photo of my working life I had ever seen.

Charles and I were lucky with the first album because the single 'She' went to number one in the British charts, helped by being the theme tune for a television series. Barclay Records were very happy and I was invited to Paris to meet Eddie Barclay. He was a man of the world, and the twinkle in his eyes told me that he had a great joie de vivre. He said that there had been many beautiful women in his life, and I thought that perhaps they were the reason for the twinkle, but whatever the reason, he kept it a secret.

Charles's songs were nearly always about love. He once said that there was nothing else in the world worth writing about. I went to see his act in a theatre, where the spotlight only encircled his head and shoulders, and his facial expressions and the way he used his hands were electrifying. He wore black clothes so that the audience would focus solely on his spotlit image, and they were spellbound. Over 90 per cent of the audience were female, their ages ranging from 17 to 70, and I think that they would have eaten him alive if they had been given half a chance.

The irony was that he became symbolic of the eternal French lover. In actuality he was Armenian and he was very proud to be so. His birth name was Aznavourian, which he later changed for professional reasons. On the second album he wrote a song called 'They Fell', ('Ils Sont Tombés'), which was a tribute to the terrible persecution of the Armenian population of the Ottoman Empire (Turkey) during and just after the First World War. In one period of three months more than two million Armenians were slaughtered. It would appear that genocide has been part of the human experience since Homo sapiens first stood upright and we have learnt nothing that has altered that practice.

I always thought that Charles was shrewd when dealing with business matters; wealth was kept in the family. His brother-in-law, Georges Garvarentz, was a prolific film composer in Europe, and they controlled the publishing and every other aspect of their endeavours. When Charles moved to Switzerland, due to a slight difference of opinion with the French tax office, he invited me to his home to meet his wife and to discuss future recordings. He had no delusions about himself. He wasn't affected by the music media hype; he was too intelligent and secure in regard to his self-worth to let the media, or anything else, affect his ego. He was not only an excellent performer, but was also an experienced businessman. In the world of entertainment celebrities, I found this to be very rare indeed.

Charles also had power outside the entertainment field. He invited me to accompany him to a small village near Nice, in the south of France. We met at Heathrow airport and I realised that had forgotten my passport. Fortunately, we had an hour to spare before take-off. He told me not to worry and that he would try to solve the problem. He went to the passport control office and I waited for about 15 minutes. When he returned he said that everything had been taken care of and we could depart. I never discovered what took place, but I was able to go to France and return to London without being stopped by any passport control personnel. Charles wouldn't discuss the matter. He nonchalantly said that it wasn't important, and I sat silent in bewilderment.

We arrived at the village and were greeted by four men, who appeared as though they made people offers they couldn't refuse. We had a wonderful meal and the business was concluded to everyone's satisfaction. It was obvious by their physical gestures, and my limited knowledge of the language, that a deal concerning a future event in Italy had transpired. The fact that I was present told me that I was to be involved. I found out later that a performance in the Verona amphitheatre in Italy was the prize for the journey.

Every summer, for a week, the Roman amphitheatre was hired by music companies to perform their latest record releases. It was the popular music version of the opera season in the famous venue. I was excited by the prospect of performing at the venue because I always associated Verona with Shakespeare. It was like a dream coming true, and I must say that I wasn't disappointed. The venue held 30,000 people and the acoustics were wonderful. Charles was a guest artist, so he wasn't in competition with anyone, and the remuneration was to be in cash, which was the Italian way of doing a great deal of their business.

The arena was used for the rehearsal, and the size and shape of the place were quite overwhelming. When we arrived at the venue, people were busy working, with scaffolding, sound equipment and pianos all over the enormous stage. The workmen had constructed a platform about 15 feet above the stage to accommodate the orchestra during Charles's performance. However, this set-up created a major problem for Charles. He told the floor manager that he wanted the orchestra next to him on the stage, so that he could hear the music clearly. Charles's Italian was perfect. The stage manager began to argue, so Charles made a derogatory remark to him and began to walk off the stage.

Remember, Charles was a guest and didn't need to be there at all. The manager began to panic and said that he would see what he could do to change things. Charles glanced at me and gave me a wink and a sly smile. I had been told that he could be very difficult when he wished to be. I walked up to him, told him what I had heard and asked him why we getting along so well. He responded, "Well, I'm hard to get, but when you've got me, I'm easy." His remark made me feel good for the evening performance. The manager came back with a red face and was very apologetic. It had dawned on him that he might be fired if Charles decided not to perform, but Charles forgave him and gave me another sly smile. We worked until everything felt good and then took a break for coffee.

This was the only time that I saw Charles in a rage. He explained that these things happen because some people who have power don't wish to be challenged. He said that if these people gave in to everyone they would feel that their power was being diminished. Charles thought that the outcome of his performance could have been seriously threatened if he couldn't relate to the orchestra, and I understood his predicament. This type of confrontation was rare in live performance situations, but an artist needed to be vigilant at all times.

The night of the concert was magical. The weather was superb and the sky was filled with stars. The theatre was full and the audience brought candles with them to show their appreciation of the occasion. When 30,000 people cheered the atmosphere was electric. They rose to their feet on several occasions and towards the end of the evening they lit their candles. It resembled an enormous birthday cake, and I felt it had some spiritual significance. As the melodies of the songs rose higher and higher the audience sang along with the artists. During the performance of 'Vado Via' ('Go Away') I thought that the arena was going to take off into space.

Much Italian songwriting had developed from the operatic tradition of Bel Canto ('beautiful singing'). The most emotional songs had sections that rose, one after the other, and the audience responded accordingly. 'Vado Via' was the only song sung in Italian to reach the British and American charts in the seventies. The Latin blood of the Mediterranean seemed to be more demonstrative than that of Northern Europeans. As the evening progressed the audience swayed to and fro, creating a sea of light that reminded me of the Aurora Borealis.

In a strange way history repeated itself. In Roman times the amphitheatre was a place of entertainment for its spectators, but the entertainment was barbaric. In modern times it is used to create beauty rather that destruction. Verona's theatre was a complete oval, and its survival was a miracle in itself. The lower dungeons were used as dressing rooms, where scores of performers would be busy getting ready for their own entrance. Performance was an essential part of Roman (and Greek) culture and they knew how to build places to maximise the effect, thus the acoustics were perfect. Contrast this to today, when baffles often need to be placed in buildings of inadequate design to improve the acoustics.

The men that Charles and I met in France did not believe in doing business in a conventional way. The question of cheques and bank drafts never arose. Before we left the building Charles and I went into a small storeroom backstage. He showed me a small, brown paper bag that was full of Italian money. Charles smiled and began to share it out - one for you and one for me, and so on. The Italians loved dealing in cash, but then so does every other nation when the opportunity arises. I stuffed the money in every pocket I could find, and Charles told me not to let the guards at the Austrian border see any of it, as they would take it and keep it for themselves. Luckily, they didn't see it and I spent a wonderful night in a quaint Innsbruck hotel in Switzerland.

One engagement I had with Charles was conducting a concert in Edmonton, Alberta, in Canada. We arrived by plane in early December, and as we went through its opened door it was like stepping into a refrigerator. The temperature was minus 20 degrees Fahrenheit, and we were told that we were lucky it was so warm. There wasn't a cloud in the sky and the ground was covered with snow and ice. It was quite beautiful and so dry that we didn't feel very cold at all.

Edmonton had its own symphony orchestra and the concert was organised by Creative Talents Association. Money was no object and we were treated to an expensive meal in a tower restaurant that was turning very slowly, about 200 feet from the ground. The view was flat, like an enormous natural ice rink, so you could see for miles. It was like a wonderland covered in white, and it was the first time either of us had seen such a landscape. Switzerland, where Charles lived, was a mountainous country. It was also beautiful, but you could see mountains and valleys, whereas this landscape was as flat as a pancake, and it seemed to go on forever.

The Association put out the red carpet for us and they wined and dined us several times. They were always immaculately dressed, which was so different to executives in Britain. The ladies wore expensive clothes and tasteful jewellery, which was unlike the denim cult in Britain during the seventies. Charles gave a great performance, and the orchestra played the arrangements with great enthusiasm. After the concert we were given a party to celebrate the occasion. They showed us tremendous politeness and invited us back, together or separately, if ever we wished to return. I felt that I could have made permanent contacts there and it would have been a wonderful place in which to settle, but commitments on the eastern side of the Atlantic made it impossible. Their hospitality was overwhelming and I will never forget their kindness.

If I had been more of a pianist than a cellist, I might have worked with Charles for many years. Singers who didn't play the piano usually had their own accompanist, who would be given a retaining fee so that they would make themselves available when required. Mike Moran was an excellent pianist and he played for Charles for many years. Keyboard players usually had an array of instruments at their disposal, and the orchestral sounds were generally created using a keyboard rather than a live orchestra. I remember Charles fondly, and I'll never forget how generous he was to me during our time together.

The Three Degrees were a very popular singing group in Britain during the seventies. They were three beautiful, black girls who had decided to record one of Charles Aznavour's songs as a single, and I was asked to produce it. Life has a learning curve and, as with George Harrison, I didn't liaise with them before the orchestral track was finished. I'm afraid that they didn't get what they wanted. They thought that the track was too slow for their rendition. To speed the track up would have changed the key of the song and also the colour of the sound. The girls were angry that their time had been wasted, which was their right, and I felt terrible because it was my responsibility to work with them to achieve a result that was satisfying to everyone concerned. Charles was in a hurry to swing the deal, and in overlooking the importance of personal communication I made a terrible mistake. Nobody wanted to be associated with the project and a potential hit was discarded.

They were an excellent group and deserved more respect,

for I was certain we would have worked well together if we had been given more time. They were very friendly in the studio in spite of their anger, which soon turned to disappointment, but the whole thing wasn't handled properly and it was a missed opportunity. I learnt that, no matter how my workload appeared, every detail should be rigidly scrutinised to accomplish a successful outcome. Second chances were very rare in the entertainment industry, and it was prudent to realise that fact.

I thought it was strange when a few weeks later I received a telephone call from one of the girls asking me if I would give her singing lessons. I was very surprised and wasn't really positive in my reply. They all sang brilliantly and I couldn't understand the reason for her call. Perhaps she had a secret motive of her own, but whatever it was it was beyond my grasp. I've often wondered what would have happened had I agreed to her request, and the old adage rings through my mind: "Nothing ventured, nothing gained." However, as far as I could see, living my life in 'if only' mode would be a waste of that life and would lead me into the dream world of Walt Disney rather than facing the world of reality.

* * *

As a friend of mine was passing a shop window in California he noticed a sign in the bottom right-hand window. Boldly printed on it were these few words: "Hats for Sale, Small, Medium and Fat".

CHAPTER 6

I had been working in the music industry as an arranger for several years before being offered a production. The first artist I was asked to produce was contracted to CBS records in London. His name was Scott Walker, who had previously had success with the Walker Brothers. Scott was born in Hamilton, Ohio, and he had worked in New York pursuing a career as an actor. He went to Hollywood and worked with Jack Nitzsche, and he played bass guitar with other bands before the Walker Brothers came to England. They had many hits in the sixties and Scott became something of a sex symbol at the time.

I used to think that Scott was every woman's dream. He was six feet tall, had a slim build, blond hair and big blue eyes. He had what I call a baby face and looked ten years younger than his real age. He loved to drink bourbon but he also used to take vitamins, and I suppose the latter helped him look so young and healthy. There was also a boyish gleam in his eyes, as if he were up to some mischief, and I never quite knew what was going to happen next. He had a tremendous talent and was absolutely sure of what he wanted and how to achieve it.

Scott came from the Midwest and always wore a denim jacket and jeans. He reminded me of one of those young characters you see in westerns, who were always long and lean, and if you stared them out there would be trouble. He was a very sensitive, bright young man though, who had complete control in the studio, and he had one of the best voices I ever had the pleasure of hearing during my production years. The material he chose to sing was always of the highest quality and not always what his record company thought would appeal to a mass audience. There were heated discussions about what songs would end up on his albums, but Scott held out for what he wanted and usually got his way.

The first thing you learnt about Scott was that he didn't suffer fools gladly. I had read many accounts about his reclusive behaviour and how difficult he was as a personality. I found no truth in this whatsoever. He always meant what he said, and said what he meant. I was under the impression that he really didn't want to be in the entertainment business. I suspected 'The Touch' gave him this marvellous voice, and because he didn't know what else to do to earn a living he just thought he'd use it! Years after we stopped working together a musician friend of mine told me that Scott would perform in northern clubs in England whenever he ran out of money. He would pay the band out of his own fee, rather than there being separate remuneration for the two, and he always kept control over what he wanted to sing.

Scott was wide open. He had a great sense of humour and a smile a mile wide. He loved playing pranks on people in a nice way and he was full of the joys of spring. He reminded me of some young children that would do something unexpected to see what people's reactions would be. He always respected the musicians he was working with, including me. He had spent years working with others before he came to London and must have felt that we were kindred spirits. He obviously didn't feel the same about executives in the music industry, however. I remember him pulling a funny face behind an executive who came to spy on us in the studio. He felt that they were the enemy, and in many ways they were.

Scott's own taste in popular music leaned towards French chanson. He loved Jacques Brel and those wonderful stories set to dramatic music. Such intensity was rarely found in British popular music, whose roots were found in Victorian music hall or American popular music, which stemmed from the folk genre and vaudeville. Scott also liked great film music and had a large collection at home, where he would constantly listen to his favourites until the early hours of the morning.

We worked together on two albums, Stretch (1973) and We Had It All (1974), in a small studio called Nova Sound. It was tucked away behind Marble Arch in Bryanston Street and only musicians noticed that it existed at all. At one time, during the five years I worked there, Tommy Steel owned it. He spent a great deal of money updating the studio, but in relation to the number of people using the place it wasn't a good business venture and he eventually sold it. The studio was very cosy and only small groups could be accommodated in the recording room, but many great rhythm tracks were recorded there.

Scott's sense of humour showed itself continuously throughout the recordings, but I particularly remember two occasions very well. My first recollection is that he was half an hour late one morning and when he finally arrived he was panting like mad. Having rushed through the doors of the entrance to the studio, he told us that three young girls had recognised him in Oxford Street and had made a dash to be with him. He gave us that boyish smile and told us that he ran down several back streets with the girls in hot pursuit. Finally he told us, laughing so much that tears were running down his face, that he saw a woman with a pram and lots of shopping bags and offered to help her. The girls lost their direction and he was free to make his way to the studio. But he said he didn't feel safe and ran all the way to get to us as quickly as possible.

He lived near Regents Park and drove an old Beetle VW car. He would park it anywhere there was a space. One day he beckoned me to follow him and when we reached the vehicle he opened the glovebox to reveal a pile of parking tickets. He smiled and explained that having foreign number plates meant that it was difficult for people to trace him, so he didn't bother to pay them. It seemed more like a boyish prank than breaking the law. He enjoyed the game, and he really saw it as that.

The second occasion happened in the Victoria Palace Theatre when Joni Mitchell was giving a concert in London. It was a Sunday and a couple of days earlier Scott had said he had two good tickets to see the show. It was an afternoon performance and we were five or six rows from the front. No sooner had we sat down than Scott produced a large paper bag. Inside the bag was a big bottle of Old Granddad bourbon and two paper cups. He put his index finger to his lips and told me that we wouldn't open the bottle until the lights went out. Joni was marvellous of course, but by the time she'd got to the interval number I was as drunk as a skunk.

I told Scott that I had to go to the toilet, and when the lights came on I made my way to the back of the theatre. Unfortunately I went through the wrong door and found myself in the street. I went to the front entrance and banged on the door. A large man in a dress suit came and gestured to indicate that the show had started and the theatre was full. He disregarded my pleading until some time later when Scott appeared and saved the day. I felt so stupid. I apologised to the doorman and we promptly took our seats. I will not say how much worse for wear I was by the end of the show. I can't even remember how I got home. Scott must have taken good care of me, and he never mentioned the incident again.

Scott was a very serious worker in the studio. He was always listening to his intonation (whether he was in tune or not), and the colour of his voice at any particular moment. If he thought that anything wasn't quite right he would stop the recording and tell Richard and me to try again. It was a joy to hear him sing, not only because he had a wonderful voice, but also because it was fascinating to watch the way he controlled every sound he uttered. I will never forget the occasion when he tried one phrase over a dozen times, just because the colour wasn't quite right. I must admit that his performance was so good each time that I would have been quite happy with any of the attempts. This self-criticism, of course, is what makes great singers great.

I must say there were many sides to Scott's behaviour and some were not always productive. Most of my life has been lived without alcohol, and in the music business this is a rare thing indeed. Scott, bless his heart, used to bring a bottle of bourbon to the studio every day. This generosity made me want to reciprocate, so on alternate days I would do the same. Needless to say, I would go home at the end of the day feeling like a wet rag. Scott, on the other hand, didn't seem to be affected at all. I put that down to greater experience on his part. Bourbon is rather sweet though, and I do have a sweet tooth, so I must admit that it was a pleasant experience for me too. The problem for somebody who didn't drink regularly was that the alcohol took effect very quickly, and all I wanted to do was sleep.

During the various recordings in the studio Scott would make complementary remarks to the musicians to let them know how much he admired their expertise. It took weeks to complete the basic rhythm tracks, and during that time it was possible to become quite close to your colleagues. On one occasion our bass player, Badger, invited Scott and me to his home for dinner. He was aware that the only fruit I thought I was allergic to was bananas, so he was determined to surprise us. Not only did he cook us a fine meal, but also the dessert was banana flambé. I didn't know what it was until after I'd eaten it, when he quizzed us about the dish.

Ray Cooper was also a fellow musician who performed on much of my work, and we became great friends. He is well known for his work with Elton John and his occasional presence in films such as Brazil and Baron Munchausen. We were having a meal in a London restaurant one evening when he surprised me with a present: a box of superb white wine. I told him that I would keep the last bottle until we met again. It was nine years before I decided that I had better drink the last bottle while I was still able. Ray lived in a converted warehouse in Narrow Street, in the East End of London. He told me that he'd bought it because he liked the name of the street. It's the sort of thing Ray would do, for he was quite unique, and an absolute gentleman. He was the most sensitive percussionist I ever worked with, and I thank him for his artistry and for his generosity of spirit. These friendships were important, and Scott and I both appreciated the gestures these people made, as they gave of themselves without selfish motives.

Richard Dodd, the resident recording engineer at Nova, was a very talented technician and we worked together for many years and on many albums. He was young and enthusiastic and would go out of his way to please a client. He worked quickly and the results he achieved were always of the highest order. After a while he was able to read my mind, and he was such a great help in producing the quality of sound that I heard in my imagination. Richard eventually became a freelance engineer and had a very successful career. I would have liked to work with him permanently, but sometimes artists or managers have their own favourites. This can be catastrophic, as you will hear when I discuss Elaine Paige. For a person who would never take a holiday abroad, Richard was full of surprises. He now has an American family and is living and working in Nashville, USA.

I really understood Scott's frustration with the bureaucracy in the music industry. Like all large businesses, record and compact disc companies had a great number of people working on various tasks to enable the end product to come to fruition. Each creative area of a company had its head of department, and all the remaining staff tried their best to give as much input into the process as possible. But you know what they say about too many cooks, and in many circumstances the saying is true. An artist's future career depended on so many decisions being made by so many people that any wrong decision could jeopardise the success of good marketing. And this was often the case.

Scott had many heated discussions with company executives about his right to choose the material he recorded. In a way it was a catch-22 situation. The company's interest was solely to make money, but Scott was more concerned about the quality of his work. Nobody could predict the outcome of sales; if they could it would be like winning the lottery with every release. Each point of view was valid, but in the end the company always wins because if it smells trouble it gets rid of the artist. This has been the reason for many artists to change their record label or start an independent label of their own.

I never saw Scott discuss anything in an aggressive way. Like me, I think he would rather walk away from confrontation than battle with people he thought unsympathetic. It was not in his nature to try to dominate; he was much too intelligent to waste his energy with such things. But his situation was full of contradictions. He didn't want to be seen as a pop idol, but the mass audience didn't really relate to the types of wonderful stories that Jacques Brel sang. He was a fine songwriter, but the media, and probably the audience at large, preferred him to sing middle-of-the-road songs like Joanna, written by Tony Hatch and Jackie Trent.

The odds against being successful were hard enough, even if artists had a clear vision of where they wanted to be and knew how to achieve their goal. In Scott's case the dice were loaded against him from the beginning. Here was a person with a voice of a quality that many singers would have given anything to have, and his nature made him a square peg in a round hole. His tragedy was that he was born in the wrong place, knowing the wrong language. Had he been French or Belgian or even from the Mediterranean, he would still be singing today, and we would have the pleasure of hearing that remarkable voice.

A friend told me recently that Scott had completed a record deal with Fontana Record and had finished a new album for which he had been given the freedom to record any material he wished to sing. I look forward to hearing it, as I am sure that Scott will have lost none of the magic he showed me so many years ago. I wish him well for the future and hope that he continues to sing until he enters that great recording studio in the sky.

* * *

A man was walking along a street when he heard a noise behind him. He turned to see what it was and, to his surprise, he saw a coffin bouncing down the street towards him. Frightened, he ran all the way home and locked the door behind him. After several minutes the coffin crashed through the door, and so the man ran upstairs and locked himself in the bathroom. Suddenly, the coffin smashed through the bathroom door and began moving towards him. Reaching out for something to defend himself with, the man grabbed a bottle of cough mixture and threw it at the coffin as a last resort. Only then did the coffin stop!

CHAPTER 7

When I received a call to work with Mama Cass Elliot I was filled with delight and anticipation. I used to listen to The Mamas & the Papas when I first got into the music industry, and they typified for me the quintessential American folk group. Cass was a warm, intelligent person with a tremendous sense of humour. It was obvious from the beginning that she had a great generosity of spirit. She was always smiling, which I found very endearing, and physically she was enormous. I never saw her have a tantrum or get agitated in any way, and the work was a gift from a higher power. She was a great conversationalist, and when we took coffee breaks we would discuss any and every subject under the sun.

The project was called The Road Is No Place for a Lady and it was engineered by David Hentschel, who engineered Elton John's Goodbye Yellow Brick Road album. We were working during the summer and the weather was fantastic. The studio was very hot, as we only had recycled air to breathe. Cass wore kaftans every day, and she never went anywhere without a pitcher of ice-cold water within arm's reach. She drank, on average, ten pints of water every session, which lasted three hours. We often joked with her about her liquid consumption, and she always received the remarks with grace and usually laughed with us.

Cass liked to talk about her young daughter, who was five, and the new house she had just acquired. It was obvious that she was very proud of her daughter, and she looked forward to both of them redecorating and refurbishing the house during the next school holiday. I was so surprised to learn that only a year later Cass had died because of a sudden heart attack. Cass never mentioned a husband, so I didn't know what had happened to her daughter. It was a tremendous shock for me because it only seemed a short while ago that we were laughing and joking together. It was another moment that made me realise how vulnerable we all are and how we should count every day as a blessing.

Cass was always looking for ways to improve her work. Even the selection of songs was constantly in a state of flux. Two of America's most popular songwriters arrived at the studio hoping that Cass would accept new songs that they had written. One was Jim Webb, author of the seven-minute-wonder hit for Richard Harris, 'MacArthur Park'. The other was Paul Williams, who wrote for films and many top American artists. I enjoyed both songs that were played, but Cass knew exactly what she wanted and she refused both compositions. No matter how good songs were, they were not always suitable for every artist. The taste or limitations of an artist often determined the choices made, and the fact that two of the four songs to be arranged by me were written by the composers meant that Jim and Paul didn't feel too bad about the decision that Cass made. It is important to remember that a songwriter's income depended on the successful placement of their material. Mama Cass sold millions of records in the States, so the competitive nature of the writers was understandable. But since they, along with Burt Bacharach, were two of the most successful songwriters on the American scene during the seventies, they accepted their rejection gracefully.

Cass's years in the business held her in good stead in the recording studio. She was always well prepared and she sang the songs with ease. Her high voice sometimes sounded like a child's voice, and it was something that puzzled me about singers. There were large people, like Pavarotti, who had a high vocal range and then there were small, thin people who were low range bass singers. It seemed that the size of their voice box bore no relation to the size of their body. Sometimes the technology in a studio did more aesthetic damage to an artist's sound than their natural voice. What was called 'double tracking' a voice - getting the artist to sing the song twice - completely changed the colour of the artist's natural sound. It was often used to add body to the natural sound, but it often ruined the natural colour of a voice. Cass often allowed this to happen, and in my opinion it diminished the beauty of her own natural gift.

I mentioned my feelings on the matter but she took the advice of her producer, Lewis Merenstein, and I couldn't intervene. The point was that a single voice, whatever the colour, would have made a more personal statement. If we consider the early records of Bob Dylan, he would almost throw away a beautiful melody in order to get the literary message across to his audience. But the words were his primary concern and there was a clarity in his execution. Had his voice been double tracked I'm certain that half the power of his statements would have been lost. I know it takes all sorts of people to make a world, but I could never understand why artists and producers didn't appreciate the quality of the natural voice. Perhaps because the technology was available it was too much of a temptation not to use it. I believe it was Oscar Wilde who said, "I can resist anything but temptation."

It is possible that Cass felt that the extra vocal track gave strength to her voice when she had to sing loudly. But I felt that the strength she may have acquired by using this technique was attained at some considerable cost. Her backing vocals were another story. Her tracked vocals were a delight. Tracking backing vocals could give them a warm sound. A good example of multi-tracking was the sound of the group Clannad. They used the technique for the title song of the television series Robin Hood, which created a veiled, mystical quality. There were moments when Cass sang softly, in her natural voice, and I was spellbound.

Without emotional expression singing has very little value. The voice may have a colour and the notes may be pure and in tune, but the communicative value would probably be zero if the artist didn't put his or her soul behind the words. Mama Cass certainly had a great soul. But some productions made it very difficult to find the real Cass beneath a myriad of techniques. Her soul was always seen when she and I went for meals. After a long day in the studio it was refreshing to leave and breathe fresh air. We used to wind down in a good restaurant and talk for hours about anything and everything. She was courteous to everyone and showed her appreciation to anyone who attended on her in any way. The stories she told at table were always positive, and it was obvious that she loved life and had many old friends that she cherished.

I loved to be in her company because she was a positive force. She joked with us and teased us until everyone was laughing. The kind of atmosphere she created in the studio was quite rare, as often the only concern was to produce the best record ever made. Many artists were so self-centred that their sense of humour never seemed to rise to the surface. Often they forgot that the best results were achieved when the work was fun for everyone, and that a dull environment wasn't conducive to elevated achievements. I know that when working with 60 orchestral players in a studio full of recycled air, a sense of humour was the only thing that got us through three hours of concentrated work.

Mama Cass knew this only too well. She had a very wide knowledge and experience of the music industry. She was an aware person when it came to relating to others. She knew that competition and conflict were not the things needed to get the work done. I had great respect for her, and in some way I was influenced by her behaviour. I am certain that wherever her spirit is now she is influencing every spirit around her in a very positive fashion, and that is really something of great worth.

Adam Faith, on the other hand, was one of the shrewdest people I ever met. Not only did he appear in films and make records, but also he thought of himself as an entrepreneur. He had the rare quality of saying what he thought to everyone he met. I never knew him to be diplomatic when dealing with businessmen, and I found this to be a very attractive quality. He was generous by nature and very unassuming, and in the music industry that was like a breath of fresh air. He was the manager of Leo Sayer and I met him in 1973. All Adam's friends and close associates called him Terry, as that was his real name. He called me because he was about to produce Leo's first album and he wanted me to write for the string orchestra he had booked for the sessions. Adam had always interested me, so I was delighted to accept his offer. He had a unique way of doing everything and I was not disappointed in the tasks to come.

Leo and Adam were a perfect pair, for they both saw their vision as a theatrical enterprise. The songs on Leo's first album were a far cry from the later successes he had as a big star in the USA. They had the flavour of the English music hall and the buskers you passed on the British streets; the one-man bands, trios and quartets who used to move slowly along the gutters, with a hat held out, in the hope that some generous person might recognise their existence. Leo Sayer, the first album, was produced by Adam and Dave Courtney (who wrote the music to Adam's lyrics). Dave was also the pianist at the sessions. There were three engineers: Tom Newman (no relation), Keith Harewood and my old friend Richard Dodd. The strings were recorded at Nova Sound Studios in Marble Arch, London, as it was a few years before I could convince Richard to take the plunge and become a freelance engineer.

Adam was very particular in the choices he made with regard to the songs and the way they were recorded. He decided on the size of the accompaniment and the instrumentation, which was generally left to me. I liked that because it wasn't always possible to know what would please the producer, and sometimes it was impossible to please them at all. Adam called for meetings weeks before recording dates so that everyone involved could discuss the lyrics. He wanted everybody to understand what he thought was important in relation to the emotional content. It really helped in getting an overview of what was needed. This was not the general practice of producers, who would usually arrive at the studio on the appointed day and be completely surprised with what an arranger had written.

It was a very productive way of working because every member of the team learnt something about the expertise of the other members. Adam was definitely the captain of his ship, and he called everyone 'love', as if he had known them for years. We all responded well to the familiarity he showed us, and his was a clever approach because everyone wanted to please him all the more as a result of his open attitude and his warmth. If certain other well-known artists had interacted with their teams in a similar way the results of their work would have been much improved. It costs very little to be courteous.

In order to bring attention to the new artist, Adam decided

that Leo should dress like a clown, and it was certainly effective. It also expressed a part of Adam's theatrical nature. The record sleeve was quite masterful. It had the open book type of cover in a subtle silver colour. The inside sleeve was also cleverly designed because we saw the clown and then behind him was Leo in normal dress, as a shadow of the clown. It seemed to me to reflect something that was probably very true of most of us.

Adam's business acumen came to the fore when he was looking for the best deal he could get from a record executive. He invited me to join him and his wife for dinner at Tramps, a well-known club in Soho, which was owned by Jackie Collins' husband. It was usually frequented by people in the entertainment business, and Adam had invited several record company executives to be there at the same time. At a specific point later that evening, he told me to watch the following events and gave me a sly smile. He left the table and began talking to one of the executives. After that he moved on to speak to another executive for a few moments, and so on, leaving each executive wondering what the others had offered Adam to procure Leo as a label artist. Adam knew that he was creating a competitive situation and they were all drawn into his web. Finally, Chrysalis Records won the deal, and history has shown that Leo never looked back. His American success was phenomenal.

Adam's wife was very beautiful, and a good deal of our conversation was about their house in the country. Leo's career was also discussed, especially the American possibilities. I never saw Adam get upset about anything. Occasionally, members of the team would have a tantrum because they couldn't get some technical aspect to work, at which point Adam would just smile and walk away. He trusted everyone to do their best for him and he gave us the space to do so. If he made an error of judgement he would quietly scrap what was done and begin again from a different perspective. Leo was really lucky to have Adam as his manager, as many managers made decisions that reaped quick financial returns and these were not always best for an artist's long-term career. Adam was in no hurry, as he was already wealthy from his past experiences, and he had the insight to know the best avenues to take in the entertainment industry. He and Leo had a fine working relationship because they liked and trusted each other. The greed of some managers had led to theft and fraudulent dealings and in the end their artists were the ones who suffered.

Adam's next production with Dave Courtney was for Roger Daltrey, the singer with The Who. Roger had his own studio in his Sussex country home. Later additions were recorded in the Beatles' Apple studio in London. There were similar theatrical elements in the lyrics, which seemed to me to be somewhat grandiose in relation to the talent. The use of Brian Cole on steel guitar, however, was a saving grace, as he was probably the best player of that instrument in the country at that time. There were Beatles pastiches in some songs and sparse lyrics in others, and one song in particular was about poverty and the poor learning to keep their money in better times. Maybe I lost some of the point, but I often found that people who wrote about poverty and the poor were the wealthiest people on Earth. Living in a beautiful home in Sussex, Roger seemed to me to have a very good life. Perhaps he didn't give too much away.

Adam's own album had lyrics that were more simple and direct. They were more universal in their content, so everyone could feel that they had experienced similar events in their own lives. They were all love songs and were sung so tenderly that they were probably about people he had known. One song was about the entertainment industry. There were many managers around who saw a potential gold mine without having to do a great deal of extraction. I remember being in Century City, LA, and a lawyer asked me for a CV and an itinerary for the coming year. Had I complied with his wishes, all he had to do, he said, was to lift up the telephone and make a few calls. For that small action he expected half of my earnings for the year mentioned. I thought the term 'leech' wasn't too strong for a person who took advantage of people in such a way.

We have read many times in the press about the greed and corruption that have been perpetrated by managers under the guise of 'managerial services'. In some cases more than a million pounds has disappeared without the artist's knowledge. If not for an annual audit the perpetrator would have taken considerably more money. When we consider that managers already get a handsome percentage of an artist's income it's hard to comprehend such behaviour. Perhaps money lying idle in a bank was too much for their small minds to handle. Casting my mind back reminds me that for 40 years the man who owned the ship-based Radio Caroline has owed me £400 for work I did for him in the sixties. I wonder what that is worth today when the interest is added to the sum? I know that the most important things in life are priceless, but I think that people who behave that way are a waste of space.

I'm certain that Adam's spirit is dealing with the angels. Adam and I parted over a simple misunderstanding and I have regretted it to this day. As I've mentioned before, these things happen in a music industry full of insecurities.

Julie Felix was a delight to work with. She was full of sunshine and was a very attractive person. I remember seeing her perform live in a theatre in West Wales, and the pure artistry and energy that she transmitted to the audience were absolutely electrifying. It was impossible to believe that this firecracker was actually 63 years old. Julie was able to balance power and delicacy in such a manner that the marriage of the two was perfect. There were very few artists that I knew who, having made a mistake in performance, would smile and make fun of themselves. She did this beautifully and the audience was with her.

One of Julie's parents was Mexican, and she felt an affinity with the people of the world who were poor and were kept in poverty by the powerful few developed countries. Many of her songs were about the underprivileged, which included male domination over women, a practice that has existed for thousands of years. Her own experiences had made her deeply aware of injustice and she portrayed this knowledge with great artistry. Although she had a young daughter, I believe she had given up relating to men in an emotional way and was quite content with the company of the fair sex.

I produced an album for her, and she told me that I was the only producer she had ever worked with. I wasn't certain whether it was a compliment or not, but her enormous smile was good enough for me. I enjoyed our time together and that is the only yardstick that is relevant. Julie had a great zest for life, which was very contagious, and when she was around you felt good within yourself. Her face used to light up with excitement at the smallest thing; it was as if she were sharing the secrets of the universe with you. Being with her was a rare experience because her generosity of spirit was always present.

Everyone in the studio loved her. She still retained a childlike wonder and curiosity about things, and the studio gave her many opportunities to ask, "What does this do?" and "What is that for?" She often made the tea for the studio team, which was generally done by the assistant engineer, and nothing was too much trouble when recording her voice and guitar. The studio atmosphere seemed new to her and she reminded me of Alice in Wonderland. She talked a great deal and was very knowledgeable about current affairs and politics. Of course, world poverty was high on her agenda, but she spoke softly and never tried to force her ideas on anyone. On one occasion a visiting engineer in the studio made a sexist remark, and two of us had to restrain her because she was about to smack his face. We asked the man to leave and I apologised for his behaviour. It spoilt the remainder of the day, and it strengthened my belief that there was never any justification for rudeness.

I remember one evening in 1975, when I was invited to the birthday party of Julie's daughter. She was four years old and Julie was so proud of her. They lived in a large, old house near Watford, which was surrounded by fields. It was just north of London and ideal for getting to town easily. Many well-known music people were invited, but the only one I remember is Mickey Most, the producer of so many hit singles and albums of the time. We all sat at a large table for dinner, and opposite me was a vivacious woman in a low-cut dress. I was very tired because I'd only slept about four hours over a period of three days due to the pressure of work. The cold soup was placed in front of us and I couldn't keep my eyes open any longer. My head went down into the soup and I heard the woman scream because she had been splashed. Someone said, "You must excuse him as he has been working hard," and that was the last thing I remember about the party. I awoke the next morning at about seven and found myself in a cosy bed on the first floor. I was so embarrassed that I left the house before anyone was up and about.

It was the last time I saw Julie until the theatre performance in Wales. There was a queue in the foyer after the show to buy various CDs she had for sale. I joined the queue and when it was my turn I smiled at her and said nothing. She didn't recognise me for about a minute and then she smiled and said my name. She asked me if I was still writing strings for people, then I laughed and we hugged each other. She was with another lady, so we had to explain our familiarity. I sensed that they were partners, but I may have been wrong, and in any case it was none of my business.

It is interesting that the emotions that swell up in people that have known each other for a long time are far greater than with more recent acquaintances. Perhaps there was an invisible bond between us that registered closeness and we reacted accordingly. Time and distance didn't seem to be important. The old cliché that "it seems like only yesterday" was really true, and I instantly felt the warmth of the sun within her. I assume that she is still performing in theatres and clubs and it would be wonderful to work with her again. But life takes us on different paths, and most of it is taken up with mere acquaintances. It has been said that if a person has one true friend then that person is very lucky. I've made many during my lifetime, and I've always felt blessed.

Another A&M artist I worked with was Peter Frampton. He was not unlike Julie in that he had the same kind of charisma. There was a delicacy in the ballads that he wrote and they were full of warmth. I believe that the work that a person creates is a window into the essence of the person. The album was called Wind of Change (1972) and the three tracks I worked on were full of sunshine. 'Fig Tree Bay', 'Hard' and 'Oh, For Another Day' were light and transparent. The playing was superb, and the production felt American and reminded me of the time I had spent in California.

Peter was very handsome and became known as 'The Face of 1968'. He was a member of The Herd and Humble Pie, and I was asked to write for his debut solo album. Soon after the album was made he formed Frampton's Camel using some of the players from the album and they toured the USA. In 1975 his album Frampton was a great success and his album Frampton Comes Alive released a year later became the biggest selling live album, selling more than 12 million copies. His work spanned many decades and the solo albums from 1972 to 1998, many of which were compilations, were usually well acclaimed and always popular in the USA. It could be said that Peter was the most American writer that Britain ever produced.

His approach to his work was more American than European, which is probably why they liked him so much and bought his work with such fervour. His music had a serene quality, which was concerned with colour and texture as well as lyrical information. The spaciousness he employed had a rhythmic structure that could only be created by a guitarist. His observations took us to places and things that were not generally in the public consciousness, such as seashells, shapes in the fire and the appreciation of being alive - "the breath of fresh air that can turn somebody on"; things that make you feel good if you are aware that they exist.

I believe that Peter's relationships were based on whether the people around him felt the power of nature. He spoke of spiders' webs after rain, red sunsets, and made many references to things that city dwellers would find hard to notice and experience living in a concrete jungle. He was a gentle soul and was obviously at peace with the world. I felt that he had leanings towards one or more of the Eastern religions, as his approach to life seemed very philosophical to me. We didn't have to talk much because the lyrics of his songs said everything about him that we needed to know.

It was probable that he studied yoga. On many occasions he sat on the floor with his legs crossed, staring into a 'somewhere' that was hard for me to detect. This activity would last about 20 minutes, and when he rose he would walk off without saying a word. I assumed that he was meditating but he never spoke about it. His privacy was something that he treasured above all things, although he was very open and friendly with the team. He told us that if he found himself in an aggressive situation he would simply walk away from it. I asked him if he studied the martial arts, but he just smiled, said nothing, and walked away.

I found his work very uplifting and simply expressed. He would have made the perfect friend. So many artists are wrapped up in themselves to the extent that they get caught up in the power game, and this leaks into their writing. They often get bitter about their early experiences in the business, or in their childhood, and the world is suddenly a terrible place. Not so with Peter. His vision was crystal clear, and I'm sure that whatever life had in store for him he would stand up and face the winds that blew. Peter would smile at what came, and then go on observing the detail of existence in his own quiet, positive manner.

* * *

A man went into a club and ordered a drink. He drank half of it and threw the other half over the barman. After the third time the barman told the man that he should see a psychiatrist. A few weeks later the man returned and did the same thing. The irate barman asked the man if he had seen a shrink and the man promised that he had. "Well, it hasn't helped you much!" cried the barman. "It certainly has, said the man. "I'm no longer embarrassed about it now."

CHAPTER 8

Uri Geller had to be seen to be believed. He visited my flat in Notting Hill in 1974 with his manager, Werner Schmid. Having arrived without warning, I was somewhat surprised by their visit. Werner explained they had been looking for a sympathetic musician to collaborate with them on an album they were about to record. He said they had seen a few people before me, but they were not happy with anyone so far. I wasn't sure whether I should have been grateful or not, since I wasn't the first person they had approached. At that time I had a young Australian girl working at my apartment part-time. She used to make tea, type, get the phone and generally tidy up after me. I asked my assistant to make some coffee and explained to my guests that I had a session with an orchestra in Abbey Road Studios in two hours' time. They settled down around a small coffee table in the centre of my living room and began to expound their requirements. Uri told me about his life and what he had been doing during his younger years. He said he had no qualifications and he had tried to make a living doing what he could do best. I understood what he was saying, so we just exchanged pleasantries for about half an hour, and then it happened.

Both Uri and Werner said they liked me and offered me the job. Uri said I was the only one they had approached who didn't ask to see him do a 'trick'. He then asked me if I would like to see something, and before I could answer he got up and went to the sink, where my assistant was drying the cups and saucers. He took a spoon from the drying board and gave it a couple of rubs with his fingers. He then asked my assistant to take over from him and told her to continue rubbing the spoon. After a minute or so he told her to bend the spoon. To my amazement it folded like a piece of hot chocolate.

He then walked over to my small coffee table, which had various things on it, including a stopwatch that I used in the

70

studio sometimes when I was recording. He picked up the watch and it exploded. The glass flew out and the numbers and hands were all mangled. The surface of the watch face had coagulated and much of it was missing. I couldn't believe my eyes. The power of the experience made me feel very strange, and my assistant had to sit down because she said her knees were shaking. Uri immediately apologised to me for destroying the watch, but my mind was elsewhere. It was like having what I supposed to be a religious experience. I looked at the watch, which I was going to use in the studio that afternoon, and didn't know what to say.

To break the mood, Werner then showed me a letter from King's College, one of the London University colleges. It was dated 17 July 1974 and stated that after exhaustive tests Uri had been found to have these extraordinary qualities, and was able to bend metal without even touching it. Professor J.G. Taylor of the mathematics department said he was writing two further papers and a book called Super Minds: An Analysis of the Geller Effect. I wasn't quite certain whether the whole experience had happened. It was so impressive that it was quite a shock to my system. Imagine it happening to you, long before the publicity about his talents.

Be that as it may, I was certainly impressed. I went to the studio an hour after they had left the apartment, and during the session I felt like I was 12 feet off the ground. I wanted to tell some of the musicians about my experience, but I felt they wouldn't believe me. Musicians tend to be very solid, grounded characters and I'm not sure they would have appreciated a story about a religious experience at three in the afternoon. They would probably have thought I'd had one drink too many the night before.

We began making the album, and I wasn't certain what to expect in the studio, but some very strange things happened. Uri's concept was to speak the words he had created over instrumental backgrounds. Sometimes a choir was involved, and at other times Maxine Nightingale sang the lyrics. Maxine had sung in Europe for a couple of years and had acted in Hair and Jesus Christ Superstar. Half of the music on the album was composed by yours truly, the other half being supplied by Byron Janis, a gifted classical pianist from the USA, who was the first American musician to be sent to the Soviet Union during the cultural exchange programme between the two countries. All the arrangements were mine.

What interested me about Byron was the fact that he was married to the daughter of Gary Cooper, the famous Hollywood film star. If you remember the film High Noon you will know who I mean. She had an uncanny way of reminding me of her father. She was a good six feet tall, very attractive in a quiet way, and had many gestures that could only have been given to her by her father. She even spoke like him, in a slow, deliberate way with lots of pauses. Whenever she came to the studio I was mesmerised.

Most of Byron's music had a Bach-like feel to it. This was not surprising considering his formal training as a pianist, for no musician who has studied music at a college has escaped the leader of the pack, J.S. Bach. The text on the album cover said he had only been composing for two years, so I wasn't surprised that he relied on a strong outside influence. He was very self-contained and didn't talk much. I got the feeling that he thought all this was beneath him, but the prospect of composition royalties was an attractive draw.

Some of my music had a 'middle of the road' feel, particularly 'This Girl of Mine' and 'A Story to Tell'. These were the two songs that Maxine sang, and she had a superb colour in her voice that reminded me of chocolate-coloured velvet. She was a beautiful woman of mixed blood and was very talented, friendly and obliging. She was used to recording her own albums and so she knew recording techniques very well, which meant she worked quickly and efficiently. She was based in Los Angeles, and I assumed it gave her more opportunities to further her career.

The tracks I particularly enjoyed writing were 'Beyond Imagination' and 'Mood', which allowed for a more imaginative approach to the words. The latter title was a background to Uri's lyrics that were trying to get the listener to bend spoons or forks at home. I don't know how successful he was because we will never know the exact outcome. I have met people, however, who said listening to Uri's voice on the record actually did give a positive result. Two technicians in the studio told me that their wives were listening to Uri talk on a radio programme. He asked the audience to pick up a fork or spoon and then rub it gently with a finger. After a short time he told them to bend the object as gently as possible. The technicians said they actually saw their wives bend the cutlery, and they were astonished at the result. I asked them if they were joking, but they both said their story was true. Having had my experience, I believed them, and it's probable that thousands of people have been affected by Uri's 'magic'.

I particularly remember one evening when we were recording Uri's voice in the studio. Richard Dodd was the engineer, and I have already mentioned how conscientious he was about the quality of his work. I sometimes got the feeling that Uri was inventing the words as the recording proceeded, as he would listen to the music in a way that made you believe he was being inspired. Richard ran the recording tape and Uri spoke into the microphone, and all seemed well. At the end of the track Richard asked Uri if he would come into the control room and listen to the playback. We all settled down and the tape was started. There was no voice on the tape. We looked at each other, and Richard assured me that the machine had been recording during Uri's effort. Richard checked the recording machine and told us it was fine, but there was no voice on the voice track. He was dumbfounded, apologised to Uri, and asked him to go into the studio and try again.

I could see that Uri was concerned. It wasn't the studio that worried him so much as the words he was actually speaking. He said he had a strange feeling about the lyrics and thought perhaps he should change them on this particular track. I said it would probably be all right now and he should try once more. Uri went into the studio, the track was started, and he began to utter the same message. At the end of the recording Richard said the dials were reading perfectly and Uri should come in and listen. This he did, but when the machine started there was no voice to be heard.

Richard didn't know what to do and assured us that there was nothing wrong technically. I had worked with him for years and trusted him implicitly. Uri said that it was not the studio, it was other forces. Neither Richard nor I knew what

73

Uri was talking about, but we bowed to his knowledge and asked him what he was going to do about the lyrics. He said he would ad lib something else and went into the studio. After giving the matter some thought he began to speak a different set of words and the recording worked perfectly. Don't ask me why this happened. To me it was as mysterious as bending metal.

We continued to work that evening, but the strangeness was not over. We had our usual break at ten, talked about the bizarre occurrences, and began working on a different track. Uri was in the studio speaking into the microphone when we heard a loud, short noise through the speakers. Richard stopped recording and went into the studio. He came back to the control room with Uri, and to my surprise he was carrying a small piece of metal, which he had found on the floor in the centre of the room. Uri said it had fallen from the ceiling as he was speaking. Richard said he had been watching Uri during the recording and he had done nothing out of the ordinary. In fact, where the piece of metal was lying, a small puddle of water had emerged. I thought someone was trying to tell us something and it was about time we stopped work for the day. I still don't know what caused these things to happen, and neither does Richard. All he could say was that it had nothing to do with him, and I believed him.

There is a track on the album called 'The Day'. It had a fast rhythmical part and the sound was quite dissonant. We used a choir of formally trained singers on the track, a full string orchestra and a synthesiser or two. When the choir had done its job and we were satisfied with the quality of the sound, we invited anyone from the choir who wanted to hear the playback into the control room. Six or seven accepted our offer and listened to the track. Halfway through the track one of the women began to cry out. She started to shake and fell to the floor. It was as if she was having an epileptic fit and couldn't control her movements. You must remember that these were formally trained, professional performers, who were certainly not behaving for effect. She was placed on a sofa and the music was stopped. It took some 15 minutes before she returned to her normal condition, and she asked us what had happened. When we told her about her reaction to the music she didn't believe us. She just said that she became cold all over, and that was all she could remember.

As with all businesses, there has to be a great deal of trust. I know that the album was released in Britain and Germany on the Polydor International label. It might even have been released in other countries, although of that I'm not certain. There's one thing I do know. Werner Schmid had placed the publishing with an American firm in New York, and so it is probable that the album was released in the USA as well as Europe. Some months after the release of the album and cassettes, I received a cheque from the publishers with an equivalent value of about £100. It seemed to me that if the number of units they sold amounted to the fee I received, given Uri's popularity at the time, they must have given away 90 per cent of the factory pressings. Werner was called the Executive Producer on the album sleeve, although I mixed all the tracks of the album. Whatever that made me, I didn't get paid for the work. Whenever you see 'EP' on a record, CD or a tape, disregard it. It means that someone who wants their name in print will have it so. It never relates to the work done to make the project a reality, as they do absolutely nothing creatively that contributes to the finished product.

I received a phone call from Uri in April 2000, telling me he had written a book and was having a book signing in Bath the following month. He said that it would be lovely for us to meet up and he would let me know when the day arrived for the signing. Strangely enough I am still waiting for his call. I don't mean to sound cynical, but haven't we all been there before? I just wish people would say what they mean, and mean what they say. If not, it would be much better if they said nothing at all. I bear no grudges. I only hope that he, Byron and Werner enjoyed the cheques they received from the New York publisher and that they, too, can sleep well at night, because for me it has never been a problem.

Maxine was a delight to work with. Weeks after recording Uri's album she called me from Los Angeles to tell me that she needed my services urgently. There were two or three tracks of her latest album that needed mixing, and there was a very close deadline for them to be finished. She said she could come to London if that was better for me, and we could work at Nova Sound with Richard Dodd. I agreed, having spoken with Richard, but it meant that we had to work during the weekend and at night because Richard was already working during the day on another project.

We worked through Friday night but felt shattered the next morning. The mixing had gone well and Richard was holding up pretty well. On Saturday night we were halfway through the second of the tracks, which by the way were arranged by an excellent LA musician, when Richard and I started feeling very tired. It was about two o'clock on the Sunday morning. Maxine took a small tin from her bag, telling us that she was worried we wouldn't finish the mixes in time for the deadline, and asked us both to take one of her little white pills. Well, I believe they were called uppers, and we had never taken that kind of pill in our lives. If you knew Richard you would have laughed until your sides were aching.

Richard at that time was so straight and predictable. He had never taken a holiday abroad because he said that Britain was good enough for him. He didn't smoke or drink, and he didn't believe anything that he couldn't see and touch. Maxine changed all that. She convinced us that the pills were harmless and explained that she only took one when she needed extra energy to do some task. We reluctantly obeyed her wishes, and I must say that half an hour later we were feeling on top of the world. I have never established what the pills contained, but they gave us a burst of energy I have never felt since, and I'm sure it was Richard's one and only pill-taking experience.

We finished the second track at about five that morning, and as it was Sunday Richard was able to go home and sleep the whole day through. We said our goodbyes and made our way to our cars, which were parked directly outside the studio. I remember driving along the road thinking that I must not drive too fast, as it felt as if I was speeding, but when I looked at the speedometer it said I was travelling at 15 mph. We were lucky there were no cars on the road, and I seemed to be home in a flash.

When I arrived home I went straight to the cupboard, got

out a bowl and a cloth, filled the bowl with water, knelt down on the floor, and proceeded to wash the floor of my apartment. I had so much energy I didn't know what to do with it, and I remember cleaning the whole apartment, which must have taken several hours. It was daylight when I finally got to bed, and it was late in the evening when I awoke. In a strange way it was a good experience, as the pill took me to a place I'd never been to before and I've never been there since. Perhaps everyone should try one thing they've never done before, providing it is harmless and in the comfort of their own home.

Our last evening in the studio was quite uneventful compared with the night before. We finished the work we were given and Richard had to package the master tapes and copies so that Maxine could take them back to America. They must have been satisfactory because we never heard from the record company, and I am certain we would have heard something if there had been a problem. Maxine was sad to leave us and thanked us for helping her at such short notice. On two or three occasions she rang me from LA at three or four in the morning, telling me she was lonely and she missed London. I completely understood how she felt. I think many musicians who go abroad for long periods of time to further their careers feel the same way as Maxine Nightingale. It is a heavy price to pay, leaving your family and friends for fame and fortune. Being a stranger in a strange land can be hard to bear, and fame and fortune may not always compensate for giving up one's roots. I don't think I could have done the same if I had been a front room boy.

* * *

When a taxpayer telephoned the Inland Revenue to ask if he could claim a certain allowance on his income tax, the answer was "No!" This was followed by, "This is a recorded announcement."

CHAPTER 9

The music industry was full of characters that were larger than life. One such person was Richard Perry. People like him tended to attract others who were larger than life. Another character with even greater dimensions was Harry Nilsson, who regrettably is no longer with us. Richard had a period of prolific production with famous artists. He once told me that he was only working in the record industry until he had earned enough money to direct and produce films. With his current artists I thought it wouldn't be long before his dream was realised. He was six feet four inches tall and very athletic in build. He had a mass of black hair, and when he smiled, which he did often, he showed a large configuration of teeth. Richard was lucky to work with successful artists because it allowed him to have enormous budgets. He would think nothing of doing 20 takes of a track and then have the time to edit them until he was satisfied with a single version for release.

Richard Dodd told me that when he worked with Perry they would enter the studio and wouldn't see the light of day for 72 hours while in the process of editing a single track. It could be compared with some international photographers who might take 200 shots of a model to get the definitive picture. It's a very laborious way of working, but if the end result was good I suppose it justified the means. I think it had an air of uncertainty about it. Anyway, I never had such wonderful luck to produce someone so successful that time and money were of no consequence.

Whereas Richard was slow and deliberate, Harry was the complete opposite. His mind was always racing ahead, and he often started sentences before finishing the ones he had just begun. He always moved around the room when he spoke; in fact I don't ever remember him sitting down. He exuded enormous energy and had a butterfly mind that was out to lunch most of the time. When you called to him for something he would look at you as if you had disturbed a dream he was having. I felt that everything was a struggle for him, as there was something very sad about his whole aura.

Richard gave me two tracks to write for on the 1972 Son of Schmilsson album. The first was a gentle song called 'Remember', and the second was a Hollywood epic called 'The Most Beautiful World in the World'. The former had a double string quartet arrangement, and the latter had a large orchestra and a mixed choir to be used like epic film music. The interesting thing about the latter song was that the lyrics treated the world as if it was a woman, which was really clever, and I thought that the idea was unique. In fact, Harry was unique in every respect. I had never known anyone think of that approach to a song lyric before. That was why Richard wanted "additional orchestration by Del Newman". The album sleeve stated that Richard conducted the orchestra and choir for the piece, but there is a story to tell about that session.

I chose CTS Studios in London for the session because we required 40 musicians and 24 singers to do the track justice. CTS had enormous space and many film-music sessions were performed there. We arranged a Sunday to use the studios, which meant that everyone who attended got double fees. Richard also thought that three hours wouldn't be enough time, so I booked the studio for two sessions, morning and afternoon. Everyone was called for ten o'clock in the morning. We began to rehearse the music and within half an hour we were ready to record. Neither Harry nor Richard had arrived by the time the rehearsal was finished, so I gave everyone a 20-minute break. I was certain that they would arrive by the end of the break, but I was wrong. At one o'clock in the afternoon the first session was over and I sent everyone away for lunch.

The players and singers returned an hour later for the second session and the artist and the producer had not arrived. I was getting worried and decided to rehearse the music again to be certain that we would be ready to perform at a moment's notice. Finally, at about 4.15 that afternoon, the door opened and in burst both of them. They were having an argument about something and Richard apologised for being a little late. Not only did they arrive, but also a complete film crew accompanied them with enough equipment to film Gone with the Wind.

Richard said that they had travelled across most of Britain to film the recording and hoped that it wouldn't interfere with the afternoon's work. By the time the film crew had set everything up, only 20 minutes of the afternoon session were left. There was time to make two attempts at recording the song and I conducted the first attempt. Richard then suggested that he should conduct the next attempt for the benefit of the film crew. He stepped onto the podium and waved his arms about as soon as the recording light shone, but it reminded me of the gesticulations people made when dancing the famous 1940s jitterbug. The musicians and singers were professional, and if Snow White had conducted them it would have made no difference. The work was finished with one minute to spare and I sighed with great relief.

Richard thanked everyone and said that he thought he had enough material to make a final version of the song in the editing room. He seemed to be more concerned about whether his image came over well on film than whether the music was what was needed to make a great record. Harry had his picture taken in his dressing gown sitting in the middle of the orchestra and Richard had his picture taken conducting the orchestra and choir. The day reminded me of Alice in Wonderland. It seemed an amazing way to work. The expense that was laid out for 20 minutes of actual work seemed extremely wasteful to me. I wondered if they both knew, or cared, how lucky they were to have the luxury of time and money to create their efforts when most other creators were working with great financial restrictions.

It was obvious when listening to the artist that he was a unique performer. There was a very thin line between genius and insanity, and often the difference wasn't recognised. Spike Milligan, the writer and actor, was such a man. I don't think that Harry ever did a live performance, but he loved making records and he was highly successful in terms of their sales. There were no boundaries for Harry, as the four-letter word in 'You're Breaking My Heart' clearly showed. What we call politically correct or poetic licence didn't apply to Harry because he was far beyond caring what people thought. His ideas were very individual, in the way that Frank Zappa's were, and the only surprise for me was that his record company allowed his idiosyncrasies to be recorded onto vinyl.

He was not afraid of making penetrating social comment, as the lyrics on 'Ambush' made perfectly clear. It was graced with a wonderful brass track arranged by Jim Price and played by him on trumpets and trombones. Bobby Keys played the saxophone for the track, and they were the most prestigious musicians in their field. I believe that Harry's candle burnt so brightly that it went out long before it might have done. So many artists died at an earlier age than expected, and although it was said that the quality of a journey was more important than its length I often wondered what kinds of creations some artists would have made had they lived to a ripe old age.

The album sleeve was full of Harry's humour. The front cover had a photograph of Harry as a vampire, and the back cover had the lyrics dripping with blood. The inner sleeve had a myriad of pictures of people who had taken part in the record's production, and Harry's picture had him posing without trousers. I'm certain that Harry enjoyed shocking people and it was obvious that he was anti-establishment. The idea of vampires stayed with him because two years later he was involved with the Apple film Son of Dracula. The film was produced by Ringo Starr and included some of Britain's best-known actors. My string quartet arrangement of the song 'Remember' was also included on the album of the film, as was the hit song 'Without You'.

The work didn't satisfy me as much as I had hoped it would, as I didn't see the movie and I found the story hard to follow. The album's structure did not have a feeling of inevitability about it, for many songs were not heard in their complete form and there were intermittent pieces of dialogue supported by dissonant music, which only confused the unfolding of the story. Perhaps it was only possible for the nature of the concept to succeed when seeing the film at the same time as listening to the record. I also found it difficult to align the song 'Remember' with the story of Dracula.

Using the same arrangements for different projects seemed to be common practice in some territories, especially if the work concerned originated from another country. It was thought that if the language was changed the companies could use the arrangements throughout the world without the consent of the arranger, or without the need to pay more money. Each project was a separate entity, and a different language produced a different product. Arrangers owned the copyright of their work, and the only stipulation with some companies was that the arrangers would not use the same arrangement with other companies for a period of time. It was an illegal yet common practice, and because the arrangers received a fee and not a royalty they were constantly abused by many companies.

It was a difficult situation because if a legal case were brought against a company the whole industry would get to know about it. This could have serious consequences for the protagonist's career. No company would wish to associate itself with bad publicity. But many of my favourite musicians were performing on the album. Ray Cooper, Nicky Hopkins, Ringo Starr, Peter Frampton and George Harrison all appeared on the disc, as Harry attracted many people and his magnetism stretched far and wide. What was it that was so attractive? During the time we spent together, about six hours, he didn't say more than three sentences to me. In fact, my observations were that most of it was spent arguing or dictating his wishes to his entourage.

I didn't know in what circumstances Harry died in 1994, but I did know that the industry, and his fans, missed a talent that was rare even in the seventies. In the new century his special kind of talent will become more rare because the industry has changed its priorities. The emphasis has moved from pure musical talent to a multimedia fashion statement. The harbinger of the change was the punk era. Managers such as Malcolm McLaren saw that the power of television and the visual image, with a sprinkling of antisocial behaviour, could become the perfect publicity machine. They spent their lives making it come true, and the rest is history.

My last work with Richard Perry was arrangements for

Diana Ross in 1977 for the Motown label. The orchestrations were for the songs 'Too Shy to Say', written by Stevie Wonder, and 'Come In from the Rain', written by Carol Bayer Sager and Melissa Manchester. I admired Diana's work, and the fact that she eventually broke away from the Motown label showed how much she desired to make her own stamp. Like Stevie Wonder, she wanted to establish an individual personality, and the Motown formula had a stranglehold on the artists' material and style that had a suffocating effect on them. They used wonderful musicians and arrangers, but far too often the fast numbers began to sound as if it didn't matter who sang the songs. The formula was rigid. The ballads were given greater independence, and this allowed the artists to show their various talents in their individual way.

I noticed that Diana moved to RCA Records in 1981 and had her top ten hit 'Why Do Fools Fall in Love'. Although Stevie Wonder and Marvin Gaye were both on the Tamla label, they had strong writing gifts. Their individual talents were allowed to develop without the need to conform to any preconceived formula. The same freedom applied to Michael Jackson, who, at the end of the seventies, moved from Motown to the Epic label. It was always important that Motown and the formula existed because they allowed an opportunity for the black artists to develop their talent. They also created a shop window for their talent to be seen and heard. A visual style was also created that became a formula for the less talented. The inclusion of a line of people dancing clone-like movements behind the main artist became a paramount requisite throughout the world.

Unfortunately, this often diverted the audience's attention from noticing that the main artist had very little talent, and the lead singer would probably not have sustained their attention had they performed alone. Throughout the eighties and the nineties this formula persisted in Britain, and I wondered what had happened to the incredible performing and writing talent of the late sixties and the golden decade of the seventies.

Paul Samwell-Smith was involved with the production of the two American artists Paul and Carly Simon. In 1971 he produced the album Anticipation for Carly, which I thought was one of the best productions of the decade. The album had clarity, space and a richness that was rarely found on solo albums of the period. It was Paul's method to piece together slowly a jigsaw of sound, listening constantly to layer after layer of colour until the finished product was crystal clear. Carly was an attractive woman and was physically absolutely stunning. She had the same magnetic aura as Joni Mitchell, and her presence always took centre stage when she was accompanied by others. I imagined that any man who met either of the ladies would fall madly in love, or in lust, with them within a few minutes of their encounter. It was frightening at times because the kind of presence that Carly had was definitely a form of power, and it left most of the recording crew completely exposed.

I found it interesting that the writing of the two women had much in common. The content of their lyrics was almost entirely about themselves and their lovers. Carly's lyrics and melodies were delicately constructed and she was an expert at expressing her innermost feelings. Individual relationships were always the topic of the moment, and having met her I was not surprised. I thought that Paul was the perfect soulmate for Carly because their sensitivities were very similar. Her writing talent needed someone who would make the sounds around her spacious, as so many producers often filled the sound spectrum to such an extent that the words of the artists were fighting with everything else on the disc.

Carly's speaking voice reminded me of dark chocolate, and whenever she spoke everyone in the studio stopped what they were doing and just listened with glazed eyes. I remember that she sang the title song for one of the Bond films and the composer telephoned me from the USA and asked me to arrange it. He was a well-known arranger and I was surprised that he had called me at all. His manner was very superior and I declined his offer and said that I didn't like the song. I didn't think that anyone should be taken for granted, and a little humility was required by someone asking for a favour.

The experience with Paul Simon was completely different

and quite amazing. I was exposed to the kind of wealth and wastage that I found when working with Harry Nilsson. I arranged a song called 'American Tune', on the There Goes Rhymin' Simon album and I never saw such opulence. Time was unlimited and a day, a week or a month was of no consequence. The studio fees were £1,000 a day, which was quite expensive in the seventies. Paul used Morgan Studios, which was owned by my favourite drummer, Barry Morgan. I was granted a free hand in choosing the number of musicians for the session. Only strings were necessary because Simon had asked a keyboard and bass player to record before the string session. Jean Roussel, who was Cat Stevens' keyboard player, was rehearsing with Paul when I arrived to discuss matters. and it sounded rather good by the time I left the studio. Chris Lawrence, an exceptional bass player, was standing by with his acoustic bass, which was lying on the floor next to the piano, still in its case. Two days later I returned to the studio to discuss some points about the arrangement with Paul. I couldn't believe my eyes. Paul was still rehearsing the keyboard part with Jean, which should have been ready two days before. Chris had not taken his bass out of its case and I could see the frustration on the faces of both the musicians. It was not my place to comment on their frustration because they could have said something to Paul had they wished to. In any event, they were being paid to be there, although in my experience musicians enjoyed playing and creating rather than being subjected to boredom.

The strings were recorded three days later. When I arrived at the studio the session was gripped by slight panic. Paul had not been satisfied with the earlier results, as Chris hadn't yet got his bass out. All that Paul had was an acoustic guitar and a guide vocal on the tape, a copy of which had been sent to me a week earlier to do the arrangement. Paul told me not to worry. He said he could record the strings and complete any additions when he returned to America. The recording of the strings went well and we all left the studio feeling satisfied.

The next time I heard the song was after I bought the album. The sleeve stated that there were three rhythm players on the track, including Grady Tate on drums. The only musician audible was Grady, who was so far back in the mix that his presence was negligible. The song became voice, guitar and strings, which I was told years later received an award. I mention this incident to illustrate how different people worked in creating an album and the luxury that some people had in being able to afford as much time and money as they wished to finish a project because they were a successful artist. Those in less favourable circumstances would have been expected to complete the recording in three hours. A month was the average time given by companies for producers to finish a project for a new artist. If the company sold a great deal of albums the artist would be allowed to take as much time as he or she wished to finish a project. This method sounded logical for good business, but had the relatively unknown artists been given more time a better product would probably have increased its selling power.

The only embarrassing situation I had with Paul Samwell-Smith involved two sisters, Maggie and Terre Roche, who were protégés of Paul Simon. They had sung harmony lines on his 'Was a Sunny Day' track. Paul invited me to his home for dinner one evening and they were there when I arrived. Simon had asked Paul to produce an album for the girls, and after a delicious meal the girls began to talk about their prospective album. They began to tell me what kind of arrangements they heard on their songs and how they wanted me to write them. All this was new to me because Paul hadn't mentioned the girls or the project before I met them.

The girls had a very confident and rather dictatorial attitude about them, and I took an instant dislike to them because I really didn't appreciate being taken for granted. I stopped the conversation abruptly by telling them that they were talking to the wrong person. They were so surprised at my comment that they never spoke another word. It was obvious that they were not accustomed to someone speaking to them so directly and the atmosphere became rather tense. I felt that it was time to leave, so I thanked Paul and his wife for a lovely meal and quickly departed.

It was always embarrassing in circumstances like that

because it wasn't my intention to hurt anyone. I felt sorry for Paul and the girls for putting them in that position, but a lesson needed to be learnt that it wasn't productive to take people for granted because it showed a lack of respect. I was pleased that Paul and I worked together after that event and things were fine between us. Paul apologised for putting me in that situation and said that it had never occurred to him that I might react in that way. He also admitted that working with the girls was a complete nightmare. It seemed that I didn't miss anything by not being involved with the project, so I sighed with relief and thanked my lucky stars that my guardian angel was still looking after me.

* * *

Two sheep were walking in a field. "Baaaaaa!" said the first sheep. "Damn!" said the second, "I was going to say that."

CHAPTER 10

It was through Richard Perry, a very successful producer, that I met Art Garfunkel. The project was Art's 1975 Breakaway album for CBS Records. Art was a very quiet, intelligent man, and it was not always easy to talk to him because you felt that you were bursting in on his silence. He had a great sense of humour, but there was a distant quality about him that made it difficult for me to break through his outer layer. I suppose, like me, he wasn't very good at small talk, and felt it was better just to say nothing than to speak and say nothing. He had a fair complexion and looked more like a college student than a professional singer. He had a gentle nature and always seemed to me to be thinking serious thoughts. I did like his craftsmanship though, and I thought the feeling was mutual.

Art's choice of material was always first class. There was a fragile touch to the lyrics he sang that was in keeping with his personality. The album had been recorded in many studios, in Los Angeles, New York and London, finally being mixed back in Los Angeles, which was the normal way Richard Perry worked. There was definitely a butterfly quality in his genes that produced movement in all directions. It is possible that Art and Richard worked well together because they were opposites. Art was cool, calm and collected, while Richard was a volcano of nervous energy. It has been said that opposites often attract each other, and it was certainly successful in this case.

'I Only Have Eyes for You' was a number one hit in the British charts in September of that year and reached number eighteen in the USA. Art had a very smooth way of singing, and I think the quality of his voice lent itself to the sensitive ballad genre, a good example being the 'Bridge Over Troubled Waters' track. Using his own voice for backing harmonies augmented the feeling of pathos on his albums, creating a consistency of colour in the sound. There was sadness in the colour of his voice that was very attractive. Using different voices for backing singing tends to create separate levels of colour and often detracts your attention from the main vocal.

There are not many artists who would choose the kind of material that is on the Breakaway album. Nearly all the songs have the quality of longing and a delicacy that is not common practice on the American rock and roll scene. Songs like 'Waters of March', 'Looking for the Right One' and 'The Same Old Tears on a New Background' were not the kind of songs your average artist wanted to record. Perhaps because Art didn't write his own songs he had a much wider range of material to choose from. It was certainly true that the problem with being a singer-songwriter was that you were limiting yourself from all the wonderful songs that had been written by other people. I met very few singer-songwriters who would sing songs they hadn't written.

Many of the best session musicians played on Art's albums. Sometimes well-known artists would also make a guest appearance because they liked what Art was doing. Guitarists Lee Ritenour and Steve Cropper, and drummers Russ Kunkel and Jim Gordon, gave their services, and on some tracks the backing singing was done by Graham Nash, David Crosby and Toni Tennille, artists in their own right, who gave their services willingly for someone they respected. The type of material Art offered me was always a challenge. I knew that the time I spent creating subtle colours for the orchestra would not be wasted on people who actually didn't hear them. Sometimes an arranger would be offered work because they had worked for well-known, successful artists rather than for the talent they possessed. In the wrong hands a person's work could be destroyed by insensitive mixing at the final stages of production.

Some 13 years later I worked on another Garfunkel album called Lefty. On the front cover was a picture of Art playing baseball in his backyard when he was a young boy. You could not mistake Art's face for any other child's, and it is amazing how little some people change physically over the years. The album was produced by Geoff Emerick, who engineered many of the early Beatles albums. Geoff and his lady took me to the Waldorf Hotel (which is similar to the London Ritz) for tea, and it was interesting to see the wealthy New Yorkers in their latest fashions. Strange as it may seem, people in the music industry that had a creative part to play always seemed to wear casual denim clothes. Regardless of their wealth, denim appeared to be the creative uniform of most artists, engineers and producers.

Always remember that our response to music is subjective, and one man's meat is another man's poison. Ten people listening to the disc would probably hear different things, for our perception is wonderfully unique and there is no right or wrong in the matter. There were critics who weren't very kind to Art, labeling much of the material as sentimental. Of course, there are critics who specialise in being negative for most of their professional lives. The two main reasons for this are that they know they have a degree of power and they love to exercise it, and their impotence in terms of talent makes them jealous of creative people.

Critics are first and foremost journalists, who have a column to write no matter what. I once read a review of a live performance of someone, and during the show the critic was in the theatre bar drinking with me the whole time. When I met him later I questioned him about his critique and he laughed, shrugged his shoulders, and walked away. The problem was that it was so easy to criticise and many people really took their words as gospel truths. On reading a reputable paper's music critic for many years, I soon came to realise that he knew next to nothing about music. Each week he would write about the costume, the scenery, the make-up, in fact anything except the music. I felt like writing to the editor, but there was no point, as it was doubtful that the letter would ever see the light of day.

Speaking of critics, there is a lovely story about the classical composer Sibelius. He lived to a ripe old age and had pupils in composition until his late retirement. In his last lesson to every class he would give a little speech to help his young composers on their way. "Now pupils," he would say, "there is only one thing of any importance I wish to say to you. Don't ever worry over what the critics say about your work .... There has never been a monument erected in the name of a critic." I thought it was a very wise statement indeed, and people who have the talent to create should heed its meaning.

There is an amusing story to tell about the last association I had with Art. It was to do with the next album Art was making. He asked me to write five arrangements for the work and told me that he would be in London in a month's time to record the sessions. I worked feverishly for two weeks to complete the arrangements, and just when I had reached the last bars of the fifth song the telephone rang. It was Art, who sounded very stressed out, and he bellowed down the phone, "How much do you charge me for your arrangements?" I told him I charged the same amount for each arrangement as the last two albums. I could feel the perspiration running down his face. "Everybody is ripping me off," he shouted. "I've just found out that many people are taking advantage of me." I didn't know what to say, and Art mumbled something about recording the strings in New York rather than London. He then slammed the phone down and I was left in mid-air wondering what was going to happen.

I decided that no matter what took place I was not going to New York and the arrangements were not leaving my hands until I had been paid. A week later I received a call from an executive of Columbia Records. He seemed very apologetic and asked me if the arrangements were completed. He assured me that Art had been under a great deal of strain lately and he meant no harm. I thought it was interesting that Art didn't call me himself, but he was probably frightened of rejection. The executive told me that the company had booked a large orchestra and a studio in New York, and the session was to take place in five days' time.

It was obvious from the phone call that Art wanted my arrangements and that nobody in the States had been asked to write more to replace mine. Yet he did not want me to conduct the American session, as then we would have to meet face to face, and that might cause some embarrassment. I told the CBS executive that they could have the arrangements provided that I was paid in advance, in cash. He said he would get back to me. I knew I was in a strong position because the studio and the musicians had been booked, and to cancel everything at short notice would have cost the company several thousand dollars.

Two days later the executive called and asked me to give the arrangements to a representative from CBS London, who would then send them express by air. There was no mention of payment. There were only three days to go before the session and I refused. He was very worried and told me once again that he would get back to me. The next day he called and said he had arranged for me to take the arrangements to the London office, where I would be paid on arrival. It was a two-hour car journey, but it was worth it to see a large company that had lost control of a situation.

I arrived at midday and was shown into a large office. The man behind the desk said that he knew nothing about the affair. I explained the situation and after an hour he told me that he had received confirmation from New York to pay me. However, he said that he didn't have enough money in the office to make the payment in cash and offered to write me a cheque. I told him that if no cash was forthcoming there would be no arrangements, simple as that. It was wonderful to see his reaction, and I'll leave you to imagine the situation. Someone ended up rushing to the bank just before closing time in order to avoid being responsible for a prospective catastrophe. Eventually the cash came and I handed over the arrangements. Had the scores not been sent on the next day's flight they would have arrived too late for the session. Weeks later I received a letter from Art written from his 'brownstone' house in New York City. He apologised for the whole affair and said that he really did prefer the London musicians (and their conductor), which I thought was a very kind thing to say. It is not every artist who will own up to being fallible, and for that reason I still have the letter today, to remind me of what a generous man Art really is.

One of the nicest people I ever met was Neil Sedaka. He was very natural, with no airs and graces, and he was always smiling and had a positive attitude. He was a true professional and I used to meet him at his apartment in Park Street, just behind London's Park Lane. The album I did orchestrations for was called Sedaka's Back. It was released on Elton John's Rocket Records label in Europe and on the MCA label in the USA. The European element was produced by 10cc at their Strawberry Studios and they did a fine job, as usual.

Neil had one of those high tenor voices that one would expect a small child, or an angel, to have, and whatever the background it would soar above it all and be as clear as a bell. Neil had his first hit singles in the late fifties with 'The Diary' and 'Oh! Carol' and had been well established for 20 years before we met. He encouraged everyone with positive vibrations and suggestions, and he never interfered when others were trying out something to improve the total performance. I always found that the people who had the most talent allowed other talented people free rein in their own areas of expertise, and Neil was no exception.

The songs that Neil wrote fell into two categories. There were the ballads like 'Solitaire', which had meaningful lyrics and melodies that one could remember after one hearing, and then there were the faster numbers, which were a product of Neil's generation and background. The latter songs had a distinctive fifties feel with a two-beat seesaw style. Much of the lyrics were about moon and June and young teenage relationships. The style had a particular coy American way about it, which was to identify the very early stages of white rock and roll. Buddy Holly's songs were a good example of the genre.

When sung by Neil, with that high, delicate voice, his rendition seemed to have an extra dimension of sadness. He told me that his young life wasn't always rosy and he had a difficult childhood, but his professional success allowed him to relax and smile with confidence. Many lyrics in his early songs related to the agony of teenage unrequited love and the problems of early relationships. Many artists that I worked with had difficult childhoods, and perhaps that's why they were attracted to music, for the medium allowed them to express some of the frustration they may have felt while growing up.

After Sedaka's Back, Neil performed a concert at the Royal Festival Hall in London. He chose The Royal Philharmonic Orchestra to accompany him and I conducted the concert.

Polydor Records thought that it would be a great idea to record Neil's performance and release an album of the evening's concert. It was a competitive move against the Rocket Records album, but there was a problem, in my opinion, with the approach that Polydor took to record the live performance. Studio recording was one thing, but live concert recording was another. When a live recording took place a great deal of preparation needed to be done. I wasn't certain how much experience the recording technicians had in recording live concerts, but I was about to find out.

A large hall, belonging to a church on the west side of London, was used for rehearsing the orchestra. This took place during the afternoon and evening of the day before the concert. People were rather tense because there was a great deal of music to rehearse in a relatively short time. I had a feeling of foreboding that afternoon because I hadn't met the sound crew. Past experience had shown me that unless the technicians were experts in live recording the slightest neglect could have disastrous results. A live performance didn't allow for errors, for the show must go on, and only once in 30 years was a performance of mine forced to stop, which I will relate later in this chapter.

I arrived at the venue in good time the next day to find that the mobile recording staff were setting up the microphones for the evening performance. I was amazed to see that the entire orchestra had only been allotted three microphones. The drum kit had five, and the remainder of the rhythm section were amply supplied with microphones. I began to wonder whether the recording crew knew what they were doing. Although I should have let sleeping dogs lie, it was not in my nature to keep quiet.

I went to the sound producer and told him about my concerns, as I thought that it would seriously limit the amount of control he would have when mixing the finished work. I cannot print what he said to me, and I was so angry that I told him to take my name off the album cover. The company acknowledged my wishes and I never heard from Neil again. I never discovered what the producer said to Neil, but it must have been more than the truth, for Neil was a gentleman and we had a good working relationship. People had their own agendas and insecurities, but it was obvious that my concerns were justified as soon as I listened to the album.

The concert went extremely well, for Neil was an excellent performer. His piano arrangements were superb and often reminded me of the artistry of Liberace. There was such a delicacy in his voice, and in his playing, that I felt they might break at any moment, but they never did. His power rose to meet the challenge of every song, for he had a way of taking the audience with him on an inevitable journey. The album, though, was a disappointment for me. Neil's voice and piano were crystal clear, but the remainder of the orchestra, with the exception of the bass guitar, were so distant in the final mix that they sounded as if they were playing in a barn 200 metres from Neil's piano. It was obvious that the sound producer didn't take advice from anyone, which suggests insecurity, or stupidity, and I thought that a wonderful performance given by all was ruined by incompetence.

The album sleeve stated that Wayne Bickerton produced the album and supervised the mixing sessions. I'm sorry Wayne, but the whole venture was a waste of money. What was more important, the project didn't enhance Neil's reputation. I never understood why a record company as successful as Polydor spent thousands of pounds on musicians, arrangers, art-workers and rhythm sections, only to destroy the quality of the work for the public. I never knew how many albums were sold, but if the company got its money back I would be very surprised.

Of course there was a hidden agenda in this story. Executives of a company should temper their egos and not jeopardise a product in order to get their name printed on an album sleeve. If the reader believes I'm being hard on the person concerned because I have a hidden agenda, the reader is wrong, because there was always more at stake than the artist's reputation. Comparing the music industry to the film industry, a musician's popularity was often only as tenable as their last association. Being linked with a product of poor quality could affect his or her future status in the industry. That was why I had my name withdrawn from the sleeve. The action cost me a great deal. If Neil ever gets to read this book I hope he will understand my preference. There was absolutely nothing personal in my decision and I have always held him in the deepest regard.

There were many who hid their light under a bush. One such person was Stéphane Grappelli. I met him in Landsdowne Studios in West London, where he was making an album of contemporary songs, which surprised me because I had only heard his jazz renditions. He was nearly 70, and a gentler and friendlier person I couldn't imagine. He spoke quietly and walked around the studio as if he was deep in thought. Whenever anyone spoke to him he would seem startled and stop walking, as though he'd been awakened from a world full of dreams.

He did things that really surprised all of the technical team, such as slipping out of the studio and buying everyone a bar of chocolate. He said it was good for the brain and helped to raise our energy levels. One afternoon, when we needed to take a long break because of technical problems, he wandered over to the piano and began to play. He displayed a brilliant technique and enormous sensitivity. I sat down next to him and didn't move for at least 20 minutes. When the technicians were ready he sauntered over to his violin and smiled at everyone, saying, "Shall I make us all a cup of tea?" I hadn't been aware that he could play the piano and I felt that people like him were rare. His outward demeanour and humility belied his hidden talents.

When I questioned him later that afternoon he just smiled and shrugged his shoulders. I knew that many musicians played more than one instrument, but Stéphane was so well known as a jazz violinist that it never occurred to me that he could be so proficient as a pianist. He wasn't someone who could just play the piano, for his technique was such that he could have been a professional pianist of the highest quality. The kind of execution needed to play jazz violin didn't show the degree of sensitivity he possessed, but solo piano playing demonstrated his musicality to the full. He played classical pieces as well as contemporary songs, and his love for music was obvious to everyone.

His attitude to everybody he spoke to was a lesson in social behaviour. He made a person feel necessary and important.

From the assistant engineer, who spent most of his time making tea for everyone, to the owner of the studio, it was plain to see that his regard for them was the same. He showed that he valued every moment he was with them, and that was rare indeed. During the breaks from work he would sit down with me and discuss all sorts of things. Music was included, of course, but he was widely read and wanted to know my opinion about lots of things. Some of his questions left me completely baffled, but I tried to keep up with his pace and enthusiasm for discussion.

Stéphane told me a story about an event that had happened years before I met him. He was taking a break from work and was touring France in his car. He entered a small village and found a quiet, unobtrusive hotel. One evening the owner told him that they were having a birthday party for his daughter and wondered whether he would like to join the other guests. Stéphane accepted the invitation, but to his surprise everyone was asked to contribute to the evening's entertainment. When it came to his turn he sat at an old piano, which was in the living room, and played a very well known French folk song. The next morning, as he was leaving, the owner thanked him for joining in the fun. It was obvious that the owner didn't know who Stéphane was and was not aware of his reputation. At the end of the story he smiled and went to get a cup of coffee. I believed it was the way he liked things.

When I thought about what some people would do to gain 15 minutes of fame, the story reflected exactly the kind of person Stéphane was and the extent of his humility. He was considered great enough to partner such legends as Julian Bream, the renowned guitarist, and Yehudi Menuhin, the world-famous violinist. There was also his lifetime partner Django Reinhardt, who was able to play his guitar so masterfully with only three fingers on his right hand. I thought these people were marvellous because after thousands of hours of practising their art their fame didn't inflate their ego. He said that he wanted to do another album with only a string orchestral background and asked me if I would be interested in working with him again. I was delighted and readily agreed, but it never transpired. It was something I have always regretted.

Stéphane's humility reminded me of Glenn Gould, a Canadian from Toronto, who was one of the greatest pianists that ever took breath. He played the music of J.S. Bach like nobody else I knew, and there was a degree of eccentricity about him. He always wore a cloth cap and mittens on his hands because he hated the cold. Even in summer he would wear a scarf and an overcoat. He really looked odd and people must have thought him strange indeed. He used to walk in the woods for hours alone, and he probably found people rather hard to digest. He had one of the brightest minds in music, and it was obvious that he had been gifted with 'The Touch' that initiates genius.

* * *

A man was having problems satisfying his wife in the connubial bliss department. He went to his doctor, who advised him to observe animals, such as cats. Three weeks later he returned to his doctor, who asked him how he was getting on with his marriage. "Well doctor," he said, "everything is fine, but we keep falling off the roof."

CHAPTER 11

Squeeze was comprised of a unique group of people and I thought that they were one of the most intelligent British bands of the early eighties. I did some arrangements on three albums: Argybargy in 1980, East Side Story in 1981 and Sweets from a Stranger in 1982. The studio was situated in a mews in London that would have been a stable in Regency and Victorian times. It had a country feel about it, with a loft, and you could imagine the straw and hay being moved around in abundance while the ever moving horses waited for their meals.

The band consisted of Glenn Tilbrook on lead guitar, keyboards and vocals; Chris Difford on rhythm guitar and vocals; John Bentley on bass; Gilson Lavis on drums; and, last but not least, Jools Holland on keyboards and vocals. The boys, for they were all very young, had signed with A&M, which was a very prestigious label, and it had the foresight to record some of the best acts in the world. Being an American company it opened the door to a vast American audience, and the band toured widely and sold a great number of albums.

Glenn and Jools wrote one of the songs, 'Wrong Side of the Moon', and the remaining ten numbers were written by Glenn and Chris. The lyrics and the music were an unconventional marriage. The stories were a perceptive observation of everyday situations and simple things that happen between people, and yet the music was quite dissonant (strange notes added to a chord to make it sound unusual) and foreboding. There was development in the structure of the songs, which put them on a grandiose scale, although the listener was not bombarded with "look how clever we are". The Shakespearean phrase, "more matter with less art" could not be aimed at Squeeze, for the content of their material was equal to the style in which they presented their efforts.

I found the mix of simple, everyday occurrences, which in themselves seemed quite boring, and the strange melodic and harmonic structures really fascinating. There was an erratic quality to the music that made me feel that I didn't know what was going to happen next. The ideas incorporated in the background sounds to the lyrics were always fresh and inventive. The rhythm was always very tight, thanks to Gilson Lavis's drumming and John Bentley's bass playing, and this acted as a firm springboard from which the arrangements could travel without ever seeming reckless or out of control.

The track I was asked to work on was 'I Think I'm Go Go'. The lyrics were quite cryptic and indicative of modern life with no real sense of direction. I asked Glenn where all these ideas came from, as I didn't know any other band that had such an eccentric perception of everyday life. He smiled and said, "Well, if you live every day, every day, you must see how crazy life can be. I think many people go through life with their eyes shut." The arrangements were spacious, symphonic and dissonant. I really enjoyed writing for tracks that gave me a challenge and allowed me to use techniques that my formal training had taught me. Cat Stevens' '18th Avenue' and 10cc's 'Feel the Benefit' were such tracks.

The band loved to work together. They joked and teased each other all the time. On one occasion someone wedged the door of the toilet, making it impossible for Glenn to open it, and he was trapped for ten minutes before he was set free. Another time salt was put in a cup of coffee instead of sugar, which made the unsuspecting drinker quite sick. But everyone took these events with good humour and their friendship was as solid as a rock.

In the studio the band were very relaxed. They waited like well-behaved children to see what goodies I had brought them. They never tried to take over and change any part of the arrangement, which some artists are prone to do. This can often waste a great deal of time. They were clever enough to know that if the writing was sympathetic to the track they could use whatever they needed. This kind of cooperation made working a pleasure, and it probably got the best results for the end product.

The second album, East Side Story, had a change of keyboard player. Paul Carrick joined the band to replace Jools, who left to concentrate on a solo career and television presenting. Every time I was asked to do something for them they had a different keyboard player in the band. Perhaps the preparation and input of ideas were so taken care of by Glenn and Chris that they felt left out of things. With regard to Jools there were so many commitments for him that it became impossible for him to find time to record in the studio. It is important to remember that making an album could take months to complete. Some mega bands can take as long as two years to finish a project.

Glenn and Paul co-wrote a song with Elvis Costello, who was the co-producer with Roger Bechirian. I wonder how much influence Elvis had in shaping the song. It had all the usual "aahs" in the background, and I'm surprised that some well-known black artist didn't snap it up and in their own inimitable style make a huge hit with it. Elvis's father was a fine trumpet player and we had played jazz together many years before. He was also a fine singer and had joined a well-known big band when ballroom dancing was the fashion of the day.

Another song was co-written by Elvis and Glenn, called 'There's No Tomorrow', and I think it is one of the saddest songs I have ever heard. Glenn's voice suited the lyrics perfectly and he created an atmosphere of pathos that made me want to throw myself off of the nearest bridge. There were some excellent backward tapes swirling in the background, which gave the track a very eerie feeling. I was always amazed at the breadth of emotion that the band's songs evoked in me, and that was the probable reason for their success. I miss the humour they displayed, for being serious about what you were doing didn't mean you had to take yourself too seriously.

The penultimate track on the album was 'Vanity Fair'. Glenn had written a song about the very essence of womanhood, concerning whether the tools in a girl's vanity box made her beautiful or not. Glenn thought beauty created that way could only be skin deep. But the girl had dreams, as we all do, and the advertising media were going to make really sure that we kept on having them. I created a truly 'classical' arrangement for this track. It sounded weird because a contemporary girl was being observed within an eighteenth-century background. The juxtaposition of the two elements was strange indeed, but nearly 30 years later it still makes me smile.

The third album had another keyboard player named Don Snow. Perhaps the demand for them was greater than for other instrumentalists and larger temptations led them away. I sometimes felt that guitar players only used the keyboard instrument as an insignificant colour in their arrangements. The guitar was self-sufficient after all, and it was capable of any melodic or rhythmic functions required. Whatever the reason for so many keyboard changes, it didn't interfere with the overall vision of the band.

The production team had changed too, and the band was sharing the honours with Phil McDonald. The first thing I noticed about the sound of the disc was the cleanness of the production. It was as if the band had been taken to hospital and sanitised. In the earlier albums the band wrapped around the voice, giving the illusion of a live performance. There was a harder, grittier sound that reminded me of Janis Joplin, which seemed to be more relevant to the bands style of writing. With this album, although Glenn's voice sounded wonderful, the dark side and the mystery were missing.

The first arranged track was 'When the Hangover Strikes'. It was one of those three o'clock in the morning, smoky nightclub kind of songs, when the blues is at its best. I could imagine Peggy Lee doing a wonderful rendition of the title, and it would have probably made a good film theme. In the last verse some muted strings enter in the good old Hollywood style and you can feel the smoke in the room.

The first track on the second side was called 'Black Coffee'. The backing vocalists were none other than Elvis Costello and Paul Young, who coo in the background in the Nashville idiom, but in a terribly sanitised way. The roughness of Sue and Sunny on Joe Cocker's 'With a Little Help from My Friends' was missing, and I know the boys were capable of delivering the goods. It was a case of being blinded by another's reputation. When the band relied on themselves to produce their work, everything was fine. When they engaged others, it wasn't always the best thing for their vision. The amazing thing was that the band split up when they were at their height and doing world tours. They packed New York's Madison Square Garden at the time, but later re-formed with Lavis, Jools and Keith Wilkinson.

It was certainly a pleasure listening to these albums again after nearly 30 years, and I will always remember their kindness. They were very courteous in the studio, and whenever we had meetings to discuss the tracks they showed an eagerness that was very refreshing. They went on to create many more albums, and everyday life seemed better because of their efforts.

I met 10cc on three occasions: at their Strawberry North Studios with The Moody Blues; at the Manor Studios, owned by Richard Branson, the Virgin magnate; and at Strawberry South Studios, where I arranged some tracks on 10cc's Deceptive Bends album. They were very experienced musicians and technicians and they had known each other for such a long time that they worked diligently without having to say a word to each other. The Moody Blues outing was quite a first for me, for the band turned up in a stretch limo, and we travelled from London to the north of England in ridiculous splendour. The driver pulled into a motorway service station to get some refreshments and we had to park in the truck parking area because the car's length prohibited us from using the normal car park. A lorry driver parked alongside us seemed to be amused by the spectacle and shouted, "My God, is this the new style of coal truck they're making these days?"

I felt embarrassed because it seemed to me that we had so much opulence amid so much poverty. I was certain that the band never gave the matter a second thought because they were used to being stared at and opulence was part of their trademark. Although the band seemed self-possessed they hardy spoke to each other throughout the journey. Some bands stayed together only for financial reasons and the lifestyle to which they had become accustomed. I felt that this was such a band. All kinds of people entered the music industry and wealth often made incompatible colleagues tolerate each other. In different circumstances the same people would probably never form an alliance.

The original 10cc had split up the year earlier. Graham Gouldman and Eric Stewart had stayed together, while Kevin Godley and Lol Creme had become partners. Eric was one of the best engineers in the business and had the great number one hit single 'I'm Not In Love'. Justin Hayward always seemed aloof to me, but Ray Thomas, with whom I worked at a later date, was a strange person indeed. He asked me to produce his From Mighty Oaks album and I was invited to his home for dinner. His wife cooked a delicious meal for us that evening, but the atmosphere was electric. Their relationship was obviously in trouble and her attitude towards him was icy cold all evening. She made many derogatory remarks to him in front of her guests, which was not only embarrassing but also rude. I thought to myself, they have all this wealth and yet they seem unhappy. There were no children, so why stay together? It was none of my business, I know, but it didn't have to be displayed.

On the first day of recording, in Decca Studios in Hampstead, I told Ray that there was a day, some weeks ahead, when I would have to be absent in order to complete another engagement. He agreed to my suggestion and we began working with the rhythm section. Ray said that we could take as much time as we needed to finish the album and if we completed one track every two weeks he would be pleased. I was amazed because I was used to finishing two rhythm tracks each day, so the luxury of being able to revise things, if necessary, was indeed a blessing. Our contract was only a spoken one and I trusted that he would keep his word. The rhythm tracks were completed and the day came for my leave of absence, but Ray told me that I couldn't leave the studio. He acted like a spoilt child who was frightened of being left alone, and the musicians were dumbfounded. I was so angry that I left the studio and never returned.

I was told that Ray and the engineer finished the album, but there was no mention of the work I had done or any payment for the weeks I had worked. Later I met one of the guitar players from the sessions and he said that I should have stayed because the sessions took ages to complete and everyone had made a great deal of money. I shrugged my shoulders and replied that there were more important things in life than money, but somehow I don't think he believed me. I've always slept soundly in my bed and that was very important to me. What we did had consequences and the actions that we took determined who we were. In the end we had to live with ourselves and that was the only criterion.

I later went to the Manor to meet the other half of 10cc, Kevin and Lol. The Manor was one of the first farm studios, situated near Oxford. The studios there had living accommodation. Many small outbuildings were turned into apartments with kitchens, or people would be accommodated in rooms in the main house with a communal kitchen. Lol and Kevin were working on their latest project, which involved sound coming from four speakers. This might be commonplace today, but in the seventies it was something new. The speakers were placed in the corners of the studio ceiling, so their effect was quite stunning.

It was at the Manor that I met my old friend and student buddy, John Cale. We had studied together at London University in the early sixties and he had made a lasting impression on me. He was a disciple of John Cage, an avant-garde musician who wanted to shock the establishment with new ideas. He was probably the first perceptual artist in music. Cale promoted Cage's works throughout our college days, but on a trip to the Tanglewood summer music school in the USA he stayed in New York and met people who were under the banner of Andy Warhol. In particular he met Lou Reed, and the band named Velvet Underground was born. The name was derived from a pulp paperback, and a significant part of rock history was made.

John Cale was a closed book. He was an excellent keyboard and viola player who, in his younger years, had played the organ in the church of his Welsh town. John said that he had always wanted to leave home and experience the big, wide world, and he certainly achieved his desire. To stay in New York when the only thing he possessed was a return air ticket to London was a brave thing to do. But luck was on his side, for the Warhol clan was the perfect refuge for John's perception of the world he wanted. Eventually, his many talents were recognised through his association with the band, and he never looked back.

The day at the Manor was pleasant for both of us because we spoke about old times. He didn't really need me to play simple percussion parts because he was more than capable of playing the parts himself. I surmised that he was feeling a little nostalgic, as I was part of the home he had left so many years before. It was also the only time I met Richard Branson, a quietly spoken young man who was interested in everything and everyone around him. He was immediately likeable, but there was shyness about him and I felt that he needed drawing out from his own perpetual observations. I don't believe that anyone had imagined that he would become the head of such an enormous empire, and yet when I see him being interviewed on television I still sense that inner shyness in him. It has been said by some psychiatrists that a person's essential nature is already formed by the time the child has reached the age of seven, for better or for worse.

I sometimes wondered what the artists and musicians of the sixties and seventies were doing with their lives in the twenty-first century. In 'serious' music and the other arts many artists continued to work and create well into their seventies and eighties, which were ripe old ages indeed. The popular songsmith, however, seemed to be cursed with a relatively short lifespan as far as creating successful work was concerned. There were exceptions, but perhaps this was because fashion in general appeared to change about every decade in the song field in terms of bands, and that didn't seem to happen quite so much in other forms of communication. The exceptions - The Stones, Elton John, Rod Stewart, etc. - were notable, but these artists were rare.

Whatever the case, I was always impressed with bands with the same expertise as the Eagles, Little Feet, The Band or Steely Dan. On the European side of the Atlantic there were bands such as The Beatles, Genesis and Led Zeppelin. Where are their like today? Is it me, or the evolution of time? After the works of Bob Dylan, who wrote meaningful songs with three chords, every potential singer-songwriter thought that they could do the same thing just as well, if not better. Mass media and television exposure (when a performer looks good perhaps the talent doesn't matter too much) encouraged thousands of people to write their own songs and learn to play the guitar. 'Tin Pan Alley' was dead. This wasn't a negative thing in itself, but I think that the standard of creativity dropped considerably.

Part of the problem was the disc jockey scene. We then had a situation where the DJ or the presenter was more important than the artist (or so many of them believed). They had become celebrities, and people were famous for being famous. Groups had been manufactured and had made great wealth and fashion statements. The Monkees and The Spice Girls are excellent examples of this new tradition. The media had created a monster that wouldn't go away, and if I'm the only person on Earth who thinks so I beg the readers' pardon. Some people in the media justified these trends by telling us that they only gave the public what it wanted. I believe the public had little choice and that the people in power gave the public the cheapest, lowest denominator. It was a question of shepherds and sheep. The majority of the public lapped up whatever it was fed. One thing was certain, the snowball was rolling down the hill and 'progress' was rearing its ugly head. No one could stop it unless we, the ordinary consumer, demanded something more substantial than the passive game show, the reality show and the regurgitation of family problems that are hung on the washing line for all to see.

* * *

My dog talks in its sleep. A friend came to stay at my house for a weekend and was amazed to hear it shout, "My name is Albert Einstein, and I wonder at the stars." My friend was so shocked that he demanded an explanation. I assured him that everything was fine and retorted, "Don't concern yourself about it, just let sleeping dogs lie."

CHAPTER 12

One of my most satisfying associations was working with Randy VanWarmer. He was an American and, like Scott Walker, he came to London to find success in the UK. So I always think of him as a European experience. His mother, in fact, lived in Looe in Cornwall for many years, and we both visited her during the making of his first album. She lived in a beautiful old cottage overlooking the bay, and the view allowed her to see the fishing boats leave and return to the harbour. When the tourist season was over and the town returned to its natural self I could imagine that very little had changed for centuries. Randy's brother, Ron, lived in the USA and we met up whenever he came to London. He always wore suits and he gave me the impression that being a businessman was his primary interest.

The amazing thing about Randy's looks was that he had an ageless face. He had curly, fair hair and wore round glasses that reminded me of John Lennon. He looked like a 16-year-old kid when we were first introduced, and when we met some ten years later he looked exactly the same. I remember thinking that whatever he was taking I would love to get some of it, but I knew he was a clean-cut young man who had never taken anything stronger than an aspirin.

Randy was signed to Bearsville Records, which took its name from a small town near Woodstock, in upstate New York. It was owned by Albert Grossman, who had managed Janis Joplin and Bob Dylan in earlier days. He was what I call a lovable rogue, for you knew immediately you met him that you couldn't trust him farther than you could see him in matters of business. Yet there was something about him that made you like him. He was a hangover from the sixties revolution. He was a big man with a long grey ponytail down his back. He always wore a denim shirt and jeans, and he would send scouts out to see if any hotels would accept him wearing such clothes. Hotels were very conservative when it came to their clients, and even their restaurants had a dress code. A suit and tie were obligatory in most places, which may have changed in the twenty-first century.

Albert knew everybody that was worth knowing in the music industry. He lived in a wonderful wooden house in a Bearsville forest that was both large and yet cosy. It was full of interesting paraphernalia and was probably built in the nineteenth century. There were trees everywhere and it felt like the perfect retreat. It was rumoured that Albert owned the town. He had a theatre built in his name and much of his wealth was spent on memorial edifices so that he would never be forgotten. The problem was that he used other people's money.

I was approached by Ian Kimmet, who worked for Albert in London, and was asked to produce Randy's first album. Having met Randy, I knew it was going to be a pleasurable project. He was such a nice person, who trusted people completely, and his songwriting had a childlike, direct expression that allowed you to relate immediately to his lyrics. Our working together created a friendship that lasted 30 years, and his wife and soulmate Suzi was his manager and kindred spirit. They lived in Nashville so that Randy could pursue his writing talents. He collaborated with other writers, and this helped him to grow and develop different styles of musical construction. He made other albums after our collaboration and he always sent me a copy of his latest project.

The first album was called Warmer. It was the only time I recorded the rhythm tracks for an album in Nashville, USA, and it was certainly a learning experience for me. Luckily, Ian and Randy agreed that Nashville was the best place to record the album. He wanted an American feel to it, and there wasn't a better place in the States to achieve such a goal. Having an American company behind Randy obviously motivated this decision, as it was closer to home and the company could easily keep an eye on things as the recording progressed.

I learnt a great deal about American musicians and about the techniques used by the engineers during the making of the album. It would be true to say that both groups were more laid back than their European counterparts. They listened to the songs they were accompanying with a great deal more reverence, taking particular care over the degree of space they gave the lyrics. Often they would ask to hear the artist sing the songs two or three times before they made any suggestions or made any effort to play a single note.

There was a great feeling of co-operative spirit in Nashville, where everybody had some input to make before playing. Perhaps in Europe we relied too much on the musical director and the written notes, which made the arranger carry a tremendous burden and also limited the possibilities. Six heads were better than one if you wished to see a song from different perspectives, and I felt so lucky to have the opportunity to work with them. Their humility, like all great players, was a breath of fresh air to a stranger in a strange land. There were positive vibrations coming from them all the time, which was not always the case with rhythm sections I'd worked with on the eastern side of the Atlantic.

Kenny Malone played drums, and his sensitivity was a joy to us all. He would listen to a song with his eyes closed and then suggest the perfect pattern for the track. He was a quiet man and a little older than the other musicians, and I got the feeling that the guys treated him with the respect that a knowledgeable elder of a tribe would receive. Jack Williams was on bass and Shane Keister was the keyboard player. They were both exceptional players and their contribution to the album was immeasurable. My guitarist was Steve Gibson and my percussionist was my old friend Ray Cooper. The saxophone playing was performed by Stan Saltzman, a well-known and excellent musician from London.

The trio of keyboards, bass and drums had worked together a great deal in Nashville. In any music centre there was a small group of players who were the best performers in their area and their reputation always preceded them. They were constantly in demand and got to play together so often that they could read each other's minds. Players of this calibre were a gift to an arranger or producer. They not only gave the project what it needed, but they also saved valuable time and money because their sensitivity and technique allowed them to work quickly. This limited the amount of physical fatigue that could result from constantly explaining what you wanted the musicians to do.

There were several guitar players, keyboard players and percussion players on the album because some extra production was done by John Holbrook, who added some backing singers to some of the tracks, which I believe were recorded in London. This was a bone of contention for me because Ian and I had argued about adding different voices to the album. I wanted the sound of the disc to be homogeneous, which would make the album more personal. The sound of Randy's voice when used as a backing voice was perfect for his albums.

Randy was very capable when it came to singing his own harmonies, as the opening track 'Losing Out On Love' shows only too well, and I wanted that kind of uniformity throughout the album. After a conversation with Ian I felt that control of the project had been taken out of my hands. I guess I gave up when I should have been more persistent, but I couldn't handle the interference. I knew deep down that Ian wanted to be involved with a project that was going so well. Apart from mentions on keyboards and percussion, Ian and John were said to be responsible for the production of 'Call Me' and 'Forever Loving You' on the album. On listening to the tracks they seemed to be very much as I had left them, but when people were 3,000 miles from each other it was better to let sleeping dogs lie.

The hit single from the disc was 'Just When I Needed You Most'. Years later Randy told me that if I hadn't been adamant about the value of the song it would not have been chosen to be on the album. In the end they conceded to it being on the 'B' side of the single. It's amazing that the people in power didn't think the song was strong enough to be on the 'A' side and it was fortunate that the disc jockeys picked up on the track. It reached number four in the American charts and number nine in Britain.

While I was in Bearsville discussing the making of the album I met John Sebastian, whom I remembered from the movie Woodstock. We were in the local restaurant where all the musicians hung out, and as fate would have it he played auto harp on the introduction and solo of the single. I

111

noticed that many people were acknowledged for supporting Randy and that showed his generosity of spirit, which would not let him forget the people who had helped him in earlier times. Randy was like a child wandering around a technology factory. He trusted everyone in the studio. He asked hundreds of questions, and I never saw him raise his voice or be rude to anyone.

I mentioned earlier that Albert was a lovable rogue, and the royalty situation demonstrates exactly what I mean by that statement. When I received my contract from Bearsville Records one of the clauses stated that I wouldn't receive any royalties until Randy's expenses had been recovered. This meant that not only were the expenses of the recordings included in the clause, but also any personal expenses that Randy may have been given, including any advances against his own royalties. This was unheard of, and my royalties should have begun with the sale of the first record after my own advance. I telephoned Bearsville from London and was passed over to the company accountant. Having expressed my displeasure, he said in a cool fashion that if I didn't like the clause he would erase it from the contract. We are talking about tens of thousands of dollars here, and if I hadn't queried it I would have lost the money to the company within the blink of an eye. The business world was a jungle for creative people.

For the single to have reached number four in the American top ten charts it must have sold well over a million copies, but when I received my first royalty statement I was informed that the single had sold four hundred thousand copies. On querying the statement, I was told that the remaining copies were given away as promotional copies. Even an idiot wouldn't have believed that possibility, and I'm no idiot. I was lucky because I didn't need the money, but think of the people who have been taken advantage of who really have needed that money. Lovable or not, Albert was still a rogue.

Sometime later I met Albert backstage at an open-air concert in New York where Randy was performing, and he just smiled at me and said, "Del!" I couldn't be mad at him because there was something in his manner that was warm and very attractive. At the same time, I knew I would never be able to trust him again. I was told years later that he was on a flight to Nice for the annual MIDEM festival and fell asleep after eating his on-board meal. He never woke up again. He had a heart attack and an important music business personality was no more. To live right up to the last moment without the knowledge that it was your last day would be like going to sleep with the next morning taking a long time to arrive. With all that happened between us I still think of him with fond thoughts. If anyone has any money where he is, they'd better hold on to their purse and beware of that roguish smile.

Rosemary Clooney was a household name during the sixties and seventies. She was a beautiful actress and starred in such films as White Christmas, and she was one of the very few singers who sang in tune. I always think of her as the most peaceful artist I ever worked with. She had a calm quality that made it easy to talk to her, as if you had known her all your life. There was also a natural honesty about her that made her very open, and I felt that whatever had happened to her in her past she never felt bitter or secretive.

I was introduced to her through United Artists Records, and she came to London to make an album called Nice To Be Around. It was a fitting title for her album because it epitomised everything about her. She had a great sense of humour, spoke with a warm, quiet voice and was no trouble to anyone. She also had a generosity of spirit that was not always forthcoming in artists. I never heard her say a negative word about another person during the time I knew her, and that included visiting her at her home in Beverly Hills when I was working for Rod Stewart.

Rosemary gave beautiful performances on the album, but in my ignorance I arranged the songs as they were on the original artist's tracks. Thus it appeared that she was doing covers of other people's work and for that I'm eternally sorry. I always assumed that the American company thought the same thing, as it didn't get a great deal of promotion. It popped into my mind now and again over the years, and I would like to say that it was only my naivety at the time that made me do such a stupid thing. Had we met later, after I had gained more production experience, the product would have been different. I thought it was a good album and Rosemary deserved greater exposure from the publicity department. But these were matters over which we had no control, and many albums never reached a large audience because of company policy or company incompetence.

Needless to say, Rosemary didn't hold this against me, and on one of my visits to California to work with Rod she invited me to her home for lunch. She lived in one of the large houses in Beverly Hills, and all her neighbours were world-famous film stars. I remember she pointed out the houses owned by Kirk Douglas, Gary Cooper and James Stewart. It gave me a weird feeling because these people had been my childhood heroes, and here I was, only a stone's throw away from their homes.

Rosemary had been married to José Ferrer and had a large family. One of her sons played the drums for her when she did live performances. She was very proud of her family and its musical talents. The house was large but it felt very cosy. The permanent sunshine in California allowed the French windows to be open at all times, and it seemed that you were living both inside and out simultaneously.

After a while Rosemary told me that we were going to have lunch at one of her favourite restaurants. This pleased me because I wondered what kind of place she would choose. On our arrival I was surprised to find that it was a cosy little restaurant with no pretensions whatsoever. The food was excellent and we chatted about Rosemary's family. Suddenly she waved to someone across the room, and when I turned around to see who it was I couldn't believe my eyes. It was Ava Gardner. I had to pinch myself to make sure I wasn't dreaming.

Ava called us over to her table and I was absolutely delighted. She must have been in her early fifties, but she looked good enough to eat. She had a mop of black hair down to her shoulders and very bright eyes. She was wearing a black polo-neck sweater and filled it to perfection. Her voice was soft and she had a permanent smile when she talked. I was lost forever. The conversation veered towards social events that would be taking place the following week.

It was obvious that Rosemary and Ava were very close friends and had known each other for years. You could see that they liked each other a great deal and I felt they were kindred spirits.

Sitting with Ava was a blond hunk that looked about six feet five inches tall. A football type I'd say, and you know what American football players can look like. He was considerably younger than Ava, but her personality was such that it didn't seem to matter. You could tell that they were sweet on each other by the way they looked into each other's eyes, and they held hands the whole time we were at their table.

I believe Ava had a reputation for being in love with love, and I didn't see anything wrong with that. She was a tremendously attractive woman who looked considerably younger than her years. Any red-blooded man would have jumped at the chance to be in her favour. Needless to say that included me, for a cat can look at a queen, as the saying goes. Being a true celebrity was not always a bed of roses. The limitations put on them, which did not affect the average person, must have been quite irksome. To go shopping in a supermarket or have a meal in a restaurant was almost impossible. The chance of interruption by well-wishers and autograph hunters was always imminent and the simple peace of anonymity was lost to them. All aspiring celebrities should be aware of such dangers.

Ava invited us to stay at her table for lunch. The two ladies talked about their friends, discussed the latest clothes fashions, and generally commented about things that only women talk about. Ava's partner never uttered a word, and I was so entranced I couldn't have spoken either. Rosemary mentioned why I was in the States and it sparked a nerve in Ava's peacefulness. She said that she remembered when her singing voice was removed from one of her earlier films and that of another woman was dubbed onto it. She thought she had sung well and it still annoyed her when she thought about it.

After an hour or so it was time to move on. Rosemary and I said our goodbyes, left the restaurant and returned to her home. We had coffee and talked at some length about the film and music industries. She said it was great fun making

White Christmas and she wished she could have made more movies. I told her that the albums she made were good enough for most of us, and I remarked that very few people sang perfectly in tune and that she was one of them. There were times when she seemed quite shy, as she blushed and didn't quite know what to say. With all her experience and talent, she showed a great deal of humility. I found the experience invigorating and didn't want the meeting to end. But time marches on and we began to say our farewells. She thanked me for my efforts in making the album, and I thanked her for being such a talented artist and a wonderful person. I think I made her blush again, but that was part of her charm.

For many years the Christmas television season showed the film White Christmas and I always tried to see it. It reminded me of our association and it filled me with positive emotions. People who had 'The Touch' were special, for they spread joy to others, and today the world really needs a bounteous, giving force to influence us, because if it doesn't transpire the future looks pretty grim.

* * *

Q. What is the difference between a rock musician and a 16-inch pizza?
A: The pizza can feed a family of four.

Steve, Gerry and Alan
in Adelaide, Australia

Gerry and Alan at the
Grand Canyon

My country cottage

Richard Dodd and Pat
in Trinidad

Above: Sir Peter Maxwell
Davies at Darlington Hall,
Devonshire

Right: Charles Aznavour in
the studio at Marble Arch

Charles' home in Switzerland

Paul McCartney and Hilary
at Abbey Road Studios

Julie Felix and Tanit on
her fourth birthday

Gordon Giltrap at my home

Brent Maher and wife
at home in Nashville

Vicki Brown and daughter,
Sam, in Rome

Victor Spinetti at home
in London

Rehearsal of the Mardi Gras
carnival in Trinidad

Above: Mike Silver and
Hilary in Corsica

Right: A small session
with string players in
a London studio

Above: The unfinished Opera House
in Sydney, Australia

Right: A band near Adelaide

Relaxing with friends in Wales

The Louvre Museum, Paris

Backing singers in Rome

A country church in Trinidad

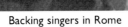

Above: Diane Solomon
at my home in
Gloucestershire

Right: The RCA
technicians in Rome

CHAPTER 13

When you are asked to work with someone that you have admired for many years it's pretty scary. So when I was asked to work with Andy Williams I was filled with anticipation. He had such a good reputation as an artist that I had built him up in my mind as being larger than life. He had been in movies and had sold millions of records over several decades. I didn't know what to expect. However, I needn't have worried, as Andy was a pussycat. He dressed meticulously and was the perfect gentleman. He spoke very quietly, he was courteous and he was an absolute professional. I believe that he expected no less from his colleagues and demanded similar behaviour.

The album was called Greatest Love Classics and we used the Royal Philharmonic Orchestra. The words set to many of the most well known themes in the classical repertoire were written by Tony Hiller and Nicky Graham. They both created the concept and structured the music. Four titles were arranged by John Cameron, one by John Coleman, and eight by yours truly. There were themes by the great Beethoven, Schubert, Chopin and Rachmaninov; even Debussy, Tchaikovsky, Fibich, Saint-Saëns and Khachaturian were included. The tunes were glorious and belonged to the group of melodies we called 'lollipops'; the sort of thing heard on Classic FM radio, which had opened the door to 'serious' music for thousands of listeners.

The atmosphere was not always good in the studio. Andy came from a breed of performer that was used to live performances. Frank Sinatra and Bing Crosby were others of that ilk. They were used to singing with the orchestra as a performance, whether they were on stage or in the recording studio. The later practice in the studio was for the artist to sing a guide vocal in a song booth (separated from the orchestra) and then sing a master vocal later, so that the orchestral tracks would remain intact if there was a problem with a particular vocal performance.

Andy found this practice quite foreign to his musicality. On more than one occasion he got very frustrated with this process and he showed his anger by shouting loudly into the air. I knew how he felt, but this was what the producers wanted. It was the normal practice in London at that time and was probably also the way things were done in most American studios. With the advances in technology it was possible to get a much cleaner sound by separating the different elements and by adding, layer by layer, various groups of instruments at different times. Andy would stop singing in the middle of a song sometimes and call the producers into an office to discuss the situation. It was obvious that he was angry and voices were raised on many occasions. Perhaps sometimes old dogs cannot be taught new tricks, as Andy didn't like the current practice and wasn't slow in voicing his opinion.

He was not only gifted with a wonderful voice; he also knew exactly how to phrase his words in order to achieve maximum effect in terms of their meaning. He showed a tremendous range of expression and a great degree of subtlety. The melodies that Andy sang were quite difficult to perform because they were all written for instruments rather than the voice. At one point I thought he was going to leave the project and return to America. He said that he needed space in order to interpret the songs according to his feelings on any particular day. But the tracks were already carved in stone and they couldn't be altered. This put his timing in a straitjacket, which was the worst thing that can happen to a performer. The producers often apologised, and Andy continued to work because he was a professional. Many artists I knew would have walked away.

Andy came from a centuries-old vocal tradition that sprung from Bel Canto in Italy. It developed in early opera and gradually spread throughout the developed world. Its very nature required a flexibility of speed, for the music of the time had to follow the dramatic action, and this was why Andy got so upset. In order for music to breathe there had to be elasticity in its speed. There was no rhythm section to prevent this from happening, so a fundamental element was missing.

Having said that, I remember watching recordings in Nashville where whole bands and rhythm sections played at the same time without any separating screens at all. The feeling of the finished product sounded much more natural and fantastically relaxed. The rhythm was tight and the sound was warm. Bands such as Little Feet, Steely Dan and Sly and the Family Stone recorded that way. It should be remembered that there was a difference between recording four or five people who could continuously record until they were satisfied, and recording a large orchestra that might only be hired for three hours due to prohibitive studio costs.

I believed that the all-inclusive method of recording was probably more natural for the artist, but greater technology allowed us to use different methods to achieve higher technical standards. It was a matter of common practice. We had invented the technology and the practice was to use it. It was the same in many walks of life, and the entertainment business was no different. We only had to think of some of the inventions of the twentieth century, such as the microchip, to see that we couldn't stop the wheels of 'progress'.

The interesting thing for me was to listen to an album that had three arrangers. Each of us gave something different to the total effect of the sound. By having three different approaches to translating 'serious' music into the popular idiom, the variety of techniques made the album more interesting for me, and for the listener too, I hope. It was always a treat for me to watch other people working with orchestras, as I learnt such a great deal about what I was supposed to be doing. I've always believed that the greatest teacher of excellence is watching other skilled people practising their art. I wonder how many popular singers today would be able to approach such a task with as much expertise as Andy possessed. He was indeed one of the greatest popular singers of all time.

I arranged some songs for an artist named Bruce Roberts. He made an 1978 album of that name, which was produced by Tom Dowd. Bruce was a very articulate young man, and I imagined him to be the perfect example of the typical

American boy next door. He wore glasses and bow ties and he used to smile almost all the time. Interestingly, his ballads were some of the saddest songs I had ever heard. Some of the titles were co-written with Carol Bayer Sager, a very distinguished songwriter, and it is always difficult to ascertain exactly who did what. But judging from the titles 'I Don't Break Easily' and 'I'd Rather Be Alone', which were Bruce's own, I would say that his smile covered a great deal of inner pain.

Bruce reminded me of a younger Neil Sedaka. His uptempo songs had that early two-beat feel and his voice had that high tenor quality that made him sound like a little boy lost in this big, wide world. It was perfectly suited to the ballads, which were generally about loneliness, and the lyrics were so well constructed that they hit that universal spot where we all live. The producer, Tom Dowd, who knew me through the Rod Stewart albums, asked me to arrange five tracks. They were all ballads, and the many musicians were some of America's finest. They included Steve Cropper on guitar and Grady Tate on drums, and the girl Roberta in 'The Car Song' was Connie Stevens. Bruce did some keyboard work, and other songs were arranged by David Campbell and Jim Horn.

While we were making the album an incident happened that made me realise that in America money is a great wielder of power. Bruce invited me to lunch and told me to meet him at a famous hotel at the southern end of Central Park in New York. It was the hotel featured in the film Crocodile Dundee. We met in the Hawaiian bar and had a long, fruity drink before eating. I then expected that we would leave the hotel because we were both wearing t-shirts and trainers. When I asked Bruce where were we eating he told me not to worry as we were eating in the hotel.

Americans were very strict in terms of certain areas of social behaviour, and many restaurants and hotels were very particular about attire. We went to the door of the hotel restaurant where a six-foot-six doorman was checking the clients as they entered the dining room. Bruce smiled at me and acknowledged the doorman. "The usual, Mr Roberts?" the doorman said, with a large grin on his face. Bruce slipped some money into his hand and the doorman brought out two ties for us to wear over our t-shirts. We put them on, walked into the restaurant and sat down at a table. Bruce told me not to worry as he did that sort of thing all the time. Everyone in the restaurant was immaculately dressed, but they didn't even look up to witness my embarrassment. I'm not certain whether this could happen in Europe.

This project was another example of the national nature of songwriting, where our environment and past traditions really do affect the kind of work we create. In listening to Bruce's ballads, which were his most sensitive efforts, I realised that the style and structure of the songs could have only come from America. There was something so personal about them and they stood with the very best of the songs we all love that came from the American theatrical tradition.

I thought of the French 'chanson', the bawdy Berlin songs of the twenties, the British music hall and the various Eastern European traditions that were founded on Arabic and Romany influences, and it wasn't difficult to see how the different styles were formed. But it was not only the musical styles that varied. If you analysed the lyrical element there were subtle differences in the degree to which these nationalities allowed themselves to express their feelings. The choice of words or phrases could considerably alter the nuance of meaning and, therefore, the emotional response of the listener. Since the majority of musical lyrics were written in rhyme, it had always fascinated me that the choices we made to achieve rhyme were related to language, culture and nationality.

If we tried to translate a song literally from one language to another it made no sense. Translators had to take the essence of the meaning of the story and then portray that meaning in their own language. Much could be lost in translation, but we did the best we could. Finally, the end result depended on the person translating the work, because the translators' creativity could change the essence of the text, sometimes fundamentally.

Michael Johnson was a young man I met in Nashville. It was my first experience in that town and I was really excited to be there, the Mecca of country music. I was making an album with Randy VanWarmer and I was approached to do some arrangements for Michael. The producers were Brent Maher and Steve Gibson, and the album, called Dialogue, was released in 1979 on the EMI America label. Brent was an engineer and had produced many well-known country artists. Steve was an excellent guitar player and played on the recording. I'm not sure why there were two producers, but it might have been politics. I've always found that two producers can sometimes cause problems because they might not always agree with each other and compromise is necessary.

Time and time again I witnessed the degree of space that American musicians allowed in their performances. It proved to me that 'less is more', and I think it's a quality that all musicians could benefit from if they were brave enough to rely on simple, memorable phrases rather than fill every available space with minutiae that get forgotten as soon as the track is played. I know it was difficult to please everyone, but to listen was not always to hear, and so many musicians just didn't hear the beauty of space. They forgot, or had never been taught, that it was the space that shaped the sound. That seemed so simple to me, but perhaps it was one of those things that was so obvious that it got lost among thousands of other rules that musicians learnt. Today's example is: where in all this information did wisdom get lost?

I was invited to Brent's home in the countryside just outside Nashville. He and his wife were charming and hospitable to me, as were their children. They lived on a six-acre plot in the woods, and they had horses and dogs. I remember that the dogs lived under a shelter next to the house and I was told that they were never allowed inside the house. It seemed strange to me at the time, because in Britain we are so mad about animals that they become children in the family. But they had their reasons and I respected them a great deal. Brent was an excellent engineer. He had produced many country artists and he had a laid-back approach that was a common trait in the southern states.

The studio was relatively small but compact and user-friendly. The Memphis Horns featured on one track and they were incredible. They drove two or three hours to reach the studio and they were late, naturally. There were five musicians in an old car that looked as if it wouldn't go another mile. They bundled out with their instruments and set up in the studio. The leader asked to hear the track and the band sat around with their eyes closed listening to every sound. Later, the leader talked to the boys in a very strict fashion, giving them instructions that they adhered to like soldiers on parade. A half an hour later they were the best brass section I had ever heard. I couldn't believe that such a dishevelled group of people could make such a wonderful sound. I thought to myself, never judge a book by its cover.

They laughed and played with each other like small children and it was obvious that they had grown up together. Brent had a good rapport with them and after a few minutes of concentration their work was done. When they left the studio they eased themselves, and their instruments, into their car. After a few bangs and splutters they went on their merry way, with smoke pouring from their exhaust. If only I could have taken them back to London I would have been a happy man. Alas, it was not to be, and what would they have thought about the English weather? The experience was a fantastic learning curve for me, and I used the information gained in Nashville during the remainder of my professional life.

A blast of wind brought Judi Pulver into my life. She and her band came to London to do some tracks at Nova Sound Studios. I remember that when her album was finished she and a young man in the band, whom I took to be her boyfriend, were so pleased with my efforts that they presented me with a pair of silver cupped pipes for smoking dope. It never occurred to them to ask me if I was in the habit of taking drugs or not, they just assumed that all musicians imbibed.

I can't for the life of me remember what I did for them to receive such an honour, but they sent me a finished album released on MGM Records. It was called Pulver Rising (1973). On the front cover of the sleeve was the famous painting of Sandro Botticelli's 'The Birth of Venus', with Judi in the centre. Airborne cherubs were blowing on her to keep her cool, and another lady with a large red blanket was waiting to dry her. Judi had an enormous sense of humour and she had asked the art department to add a small white towel with the monogram 'Halfway Inn' around her middle. The back cover showed Judi lounging on white wicker furniture in a gorgeous white satin dress with a smile that would put the sun to shame. By her side was a white swan, and there was a parrot in a white cage on the table. She had a style about her that reminded me of Liza Minnelli, for she was larger than life. Her singing voice was very gritty, a little like Janis Joplin's, and her lyrics were really kooky and quite unique in the way she expressed how she felt about her relationships.

She wore outrageous clothes and she changed them every day. The colours made the rainbows weep, and the twinkle in her eyes told you that she didn't give a damn about the opinions of others. They were open, humorous people, so working with them was like being on holiday. Judi brought an excellent drummer with her named John Guerin. He was a gangly youth who played the drums superbly and had recently played with Bob Dylan. He was all arms and legs when he played, but his technique created a wonderful feel to the music. He was unforgettable because the actions of his body when he played were unique.

Everyone in the band smoked constantly and I was at a loss to fathom how they could function when under the influence of illegal substances. Perhaps familiarity breeds perfection or they just liked being on cloud nine. They certainly performed well and deeply enjoyed what they were doing. There were no problems with the engineering staff; in fact they joined in with the festivities most of the time. Nobody seemed bothered about alcohol, which was a good thing, and their substitute, the weed, must have been very satisfying for them. Judi gave us a tremendous party before they departed. All in the studio had a great time and we were sad to see them leave. The next day we felt like nothing on earth. I didn't hear what happened to their efforts, but I'm sure that their lives were positive, for they were free spirits and nothing seemed to get them down.

Nicky Hopkins and I go back a long way. He is a superb

keyboard player and has probably played on more artists' albums than any other pianist. He was British but was in such great demand that he made the USA his home for many years. He had a house on the bay in San Francisco. When our paths crossed I was working in the USA, but I suspect he had family living in England. We would meet from time to time when I was asked to do some orchestrations for projects he had worked on, and it was always a pleasure to see him. He was such a gentle person and I always believed he was special, as if a guardian angel was watching over him. Who knows, perhaps many of us were as lucky as Nicky and were getting help from external forces.

The album he made was called The Tin Man Was a Dreamer, and perhaps this summed up Nicky's perception of life more than anything. He signed a copy and sent it to me in April 1973 and I still have it. I haven't seen him since the late seventies, but other musicians often speak of him, which brings back fond memories. Nicky wasn't the best singer in the business, but his tremendous musicianship helped him create beautifully crafted paintings in sound. He was tall and lean and was a remarkable pianist. He was rather shy and never spoke about his talent, but he was always quick to praise others. He was a good listener, which was the essential requisite in the art of good conversation.

Most of the lyrics were simple statements about everyday situations in relationships. A slight hint of depression ran through some of the songs. It was probably true that professional musicians who moved around a great deal on tour had a hard time keeping relationships together. Perhaps that was why the majority of lyrics tended to be about love that was lost rather than love that was found. Writing in the first person always created more exposure for the artist than writing in the third person. As an observer they could distance themselves much more and create an atmosphere that was not necessarily related to their own experience.

Nicky had some of the best musicians working with him on the album. Its broad spectrum was due to the vast experience of Nicky's professional life. I suspect that his musical training, the myriad of artists he had worked with, his own musical taste and his perception of his relationships all went into expressing what he achieved on the album. As they say, we all have a book inside us waiting to be written. This was Nicky's, and to answer the inscription that he wrote on the copy that he gave me – yes, Nicky, it turned out fine!

Rick Springfield was another matter. He was Australian and had moved to the USA to make his fortune. He was young and very pretty, and was the only male artist I ever worked with who put powder on his face. It was possible that he wanted to cover some spots that he had, but I never asked him. What does one say in such a situation? He was represented by Steve Binder and Robbie Porter of Beverly Hills, and Robbie produced two albums for which I did arrangements. He also played Noah Drake in the television series General Hospital.

I remember he was a quiet young man and he and Robbie had a good working relationship. Rick played guitar, banjo, organ, harpsichord and piano on the album, which was recorded at Trident Studios in London. Robin Cable was the engineer. A considerable amount of money was spent on the first album because we were allowed a great deal of time to get things the way Robbie wanted. I believe lots of time was spent on the mixing process, the crucial part of making records, and no expense was spared on the album sleeve.

I had an embarrassing moment during the recording of the brass section, trumpets and trombones. They were sat in their groups and we had rehearsed the music that was to be put on the track. I hadn't noticed that one of the trumpet players was pickled in alcohol, as there wasn't a problem with the overall performance. At a particular moment Robbie's wife walked into the control room, which was high up near the ceiling of the studio, and a large, glass plate window allowed everyone in the studio to see her. She was a very pretty woman and Robbie had brought her to Europe while making the album. Suddenly, the player in question let out an enormous roar of abuse, which was aimed at Robbie's wife. Everyone in the studio was silent. Had there been a hole in the floor of the studio I would have gladly jumped into it to elude and alleviate the embarrassment I felt. I quickly spoke to the contractor (a person who books the musicians) and the player was removed.

The contractor told me that the player was a wonderful musician, but since his separation from his wife he had gone to pieces. Although I sympathised, I told the contractor not to engage him on any of my sessions in future. I then had to go to the control room and apologise to Robbie's wife and Robbie for such an unfortunate incident. They were very generous in their response, but it ruined the rest of the session, as everyone was conscious of the fact that it should never have happened.

On listening to Rick's works many years later, certain criteria revealed what I had been told time and time again by people who were much more experienced than me. "A song, is a song, is a song." This phrase meant that a strong, universal song with meaningful lyrics and a memorable melody would stand the test of time. Whether it is sung unaccompanied, with a good or bad arrangement, or just with a piano or guitar, it will go straight to the heart. People need to identify with the story being told, and if they don't the song's wrapping means very little to them.

Songs in the first person often seemed as if the writer was contemplating his or her navel, and to make self-indulgent lyrics related to others was a hard task indeed. When we think of the great stories of the past, or the great songs of the past, nearly all of them were told in the third person. The observer told the tale in an objective fashion, setting a scene that the listener could be drawn into. Nobody really wanted to be drawn into an outburst of negative self-indulgence. I say this because nearly every song I'd heard that was in the first person was about unrequited love. I'm sorry, but life was hard enough without having to wallow in someone else's mire.

For me, Rick's first album came into the 'wallowing' category. The second album was more adventurous, with many of the songs having large structures but little content. I longed for more content in less complicated structures. Two waltzes, 'The Photograph' and 'Born Out of Time', were much more simple and more direct. They showed that Rick was not without talent, but he seemed to need to be grandiose and added "Na na na" sections on three consecutive songs. I also felt that he pitched his keys too high, and most of the time he sounded as if he was really struggling to sing his melodies on the large-scale songs.

I know that when we were young we were still trying to find our identity. We were looking for the best advice we could get. Possibly we wanted any advice that was on offer. The people who guided young artists played a similar role to their parents. If an artist was lucky, he or she got a manager or an agent who really cared about their future career. If they were unlucky, the artist could be led down a one-way street to oblivion. It was so easy for some of the young, aspiring talent I met on my travels to fall into the net of a ruthless plunderer; someone who was only interested in making a quick financial gain without any thought, or feeling, about the future of the person in their charge.

Having said this, I do think that Rick was a lovely, gentle person, and he deserved the later success he had in the early eighties. His role in the television series was a success and I have seen him in movies in recent times. To be a success in rock and roll you had to deliver the songs that everyone identified with. Many would-be 'stars' have found that even with a great voice and lots of personality, without immediate, memorable material, they were doomed to disappear into that distant fog that claimed all those who just couldn't write memorable material.

It is more difficult today than in earlier decades to clinch that opportunity to be discovered, as there are more young people aspiring to stardom now than ever before. Even with television programmes in Britain such as The X Factor, it must be remembered that hundreds, if not thousands, of hopefuls send in applications for auditions. The fact that it is much more expensive to manufacture the finished article now with the advance of technology means that many companies are not prepared to take as many calculated risks as they did in the sixties, seventies and eighties. I remember when the Middle Eastern countries dramatically increased the price of oil, which affected the production of records, artists' contracts were being cancelled if they were not top sellers for their respective companies.

Many of the heads of companies today are suffering from the 'quick profits' syndrome in Britain. The age of nurturing an artist for years, if necessary, has long disappeared. Joni Mitchell is a good example of the norm in earlier times. She was a Canadian from Alberta who first studied art and whose songs were exposed on Judy Collins's Wildflower album. She was brought to England by Joe Boyd to show Europe her talent. She was not an overnight success, but paid her dues by performing in all sorts of small places before becoming an international star. This is not the case today. People seem to spring from nowhere, with little talent, and expect to perform on television before millions of people. It might be good for the judges and presenters of these programmes, but does it do much for the art form?

I remember being told that you could take anyone off the street and turn them into a 'star'. When I thought about the development of musical technology over the past four decades I believed it was true. The equipment in recording studios moved from the early four-track mixing desks of the sixties through the increasingly higher capacity analogue machines of the seventies and eighties and on to digital machines. Rod Stewart's producer often used two 32-track mixing desks coupled together, making 64 tracks available.

What did this mean with regard to the process of production? It meant that each track was capable of having one or a dozen voices or instruments on it if need be when the recording process was in operation. Producers were able to record many lead vocal attempts on different tracks and, like editing a film, they could use a syllable, a word or a phrase from any of these recordings. Piecing the attempts together to make one rendition was quite easy, and to the public the result would appear to be a seamless single performance. Rod's producer often used one of the coupled 32-track desks mainly for his voice, and this was common practice throughout the industry for all artists.

When the double or triple tracking of a voice mechanically was used, and the right amount of echo was applied, it was possible to change the sound and quality of artists so that they seemed to be wonderful singers, when in fact some of them had hardly any singing experience at all. Various techniques were used that the fans weren't aware of, and didn't need to know; after all, we don't need to know the ingredients of a meal to enjoy it. The point was that what we saw and heard wasn't always what it purported to be. Good examples of this were when an artist was miming to a tape at a live concert, or miming on television when a backing tape was being played.

Were these the giants that we revered in the popular music industry? Yes they were. But it should have been expected, and the media that criticised them for doing it conveniently forgot that we were living in the age of technology. Anything was possible and everything was done to improve the quality of the artists. I wondered how the popular entertainment industry would develop in the future. Would there be a hundred dancers behind a singer who can't sing? Would there be six presenters (three men and three women) reading the news that was displayed under the camera? Would television consist entirely of game shows and reality programmes? These were some of the things that I found interesting, and I wondered whether others felt the same. I did hope that the public would revolt and stop subscribing to the junk they received on television. But so far nothing has changed and the junk continues to be thrown at them in an ever-increasing volume.

* * *

Pulling over a motorist, a policeman from San Diego told the driver that as he was wearing a seat belt he had just won five thousand dollars in a safety competition. "What are you going to do with the money?" the officer asked. "I'd better have some driving lessons and get my licence," the man answered. "Don't listen to him," said his passenger. "He's a smart cookie when he's drunk." This woke up the man in the back seat, who exclaimed, "I knew he wouldn't get far in a stolen car." Suddenly there was a knock from the boot, and a voice uttered in Spanish, "Are we over the border yet?"

CHAPTER 14

In 1985 I received a call from Bernard Theobald, Barbara Dickson's manager, asking me to produce an album of Andrew Lloyd Webber's songs called Ovation. K-Tel had closed a deal with Bernard to release the finished product, and Andrew had to give final approval of the work when everything was completed. What I didn't know was that Lloyd Webber had a darker side. It is said that power corrupts, and absolute power corrupts absolutely, and to me he was a wonderful example of this. The project was an exciting one because there were various artists involved in performing the songs and, as you know, variety is the spice life.

Barbara Dickson performed on four titles, the most well known being 'Don't Cry for Me Argentina'. I believe that Barbara came from the folk song tradition, and because of this she had an acute sense for controlling the nuances that a song called for. It was always a pleasure working with her because she was ready at all times to get the best out of her performances. There was never any 'prima donna' attitude when she worked, and she would listen to any advice reservedly and take the best from the opinions of people around her. She was very decisive in her manner and said exactly what she thought, so there were never any misunderstandings with Barbara. It was no wonder that she had been popular for many years, for her audiences identified completely with her interpretation of a lyric.

Rebecca Storm performed on two titles, and 'Tell Me on a Sunday' was a really fine performance. She was discovered by Willy Russell, the author of Blood Brothers, and her sensitivity in the rendering of the above track showed an artistry that was quite rare in my experience. She was diminutive in size and yet she had a large, powerful voice with a rich quality. She knew her material very well and it didn't take long to get the vocal tracks that we both felt did justice to the songs. She was always cheerful and smiled a great deal. She often told funny stories about things that happened to her in her everyday life, and all the technicians liked her and said she was like a breath of fresh air. Unfortunately, I never worked with her again after the completion of the album, as people who were amusing were a joy to be around.

Paul Nicholas sang two solo songs and a duet with Paul Jones. He had enjoyed success in films, television, music and the theatre; and at that time he was basking in the popularity of the BBC television series Just Good Friends. Paul was very flexible and his talent allowed him to adapt his voice in the same way that a character actor would change his whole demeanour to suit the part he was playing. He had a great sense of humour and he would exercise it at every opportunity. He lived in Highgate with his beautiful wife, where he had an enormous view of London from the patio of his garden. We had dinner and talked about his songs, as he was anxious to get his performances right, and I felt the project meant a great deal to him.

He had a considerable experience behind him and this allowed him to be very relaxed in the studio. He was very easy to work with and reminded me of the professionals of earlier generations who had everything under control. All three songs required a different texture and approach, and Paul was able to capture the spirit of each song with ease. He joked with everyone, especially in the duet with Paul Jones, which made the session enjoyable, and also showed his knowledge about getting the best out of relaxed colleagues.

Denis Quilley sang 'Old Deuteronomy' and his expertise was obvious from the start. He was a seasoned stage actor who had performed with the National Theatre, had taken part in many television productions and films and had sung in many musical productions. He was a large man with a deep, soothing voice, and the quality of his voice was perfect for the contribution he made to the album. I remember him as the Italian in the film Murder on the Orient Express, which showed just one side of his versatility. One of the things that impressed me in the studio was the way he took his time in phrasing the lyric of his song. He was completely at one with the spirit of the piece and it was a great pleasure working with such a multi-talented person.

Paul Jones sang 'Pumping Iron' and the duet 'Starlight Express' with Paul Nicholas. He had a close association with Lloyd Webber, having starred in Joseph, sung the part of Perón on the original recording of Evita and deputised for Nicholas for one month in Cats. He was, of course, a seasoned blues singer and sang with Manfred Mann's R&B group in the sixties. After a period of stage and film appearances he formed The Blues Band, which became a very successful unit for many years. Today he hosts two weekly blues/gospel radio programmes and shows he has gained a great deal of knowledge of the genre. I was very surprised to see him play the harmonica in the studio. I was not aware of his blues band efforts and I must say that I thought he was an excellent harmonica performer.

I must not forget to mention the backing singers on 'Pumping Iron'. I was very lucky to have the services of two excellent actresses, Belinda Lang and Fiona Hendley, who are well known for their television appearances in popular soaps, together with Linda Hayes and Betsy Cook. They made a formidable quartet that gave a great deal of energy to the track. Belinda and Fiona also took part in Trouble in Paradise, a musical devised by Susan Cox, which celebrated the music of Randy Newman. Fiona was married to Paul Jones and he suggested that they should take part in the recording of his song. I'm glad he did this because they were a great asset and contributed a dimension that would have been sorely missed had they not taken part.

Raphael Wallfisch is one of the leading classical cellists in Britain and he seemed an unusual choice to play the difficult part in Lloyd Webber's 'Introduction, Theme and Variations'. I was surprised because the cello part was written in a funky rock and roll style, and classically trained musicians are not naturally disposed to feeling the essence of that style of playing. He executed his performance exceptionally well, which is quite rare in my experience. I don't believe that labelling music is very productive, but I know we tend to feel safe once we have named and tagged things. The same 12 notes are used to express all styles of music, and in each and every one of the genres there are works that have captured the imagination of their listeners and ones that have not. A work that doesn't move us emotionally is useless and might as well be labelled 'muzak' if we can't resist labelling things. I'm sure that this labelling has its roots in an elitism that springs from a class-conscious society, which has created an environment that destroys creativity rather than nurturing it. I'm certain that a Leonard Bernstein, who had his feet firmly planted in the classical and the popular traditions (West Side Story), would not have been received in a serious manner in Europe, and certainly not in Britain.

Last but not least, we come to the 'Requiem'. The movement was being recorded around the same time as its first performance in New York and this created a slight problem. The 'Pie Jesu' had already been published and Lloyd Webber didn't seem to have a problem with the fact that we were recording the piece. The 'Hosanna' was a different kettle of fish. Andrew didn't want our version to reach the public before his performance, or before the work's publication.

I was very lucky that someone had arranged to have The New Scottish Concert Choir on our recording, as Andrew had used the choir for the rehearsal of his version. I had transcribed the movement from a tape I was given and all was set for the studio. The arrangement was performed successfully, and it was the choir's turn to put their voices on the track and complete the title. When I arrived at the studio the choir were waiting and ready to record and their parts had been given out to them by someone from Andrew's office, whom I assumed was looking after the singers. We had a run through the music and then made a superb performance for the record. Everyone was pleased with the session and we parted feeling that we had spent a good day in the studio.

Some weeks later I received a phone call from an obnoxious man claiming to be Andrew's musical director. Before I could utter a word about the subject matter of his call he proceeded to list all the qualifications he had gained at his music college. He told me, in a very superior manner, that he had listened to our version of the 'Hosanna' and I couldn't possibly have heard the choral parts on the tape enough to copy them. He implied that I had stolen the original parts from somewhere and he wanted to know what I was going to do about it. I was flabbergasted. I was so angry that I thought the best plan of action was to hang up the phone.

In all his pomp it had never occurred to him that there are musicians who have a pair of ears that can actually hear music. It had also never occurred to him that there are other musicians who have had formal training and may have had six years post-A level tuition. The next day I got a call from Bernard, the catalyst for the album, and he told me that Andrew was very unhappy. The 'Hosanna' had not been published, and I assumed that there might have been a little competition somewhere. The next thing Bernard told me was that the young man who was looking after the choir had been sacked because he had brought the original choral parts to the studio. Apparently they were in boxes in a small outer room. The crux of the matter was that Andrew and his flunky wanted Bernard to get me to admit that I had used their choral parts, and they wanted an apology.

I told Bernard that aside from the insult I was not going to admit to something I had not done. In the end Andrew told Bernard that if he wished to release the album he would have to give a percentage of the royalty money to charity. It seemed to me that this was an exercise in power, and I wasn't very impressed. The man who lost his job over a simple mistake was the loser in this tale, and I felt terribly sorry for him. Bernard told me later that the album sold very well, so the gift to charity was a blessing for them, and Bernard didn't do too badly from the project.

At the same time as the Lloyd Webber album was being recorded Bernard asked me to produce the next Barbara Dickson album, called The Right Moment. Barbara was pregnant and sang her master vocals three weeks before she gave birth. Strangely, her condition gave her voice a coarse quality that I found very attractive. It seemed to allow us to get really close to her emotional self, which I hadn't heard very often before. Considering the pressure of her condition on her psyche, Barbara showed just how professional she was. The work, at times very gruelling for her, went smoothly. There was never a complaint, and I have the greatest regard for her professionalism. The album was recorded at the Chipping Norton Studios, which had accommodation for the crew, so it was possible to work at any time of the day or night. The musicians used were the band that played for Barbara when she gave a live performance: Ian Lynn (keyboards), Bob Jenkins (drums), Andy Brown (bass), Richard Brunton (guitars) and Pete Zorn (horns, wind and percussion).

Barbara was beguiled by their proficiency, and I thought this made her somewhat vulnerable. Sometimes musicians have agendas of their own, and this can lead to the work going in the direction that the musicians want rather than what is good for the artist. I say this because I have sometimes heard albums where the artist is singing along with the band rather than the band accompanying the artist. Many British musicians are frightened of space. They are trained that way, so they can't resist filling every available space that the music dictates should be there. I think that American and European musicians are much more aware that it is the space that gives the music its shape and dimensional nature, whereas many British musicians seem to think that the instrumental arrangement is the most important thing, at the expense of the artist.

Barbara co-wrote four of the songs with Charlie Dore, the title song was written by Gerry Rafferty, and Alan Oday's 'Angie Baby' was included. For me, however, Barbara's greatest performances were the traditional 'She Moves Thro' the Fair' and Jacques Brel's 'If You Go Away'. Barbara's artistry really shines in these two tracks, and had we done nothing else together I would have been satisfied that I had met such a talented artist.

The people in power in the British music industry (the heads of record and CD companies) have developed attitudes towards artists, and those who work with them, that are quite different from the attitudes of the people in power in the USA. The manufacturers and the market place are also different. In very general terms, the degree of greed is much higher in Britain than in the USA.

An excellent example of this is seen when we consider the case of Rod Stewart versus his parent company, Sony, some years ago. I can tell you that not only has nothing changed, but also the degree of greed has increased, and the British public puts up with the situation in its calm, civilised way, as it does with all things. Rod was going to take his parent company to court on the grounds that it was interfering with his ability to earn a living. The premise was that, as the British shops were selling his product at almost double the American price, the number of sales in Britain was being seriously affected and his income was suffering as a result of this practice. I think they eventually came to some agreement, but what Rod had stated was correct.

When CDs first appeared in British shops they cost around £10. In the USA they were $10, at a time when the exchange rate was $2 to £1. The price gradually crept up to £12, and a short while ago the Monopolies Commission was asked to look into the matter. They decided that nothing unfair was happening, which left the door open for the mark-up to show its teeth with a vengeance. When I browse in the music shops now I can see CDs costing £16 and more, and the jolly old public buy, buy, buy! As Hamlet said, "There's something rotten in the state of Denmark," and I leave that thought to your imagination.

I first met Deke Arlon in 1973 in Tramps club, in London, while I was dining with Adam Faith. He later asked me to arrange an album for Ian Page, who was an up-and-coming young man with a great deal of songwriting talent. His lyric writing was particularly brilliant. He painted beautiful pictures in words and he could draw you into his world so convincingly that you couldn't resist his charms.

There were ten songs on the album. Four were co-written with Nat Kipner and two with Gerry Shury. I orchestrated nine tracks and Fiachra Trench did one. The rhythm tracks were recorded in Columbia Studios in New York and the orchestra was recorded in Nova Sound Studios in London. The recording engineers were Don Puluse (USA) and Richard Dodd (UK). My favourite tracks were 'Dream' and 'Everybody's Singing Love Songs', but I've always been a romantic and the ballads go straight to my heart.

Ian had American connections and the album was released on American Columbia Records. I was told some time later that Ian did very well in the States. He met some rich benefactor who became his patron, and he was asked to write musicals, which I understand were very successful. I remember him fondly. He was the only person I worked with who openly asked me if he could use some of the themes from my orchestrations to create further songs. I appreciated this gesture because taking other people's ideas is common practice in the music world, and here was somebody who actually had the decency to ask permission.

Deke Arlon was the manager of Elaine Paige, and many years later, in 1988, my old friend Mike Moran was producing The Queen Album for Elaine. There were ten tracks on the album and I was asked to arrange two ballads using a string orchestra with no rhythm section. I took this as a great compliment indeed because Mike was an excellent arranger and composer and it was an unexpected gesture. Most of Queen's great hits were included and I was given 'Love of My Life' and 'One Year of Love' to arrange. I think the former song was one of my favourites.

Without the restrictions of a rhythm section I was able to support the natural nuances of the lyrics, and this allows the music to breathe in a way that is impossible when a constant drum pattern is present. Mike sent me a guide tape using the piano and told me that the piano would be withdrawn when we recorded the title in the studio. I arrived at the studio on the recording day and Elaine and I rehearsed the songs. She was standing next to me in front of the orchestra and very soon adjusted to the string sounds around her. It isn't easy to absorb an unfamiliar arrangement without rhythm, where the speed fluctuates and there are occasional pauses. After a couple of plays she was relaxed and confident, and she showed everyone just how fast she was at picking up a new arrangement. The recording went well and everyone was satisfied. When the recording was over Elaine, Mike and I went to the restaurant to relax and have a chat. Mike did a splendid job with the production and I'm sure that the company was pleased with the result. The record was released on the Siren label, which was a Virgin company.

If only all our work was as pleasant as that occasion. The next time I got a call from Deke Arlon it was for a meeting at Warner Records in Kensington, London. Elaine was preparing for a musical production based on the life of Edith Piaf. Deke said that it would be a perfect time to release an album of Piaf's material and he asked me if I would consider arranging the songs. I was very interested because French chanson had always been one of my favourite genres and I already had a few records in my collection. During the meeting Deke and I discussed my fee, which was agreeable to him, and that's when I made the biggest blunder of my career. I asked Deke who was producing the album and he replied that it hadn't been considered at that point. I asked him if I could produce the album, as I knew what a 'deaf' producer could do to my arrangements. What a mistake to make!

Deke told me that Elaine needed a great deal of help with her vocals and that was the area that I would have to concentrate on in order to get the best results. He said if I could do that I could be responsible for the production. As there was nothing out of the ordinary in his request I agreed, and I looked forward to the assignment. He also said he wanted me to work with an engineer that Elaine knew well. He would be my right-hand man, the most important other person in the triangle. I had not worked with him before.

The writing was on the wall and I didn't see it. And there were other things I did not see. Elaine did not speak French and some of the songs on the album were to be performed in that language. She was having lessons from a French coach during the making of the album, which took up a considerable amount of time. She was also on tour with the musical before it got to the West End of London. This meant that the engineer and I had to travel to different parts of the country trying to record Elaine's guide vocals so that the orchestrations could be written in the appropriate keys. This meant hotel bills and other expenses that would have been unnecessary in normal circumstances.

There was also a problem regarding the rehearsal pianist. David Katz was my contractor, who booked the musicians for me, and he sent me a fine pianist to do the work. The pianist was fond of Rachmaninov and he would play excerpts from the concertos during our break periods. Unfortunately, I told him not to be too flamboyant while he was playing for Elaine, and at the end of the first day Elaine said that he didn't help her enough when she was singing and she wanted her own pianist to play for her.

I think she would have asked for her own pianist even if God himself were playing for her, for I learned later just how much she depended on this person. This was another problem for me. The pianist that David had sent told me that he had been promised £1,000 as a minimum fee and he needed the money. I felt so sorry for the poor chap that I paid him out of my own money. It didn't occur to me to check with the contractor. Later, of course, it dawned on me that no contractor would have promised such a minimum fee, but I still felt sorry for him and I let the matter go without mentioning it to David Katz. It is quite probable that the pianist got money out of David too, but that's the way things go sometimes.

My biggest surprise came when Elaine's pianist told me that he never worked for less than £250 pounds each time he played. This meant that even if we only did 15 minutes' work he charged me that sum of money. You can imagine what this did to the budget I was given. There were many occasions when Elaine had to sing after her musical performances when she was very tired, which meant that if we got one song from her that was adequate for the purpose we were very lucky indeed.

I was informed that her pianist had designs on producing the album and had done some work with Elaine before I became involved. I do believe this had something to do with the animosity I felt from him from the beginning of the project. Also, years earlier, I had done some arrangements for his wife for a television show and there were problems during a rehearsal because the musical director had not done his homework. You can see that the writing was on the wall in large letters. With regard to the engineer, I had been spoiled working with Richard Dodd. He would arrive in the studio to set up a master mix of a track at ten in the morning.

I would arrive at midday and we would have the definitive mix by two in the afternoon. We would do two mixes each day and go home happy. The engineer on this project told me that he only did one mix a day. I would arrive at the studio soon after midday, but the track was not ready for me to approach it until seven or eight in the evening.

The problem with studio work is that the air in the studio is recycled rather than fresh, so you get very tired after a reasonable length of time. What is worse is that your hearing gets impaired and it is difficult to trust your judgement. It is very important to find coworkers who understand what you are trying to achieve and who know how to give you what you want. These people are worth their weight in gold and I take my hat off to them.

It was my fault, of course, as I should have changed the situation, but like many people who went before me I would rather trust that somebody knows what they are doing than spend a great deal of time telling them what I need and want. The vocals never reached the quality that I had hoped for because the musical Piaf took preference over the making of the album. Elaine and I had different conceptions of what makes a great performer, and we both had a right to our opinions. Finally, I was told by Deke that I was well over budget and that he was going to replace me with my old friend Mike Moran who had finished The Queen Album. Mike finished the album and Elaine was in safe hands.

I learnt a great deal about the difference between talent and mediocrity during the making of that album, and it allowed me to grow. Elaine was more concerned about singing an accented word exactly at the point of a downbeat than singing a phrase with emotional expression, wherever the words might land. I did not tell her she ought to listen to Frank Sinatra or Barbara Streisand, whose phrasing was impeccable when it came to rendering the lyric of a song. Their phrasing weaved in and out of the beat, making a beautiful tapestry of feeling. A voice is just a voice, and it is what you do with it that allows the listener to relate to common experience. There is an old saying, "you cannot give ears to the deaf," and that is so true.

Much of the problem was my fault because I didn't pay

141

enough attention to Deke's words in the first meeting. Elaine needed a great deal of attention, and I was used to working with artists who knew exactly what they wanted to do and how to do it. The moral of that episode of my life was that you had to be armed with all the facts before you committed yourself to any project. Believe me, I wasn't entirely equipped for what happened, and I blame myself for jumping into the frying pan without knowing what high temperatures were to be bestowed upon me. It just shows that we have to be prepared to take the rough with the smooth. The rich tapestry of life is not always what we would like it to be, and we have to go on and grow from the experience. I think inner strength is shown at its best, not when everything is going well, but when we get through difficulties and face the future with a positive frame of mind.

I remember going to a party some years ago because the host was celebrating her birthday. During the evening I found a quiet corner and took advantage of some floor space, for the house was packed with the host's friends and relations. A young woman approached and sat down beside me. I thought she was very attractive. She had a pretty face, long, flowing hair and a well-proportioned figure. I made the mistake of asking her how she was and whether everything was right with the world. She spent the next hour telling me about every man she'd had a relationship with and how badly they had treated her, and basically she did nothing but moan about her life in the most negative way.

After our conversation she stood up and thanked me for being a good listener, smiled very sweetly, and walked across the floor with the air of a conqueror. I felt quite miserable for at least five minutes, and then her message suddenly hit home. She needed to unload her baggage onto someone in order to feel relief, and she sensed that I was the most suitable dumping ground. I relate this story only as an analogy to many singer-songwriters. She reminded me of those who demonstrate the 'I' syndrome. I believe it is natural to want to hear good, positive news from people if at all possible. Surely bad news leaves a nasty taste in the mouth? I don't understand why the performers of self-indulgent songs don't realise the trap they are laying for themselves. I'm aware that there are parts of life that are very sad indeed, but a safer route to success comes if they are viewed in the third person so that we can all share in a communal, human experience. The Beatles' 'She's Leaving Home' is a sad tale, but there is a universal truth in its message. It is a story that is meaningful to anyone who has experienced loss. Young hopefuls of today - beware!

* * *

Tarzan swung through the trees to get home. Greeting Jane, he asked her for a cold martini. He drank it quickly and asked for two more immediately. "Hold on," cried Jane, "isn't three martinis too many for you at this time of day?" "You don't understand, Jane," said Tarzan, "It's a jungle out there!"

CHAPTER 15

Paul Samwell-Smith introduced me to Chris de Burgh. His debut album, Far Beyond These Castle Walls (1975) was being produced by that sought-after engineer Robin Geoffrey Cable. Richard Hewson, an outstanding arranger, was asked to do two tracks, and I was also asked to do two. My titles were 'Hold On' and 'Satin Green Shutters', and until listening to the album recently I had forgotten how eloquently Irish his lyrics were. They had an element of sadness that reminded me of the Celtic epic stories of time before recorded history. I must say I thought his real talent lay in the genre of the mystical past rather than the modern 'pop' song such as 'The Lady in Red'.

Chris's early work had a delicacy that was rarely found among songwriters of the seventies. It took nearly 11 years for the British to appreciate his talents, while he was very popular in many other parts of the world. The 1986 hit 'The Lady in Red' firmly established him as a world talent worthy of attention. I particularly remember a track I arranged on another album about a country graveyard. It was almost Dickensian in the way he described the scene and unfolded the story. It was obvious to me that this young boy had something to say that was worth listening to.

Chris was a quiet young man who didn't say a great deal. He knew exactly what he wanted and only spoke when he had something to say about the development of his work. He didn't appear to enjoy 'small talk', and when the others in the studio were exercising their humour he would sit quietly observing our antics. I often felt that he was gathering material for future songs, as his eyes were everywhere and I was certain that nothing escaped him.

He preferred considerable amounts of space on his tracks rather than busy lines or layers of different musical sounds. I never heard him raise his voice. In fact he had a high, squeaky voice, which he delivered very softly but with an air of authority. Perhaps this was due to his background. He was born in Argentina, as his father was a diplomat, and I shouldn't imagine there was a great deal of shouting in the diplomatic corridors. The technicians liked him a great deal because he was always precise, always completely clear in his meaning, and there was never any misunderstanding about his desires. This wasn't always the case with artists, for some had real difficulty in expressing what they wanted.

Robin, the producer, used some fine musicians to accompany Chris. Barry de Souza on drums, Brian Odgers (known as Badger) on bass, Ronnie Leahy on keyboards, B.J. Cole on pedal steel guitar, Phillip Goodhand-Tait on harmonium, and three lovely ladies for the backing vocals, Liza Strike, Joy Yates and Madeleine Bel. Chris played acoustic guitar and Ken Freeman played the string synthesiser. It was the first time I had seen a string machine, which could reproduce a metallic version of violins, violas, cellos and double basses, used in a studio in place of live musicians, and it was a harbinger of things to come.

Technology had reared its head and was telling the musicians and arrangers that the writing was on the wall. The introduction of synthesisers into the recording scene was the thin edge of the wedge waiting to explode. Technology in music caused many musicians to lose their livelihood, just as it did in many other industries. In recording albums, CDs, background music to advertising jingles and film, technology took a heavy toll. Rhythm sections (piano, bass guitar and drums) were particularly hit with the introduction of synthesisers and the drum machine, and string players were superseded by people like Ken Freeman. It was a question of economics. If one or two people could programme machines to do what many people had done before, the cost was considerably less. What nobody seemed to worry about was the fact that the sound would be different. It was like home-grown fresh food being substituted by tinned processed food on the supermarket shelf. I know we adapt to anything, but gradual changes are not always for the better.

There was a strange predilection for death in Chris's lyrics. Although they were beautifully expressed you felt he had a dark side to his personality. Perhaps this was why it took so long for him to be recognised in Britain and the USA. South America and Europe loved his work, but they had to cope with the English language, for it was a second language to them. I suppose the emotional power of the work drew the fans to him. Only in Canada and South Africa were his records selling to English-speaking nations, but Chris relentlessly toured for ten or more years until he was fully recognised.

It was interesting to note what effect language in music and literature had in different cultures. The English language in 'Rock and Roll' had practically pervaded the entire planet, but what of other languages? I went to Rome to work for a month and ended up staying for three years. The quality of the songwriting and the art of the production were second to none, but the sale of 200,000 records in Italy was considered excellent. In the USA and Britain millions of records were sold by many artists and this was considered normal. The only time that English-speaking people will listen to different languages in music is when they are listening to opera. The only Italian song that reached the British charts in the seventies was 'Vado Via', and I assume that this was because of its powerful melody and rhythm.

I learnt, from the experience of producing artists whose lyrics were more negative than positive, that to sell records you needed to express the bright side of life. People wanted hope and they loved a happy ending. The success of Walt Disney testifies to that fact. The artists I worked with who expressed negative perceptions of events never became popular with the masses, especially those who wrote in the first person. Nearly all the great works come from the thoughts of observers; people who look at the world and express what others are doing. Egocentricity was generally thought of as a negative quality and, if nothing else, it was so boring. So many people wanted to tell us about their pain, but they didn't realise that the public had their own problems and were too busy living to worry, or care, about them.

Of course there were exceptions. Joni Mitchell was a fine example of someone who constantly told you about her love affairs, but she showed such great artistry when she related her tales that you were mesmerised into listening to her stories. The only successful artist I knew who made me want to jump off the nearest bridge was the Canadian artist Leonard Cohen, of 'Suzanne' fame. He was a novelist before writing songs, and his books had moments of despair and black humour. The sound of his voice on disc was so melancholy to me that I could only listen to one side of an LP at any given time. But there was something attractive about his renditions that made you want to listen again and again. I remember being told that young girls in their teens loved to hear songs about unrequited love, and in America they bought millions of his albums.

The fact that Chris de Burgh was signed to A&M Records and released work between 1975 with his debut album and 1995 with Beautiful Dreams shows how prodigious he was. He never pandered to the changing fashions that happened during more than 20 years of his career. In fact he was once quoted as saying to the A&M Records chairman, "There is life after the Sex Pistols," which is a wonderful tribute to an artist who didn't ever feel the need to reinvent himself because he knew who he was, and I take my hat off to him.

There haven't been many artists who have felt the need to reinvent themselves. But a wonderful example was David Bowie. He was David Robert Jones, and he was probably the greatest magician in the whole of the popular music world. He went through a myriad of changes before he became an international star, and sometimes it was difficult to keep up with his various images after he was famous. His eyes were different colours, which in itself was a remarkable gift, as while at school one of his eyes was damaged in a fight. He was involved with many groups during the sixties, and because of Davy Jones of the Monkees he decided to change his name.

I believe he studied mime, which was very useful for any performer on the stage. In 1969 he had his first big success with Space Oddity. In the seventies he changed management, and Tony De Fries took over the driving seat. His vocal style changed, the band sound got heavier, and the dark side of his nature created some strange and telling lyrics. Dressing in female clothes and admitting his bisexuality also added to the mysterious nature. David's career was certainly a unique one, and it spanned a considerable number of years. And if reinvention was necessary for fame, who among us had the right to cast the first stone?

The album I worked on for Peter Sarstedt was called Every Word You Say. It was released on the United Artists label in 1971 and was produced by Vic Smith (later known as Victor Coppersmith-Heaven), Peter and his brother Clive. I believe that the orchestra I was asked to use, The Harry Smith Orchestra, was in fact Vic's father's band. Peter was the brother of the 1960s pop idol Eden Kane, who occasionally played bass for Peter. It seemed that all the children in the Sarstedt family were musical, but Peter never discussed his parentage, so it was difficult to know where the musical genes came from.

Peter reminded me of a poet rather than a musician, in the same way that Bob Dylan's words were more important to him than the music. In Dylan's case this was obvious by the way he would throw away the melodic element of his songs in order to get his message across to his audience. In fact it was only when I heard 'Lay, Lady, Lay' sung by another singer that I realised the beauty of the melody. The same could be said of many of Bob's songs when covered by other artists.

In Peter's case I got the same feeling. He was what I would call a philosophical poet. His lyrics on this album were all about the plight of man. He was very observant of those who had wealth and those who were poor, and it was very obvious whose side he was on. He was anti-establishment as far as I could determine, and there was the same kind of bitterness that Dylan had. I don't mean this in any derogatory way because his perception of what he saw was as valid as the next person's. I think it was this bitterness that gave his songs an edge that many other writers lacked. He was very quiet most of the time, which surprised me because his lyrics were so full of ideas that they begged for conversation to resolve his thoughts.

In the song 'Mind of Man' he stated, "It's only a dream, a fantastic scheme, that's captured the minds of man." He could also be incredibly sensitive, as in the song 'Rain', which could reduce me to tears. There aren't many songs I can think of that had that kind of effect on yours truly. 'Every

Word You Say' had a kind of Shakespearean truth about it. It's first line, "Every word you say is written down, somewhere," seemed so perceptive to me. What we said to young children in the home, or at school, formed their minds, and this created our future whether we wanted that future or not. It was as if the snowball was rolling down the hill, getting larger and larger, and we weren't even conscious of the direction the ball was taking. But amid the serious nature of the lyrics there were rays of hope. I thought Peter was an optimist at heart, and if only a few people were moved to see the importance of what he was saying, our species had a chance of surviving. With climate change, his words have more significance than ever.

There was a lovely faux pas on the sleeve of the album. I guess it doesn't pay to try to be too clever. One of the greatest American jazz players, Gary Burton, played on three tracks: 'Rain', 'Down on the Flesh' and 'Let the Music Flow'. He was in London playing at Ronnie Scott's club, and I was very fortunate that he agreed to find the time to play for us. At the bottom of the sleeve, in small letters, there is a line of print without gaps that is difficult to read. Its message thanks Gary for his work and names the tracks. The last two words in the line were his name. It read, "barryeurton," and I hope that Gary never read it because he would probably think twice about accepting another engagement.

The expertise with which Gary performed was awesome. His roadie arrived with his instrument, a beautiful, gleaming vibraphone, an hour before the master. Before each track Gary only wanted to hear the music once. He didn't want to see the music of the songs, just hear them. He accompanied 'Flow' throughout as if he had rehearsed with Peter for hours. It wasn't only his fluency that was amazing, but also the sensitivity with which he played, leaving spaces exactly where they were needed so that the accompaniment fitted like a hand in a glove. At times the speed of his playing reminded me of the cascade of a waterfall. I had never heard anything like it before, and it stayed with me for days afterwards.

I noticed that Gary always had four sticks in his hands rather than the usual two, and this allowed him to play four-note chords as well as using two sticks for solo melodic work. On 'Flesh' his rhythmic work was a joy, and on 'Rain', which only had a guitar as the track, he supported Peter beautifully. The technique of improvising in the jazz idiom develops the ear in a way that reading music in a formal way does not. The memory of a jazz musician is also developed to a high degree because the chord sequence, upon which the song is constructed, has to be memorised. It must be remembered that these musicians know hundreds of standard sequences by heart, and their ear tells them where they are in a song at any particular moment.

In 1973 Rocket Records asked me to produce an album for a band called Longdancer. I had not met the band, or even heard of them, but I was in for a very pleasant surprise. The boys were young and vibrant, and their long hair (which was the fashion at the time) seemed to be everywhere. The band consisted of Matt Irving on keyboards, guitar, bass and vocals; a very handsome young man on guitar, harmonica, recorders and vocals named Steve Sproxton; one of the leaders named Brian Harrison on guitar, bass recorders and vocals; Charley Smith on drums and vocals; and another leader on guitars, bass and vocals named Dave Stewart.

Dave was an excellent example of a person who was in the right place at the right time. It was at this time that Dave met Annie Lennox, who was an ex-Royal Academy of Music student, and they lived together for some time. After forming The Catch and The Tourists, which had minor hits, they formed the Eurythmics, which became one of the most successful bands of the eighties. Dave also became known for his production acumen, and he worked with Bob Dylan, Feargal Sharkey and Mick Jagger. It was obvious from the beginning that Dave had a special gift. He had a quick mind, and the members of the band, talented as they were, looked to him for leadership.

The album was called Trailer for a Good Life. It was the title of one of Dave's songs, but every member of the band wrote and performed their own songs. There was a strong American influence on some of the material, such as Steve's 'Country Song' and 'Mother Nature', but the standard was always high and I was reminded at times of the Eagles and

Neil Young. Brian's songs were more European and they had an epic nature about them, such as 'The Ship' and 'Take a Song'. Dave's work always seemed philosophical to me and it had a tinge of sadness about it, which came from a keen, perceptive mind. The tracks 'Cold Love' and 'Trailer' were good examples of keen observation, and for a man of 20 they were very perceptive indeed.

Dave was quite small with a round face and big eyes. He was always smiling, but behind the smile I knew he was observing everything that was taking place in the studio. Although the band appeared to be a cooperative unit I believe that Dave was the guiding force and had the strongest personality. He would sit and joke with the boys and then suddenly shout out, "I've got a great idea that ought to be tried out," and the band would gather around him as if he had something to say that was earth shattering. There was never any tension between the musicians, for they were young and they were about to start out on their long, musical journey with great hopes for the future.

We recorded the album at Nova Sound Studio behind Marble Arch and Richard Dodd and Steve Allan were the engineers. The music was published by Island Records, which also distributed the record for Rocket. Additional artists were brought in for specialist work: Viram Jasani on sitar for Dave's 'Sweet Leaves'; Judd Proctor on banjo for Charley's 'Sandy's Song'; The Bones backing vocals group for Brian's 'Hard Road'; the Charles Young Choir for Steve's 'Mother Nature'; and Uilleann pipes played by Tommy McCarthy for Brian's 'The Ship'. As you can see, the sounds were varied, and the feel of their songs was often more from the folk genre than the current rock fashion. There were Celtic influences from the western regions of Great Britain as well as shanties from the depths of the sea.

All the boys were talented, and I can never quite understand why certain people were destined to be successful and others fell by the wayside. Perhaps it was lost opportunity, wrong personality, or just that some people are hungrier than others. I feel there was a mystery in it somewhere, and the title of this book might have given us the answer. Dave went on to bigger and bigger things and the remainder of the band, for whatever reason, were probably never heard of again.

I enjoyed my association with the band very much because they were a joy to work with. It wasn't that the band were great singers either, for they had young, clear voices that were almost spoken rather than sung, but their efforts were direct without any frills and their messages went straight to the heart. They had the energy of youth and they were full of enthusiasm. All the lyrics expressed deep feelings that made you sit up and think about your own situation. There weren't too many songs that could do that, and only the best artists had the talent to create simple, universal experiences that touched us all.

The boys really liked each other and showed it at every opportunity. They supported each other's ideas, which made the atmosphere very positive. They said ridiculous things to each other all the time, but they enjoyed the bantering. It made me smile more than once to see such harmony between band members. The songs were in the third person and showed a very positive outlook. There were love songs, anti-establishment songs, philosophical songs and epic folk tales, and their playing was always in good taste. Had they stayed together, who knows what kinds of albums they might have produced. Certainly Dave's later work shows that the band would have benefited from his input if the chance had been given to them. I feel it was another case of being in the wrong place at the wrong time for all but Dave. As one of their songs rightly states: "Mother Nature is sound, but Father Time wears the crown."

One of the strangest but interesting bands I worked with was Max Merritt and The Meteors. They were Australian and they made an album for Arista Records (a subsidiary company of Columbia Pictures) in 1975, which I produced. They were as diverse a group as you could find, and being musicians that is quite a statement. The leader, a very good musician, had lost an eye in a terrible accident. The band were coming home from a gig one evening when a car joining the motorway from a slip road drove into the side of their transit van. The car was going so fast that it pushed the van off the motorway and down a ravine. The van rolled over several times and it was fortunate that nobody was killed.

Max played acoustic and electric guitars and he had a great voice that was so sharp you could cut paper with it. He was like a male Janis Joplin, with an edge to his sound that was like the rasp of a machine tool. Stewart Speer was on drums, and he would have made the greatest Father Christmas ever. He was old enough to be everybody's father and he was rotund, with long grey hair and a long, bushy grey beard. His smile was a mile wide, and he was so powerful that every time he played I thought the kit was going to break. Barry Duggan played saxes and flute and sang backing vocals. He looked like the proverbial preacher from the Mid West two centuries ago. He was tall and lean with a dark beard, and you could imagine that at any minute he might pull a gun from his pocket and hold you to ransom. The other two members of the band looked less extraordinary. Martin Deniz played bass and sang backing vocals, and he looked like there were some Hispanic connections in his family. John Gourd, like me, had African blood in his veins, and had the best head of hair I'd seen in a long time. He played lead electric guitar and sang backing vocals.

Whoever thought that being in the music industry was all chocolate cake really got it wrong. Sometimes things happened that made you want to be a thousand miles away from the studio. I remember on one occasion Max wanted to put some guitar down on one of the tracks. He'd tuned his instrument a couple of minutes before going into the studio and all were ready for him to record. The engineer, Richard Dodd, played the tape, and after 30 seconds or so Max said that his guitar wasn't in tune with the track. We stopped the tape and Max did some tuning. We started all over again and the same thing happened. I told Max that the tuning was good and that if he put his part on the track and came into the control room and listened to it he would find that the tuning was fine.

This he did, but he said the tuning wasn't right. You may not believe what I'm going to tell you, but this tuning and retuning went on for six hours. Yes, we spent the whole day listening to Max tune his guitar. At the end of the day I'd had enough and I politely said goodbye and went home. The next day Max went into the studio and played his part in ten minutes. These things happen and there is no rhyme or reason for them. Max didn't even mention the day before; as far as he was concerned it never happened.

You can see from this that the producer has to be very diplomatic in the way he behaves with the artist or anyone connected with the recording. I had been in situations in my earlier days when I had become so frustrated with people that I just walked out of the studio. I know now that this wasn't very helpful to anyone, but there are times when we have to let the steam out of the boiler or we'll burst. I also know that had I stayed I would have said something that would have ended the relationship, and on occasion I did just that.

All the titles were written by Max except for two: 'King-size Redwood Bed' written by Charlie Daniels, and 'Mr. Horizontal' written by Miller Anderson. 'King-size' was one of the best tracks I have ever produced. It was arranged by Max and was really a very tight blues. It was spacious, with a wonderful bass and drum pattern pervading the whole track. Max's vocal ran shivers down your spine. It is not often that I look back on a track and know that I would not change a single note or mix it differently. I thought that the band's material was more suited to the American market than the European scene, so it was a shame that they headed for Britain rather than the States.

Max was the king of his castle. He ruled with a rod of iron and what Max said was law. The band accepted his leadership because he had a very good musical instinct for what was right for a particular song, and this wasn't always the case with some band leaders. The material was also diverse. Max's writing had a variable quality about it. He penned songs like 'Slipping Away', which had a wide open feeling about it and sounded like the songs that later came from the Canadian writer Bryan Adams, and 'Coming Back', which was a wonderful ballad in the same vein, but he also wrote titles like 'Find a Home' and 'Wrong Turn', which indicated that there was something rather sinister going on in his mind.

I remember in one session the studio turned into a circus. The title was called 'A Little Easier' and the first line was "I'm gonna walk out that door." Max said he wanted the sound of feet marching, which would give the track impetus and give the feeling of a never-ending search. Well, the whole band came to the session and they were asked to stand in the middle of the studio. Richard recorded their feet stamping and had plenty of ambience microphones hanging above the guys. We started the tape and told the boys to pick up their feet and march as if they were tramping through a forest.

It was all we could do in the control room to stop ourselves bursting with laughter. Here were five men, pretending to be in the Foreign Legion, puffing away under a barrage of studio lights for at least five minutes. They were all perspiring like mad, and because of the recording they were unable to utter a word. When the track was finished they came into the control room to listen to their efforts. They all laughed, but the effect was tremendous. It was the first time I had been called upon to do such a thing, and it was great fun.

They were a very good band and deserved success. Perhaps, like many great musicians before them, they were more interested in playing good music than being commercially successful. That may seem a strange thing to say, but the two things were not always synonymous. Commercial music related to what the wider public liked, but there was 'pop and rock' music, and there was 'classical' and 'jazz' music, which had a more limited audience and brought less money to the audio companies. Their tracks were a little too long for Radio One, and their solos would have probably pleased musicians more than the population at large. I suppose they returned to Australia and continued music-making down under, but while they were here they were a joy to listen to.

Another interesting artist I met was Asha Puthli. It was in the same year as my work with Mama Cass, and the world seemed to be turning on its head. John Hammond, the legendary critic and promoter, said wonderful things about her in a New York publication and everyone was buzzing with anticipation. It isn't easy to know where to begin when talking about Asha. She was certainly one of the most beautiful women I had ever met. She could have been, and may have been, a New York model. John Kobal, the American author and broadcaster, wrote the following for her album sleeve: "Asha from the East, Kali, Temple Bells, Peace, [for she came from India] Asha from the West, New York, Ornette Coleman, Warhol's factory, Now ... She belongs to the world."

This was quite a great deal to live up to. She did have a wonderful voice. It was like cream in your coffee when she sang in her best range. She had a soft, husky quality that was as seductive as you could imagine, and when she didn't go too high she was perfectly in tune. The problem for me was her natural inclination to sing in a florid style all the time, and the melody of the song being performed got lost in the cascade of notes coming from her throat. The production of an album for her became an inner conflict for me. I had always believed that a producer's role was to help bring out the best an artist had to offer. There were some producers who wanted the artist to comply with their vision of things, but I didn't subscribe to this view. However, I knew that in giving Asha her head in the studio we would end up with nine tracks that nobody would recognise.

I decided to be strict for her own good and we argued about the approach to every song. I like to think that I did the right thing in order for her to make other records. On one occasion I nearly walked out of the studio during one of her renditions. She pleaded with me not to leave and I took this to indicate that she knew I was trying to help her. I didn't enjoy those confrontations with her, and it was the only time in many years of producing that they had been necessary. She was such an individual artist that making the disc was a challenge to us both.

When Asha was recording I used to stop her singing in mid-phrase and then ask her to come into the control room to discuss a vocal problem. She would go absolutely crazy, as she was very emotional in everything she did, and I would try to calm her down. She wanted to please everyone and she always forgave me after her outbursts. She always complimented the technical staff and showed great respect for their expertise. Although I've never mentioned assistant engineers, during the five years or so that I worked with

Richard at Nova sound the assistant was always Steve Allan, a wonderful engineer in his own right and a very generous person. He was always ready to supply whatever was needed, and I never saw him in a bad mood or without a smile to greet the day.

Asha had some great songs to sing, the writers including J.J. Cale, Jim Webb, George Harrison, Bill Withers, John Lennon and Neil Sedaka. She knew her words backwards and had a wonderful ear for phrasing, which made me soon realise that the jazz style was where she probably felt most at home. She would weave in and out of the structure of a song with ease and captivate anyone who was listening to her. The studio boys would stay near to the vocal booth when she was recording just to hear the wonderful voice she had, which was quite uncommon in my experience.

I couldn't understand why she didn't practise the axiom of 'less is more'. It was practised by some of her greatest role models, including Billie Holiday. I know that we are all creatures of habit, but somewhere along the line someone should have pointed this simple fact out to her. I guess I always expected too much from the artists. I assumed that they knew the basic rules: say something simple, and always create space so that the creation has a place to breathe. With hindsight I know I shouldn't have been surprised because our knowledge is always acquired from the people and information around us. But I was frustrated because she had such great potential and, like Walt Disney, I wanted everything and everyone to have a happy ending.

The first track, J.J. Cale's 'Right Down Here', caused us to argue for hours over the need for a simple vocal. The mesmerising two-chord structure was like a seesaw, and the only thing that Asha had to do was give a convincing rendition of the lyric. She finally agreed, and the difference between her first efforts and the final master vocal was amazing. There was a directness and clarity in the last take that went straight to the heart. I did get the feeling that, in the ballads, it was like a powerful creature being constrained and that at any moment it would shake off its shackles and consume us all. 'Neither One of Us', written by Jim Weatherly, was an example of this. At times, the spaces were so tempting for Asha to fill in that I almost burst a gasket waiting to see what would happen. In retrospect, I feel guilty about the control that I wielded over her, but I did it in good faith, believing that it would help her to be accepted by a wider audience.

She displayed her sexuality to an amazing extent in Harrison's 'I Dig Love'. I had never heard such sensuality expressed by a singer before the making of this album. I was never quite sure what it was she really wanted. A small guess would have suggested stardom, of course, but she was beautiful enough to be an international model. She had the voice of an angel and the intelligence to be a fine actress. She didn't socialise with me much because of the situation between us. She was a closed book because I didn't allow her to be self-indulgent. I take full blame for this, and looking back I regret not being kinder to her. I know I became the kind of producer I detest, but had I been kinder it would have been a different album.

On the other hand, after a great deal of consultation, she sang Jim Webb's 'This Is Your Life' and Lennon's 'Love' as well as anyone I could have thought of at the time. Asha obviously loved to sing J.J. Cale's songs because there were two of his compositions on the album. The second one, 'Lies', was sung a little too dramatically for my taste. She wanted two voices at times, and actually asked for more. There were shouts and screams in the outro (the last few bars of the piece), which didn't really add to the overall effect of the rendition. It gave, though, a good idea of her performance when unbridled.

In 1975 Asha made another album in America. It wasn't a very expensive sleeve, but the back cover had a beautiful black and white photograph of Asha that was absolutely incredible. She held her head in her hands, pulling her hair back, and her eyes were closed. It seemed like a magical picture that only a great photographer could have taken. That man was Richard Avedon, and I take my hat off to him. There were three producers mentioned on the sleeve, including yours truly. The others were Tony Macero and Paul Phillips, the latter being a CBS executive, which is interesting. It seems I wasn't the only one who found the lady difficult to work with. I read in the music press that they had both had their moments with her, but perhaps a truly talented person might be forgiven for an outburst now and again. I now think of her fondly and sometimes wonder how her career developed. She was definitely larger than life, and if there was a special man around he would need to be a giant among the species.

* * *

One of the assistant engineers shared a lovely concept with me: 'Heaven is having a British home, an American salary, Chinese food, a German car and a Latin lover. Hell is having a British lover, an American car, a Chinese home, German food and a Latin salary.'

CHAPTER 16

The interesting thing about the Linda Lewis album called Lark was that I had two copies and they were different. The first copy was released in 1972 and had 12 titles, and the second copy was released in 1973 and had a baker's dozen - 13. The reason for this was that the album needed a hit single to sell greater numbers. It was always common practice to have as many hit singles as possible from an album because this kept the album in the public eye, and this in turn, of course, increased the total sales of both the singles and the albums.

The track that I'm referring to was called 'Rock-a-Doodle-Doo'. Jim Cregan asked me to write an orchestral arrangement for the title, and it was probably through him that I was asked to work with Rod Stewart some years later. Jim was Linda's husband and he co-produced the album with her. It was recorded at Apple Studios, which was owned by The Beatles. In fact the studio was situated in the Apple building where the Beatles Empire was located. The engineer was the famous Phillip Macdonald who worked on many great albums, and it was released by the Warner conglomerate.

Linda looked like a child angel. She was petite, with a beautiful smile and long, black, curly hair. Her singing voice was high and childlike, and she was a joy to work with because she was so laid back. Jim was just a really nice person. He was a fine musician, and it was obvious that he wanted to care for and protect Linda, both as a person and for her natural gifts. Linda and Jim were easy to get along with, and in their quiet way they knew exactly what they wanted and how to get it. At that time their relationship was fine, for they supported each other with every gesture. But the horizon was looking stormy, and geographical distance would play a crucial part in their separation.

The musicians on the album included some of the lads who

had toured with Cat Stevens a year earlier. Old friends Gerry Conway and Jean Roussel played drums and keyboards respectively, and Pat Donaldson played bass. Poli Palmer played vibraphone, marimba and flute, and Emile Latimer played percussion. Linda and Jim played guitars and a variety of other instruments, and Paul Williams played guitar on 'Waterbaby'. One of the real pleasures in the industry was knowing so many fine players and feeling that you just had to ask them for help and they would be there for you.

The album embraced a tremendous variety of styles and moods. There were tracks with high harmonies, touches of the Deep South, Appalachian Mountains ditties, and Linda's own laid-back islands feel about them, which always made me want to dance. Her smile had the warmth of the sun in it, and so did her writing. The attractive thing for me was that her lyrics always showed the positive side of relationships in particular and of life in general. As most of us were aware, there were many songwriters who wrote about love in an unrequited way, as if it was always the partner's fault, and we knew it took two to tango. Not so with Linda. Even when times were hard she offered hope to her partner. I found this rare and endearing and a manifestation of her personality.

Linda was also very philosophical in her tender years. Such songs as 'Reach for the Truth', 'Gladly Give My Hand' and 'Lark' had a message that everyone should hear. They were full of wisdom, an element that is sadly missing in many songs, and they made me feel two feet taller. Linda and Jim's response to each other was quiet, as if they had more on their minds than the recording. Perhaps the seeds of discontent had already been sown, and in hindsight it was a sad thing to witness, for they were both lovely people. Sadly, I didn't see Linda again to bathe in her sunshine. I know that Jim went to America to work with Rod Stewart and Linda stayed in Britain. Meeting them was a pleasant experience, and I will never forget the warmth they showed to me during our collaboration.

Around the same time as my association with Linda I was contacted to do some arrangements for Hudson-Ford. They made an album called Nickelodeon, which I think was one of their best works. Richard Hudson and John Ford were your quintessential English duo. I believe their roots stemmed from the British folk tradition, although they were capable of assimilating many of the influences around at the time.

Richard was tall and slim, with reddish hair and a medieval beard. He had piercing, hazel eyes, and in olden days would certainly have been a knight on a white charger. John was like a cuddly bear, with long, curly, fair hair and dimples when he smiled. I never saw him without tinted glasses and assumed that his eyesight was not very strong. Their work was attributed to both of them, and I took that to mean that the lyrics and the melodies were a joint effort. It wasn't easy to discover the amount of input by individual artists when the writing was attributed to two people. Lennon and McCartney were a good example of shared writing where it wasn't always certain who had contributed what.

I remember that John lived in an apartment that was only a stone's throw from my own, in Notting Hill, London. On one occasion I was invited there to attend his wedding. Having lived with his partner for seven years or more they had decided that it was about time they became husband and wife. It was a very happy day for them and their guests, but I always wondered why they bothered to tie the knot having lived together so successfully for quite a considerable time. In retrospect, they obviously did the right thing for them, and any doubts I may have had were my problems manifesting themselves. Sometimes it benefited people to legalise unions, especially if children were involved, as inheritance matters needed to be taken into consideration. I just felt that I knew several couples who were quite happy together as partners and then not long after their marriages they split up. Perhaps expectations change with legality and the degree of commitment takes on another dimension.

The nature of their folk roots was seen in songs like 'The Dark Lord', which was an epic tale about an old, blind man whose fearlessness defeated an evil force. The lyrics conjured up an image similar to the figure in 'Night on Bare Mountain' from Walt Disney's Fantasia. They were able to get to the heart of their subject matter with wonderful imagery and their melodies were always memorable. In a simpler vein, 'Solitude' had a medieval feel about it because of its parallel harmonies (the same melody sung at an equal distance apart). It had a section where the voices sang "ah" in a style that reminded me of monastery chants of long ago.

On the other hand, 'Crying Blues' was an uptempo, electric, funky track that was equal to any of its American counterparts. 'Angels' was a delicious little ditty with layered voices and a chorus that stated: "You'll only meet angels in heaven … if you believe." They could be as powerful in their simple structures as they were in their more complicated ones, and I believe this is a real sign of talent. To be able to express a universal truth in simple terms is one of the hardest things for songwriters to achieve, and without a doubt Hudson-Ford could do just that. They had a great deal to say that showed their common sense. They said that bad news can be taken easier if sweetened, or if told with humour, but it could also be lost to those who saw no further than the surface. The films of Mel Brooks and Woody Allen are wonderful examples of this philosophy.

The boys' philosophical nature was seen in the last two tracks of the album. 'I Don't Understand' was a political statement about the state of the world in the hands of politicians: "But I don't understand … Why the world is in your hands … Is it still here … Or is it dying." The last track had the feel of a David Bowie song, and was called 'Revelations'. It was a message to the young, who were taking a trip into space because the Earth was no longer a fit place on which to survive: "You, my children, are the new ones, who will help man decide, please don't make the same mistakes, if you survive the ride."

I would have liked to be involved in other Hudson-Ford projects, but alas it was not to be. I did enjoy my time with them, and John once told me a humorous little story:

A queen from some faraway country awoke on the first morning of her honeymoon. She was singing to herself, for the night before with the king was so amazing for her that she couldn't contain her joy. She turned to her beloved husband and asked, "Tell me, darling, do the common people do what we did last night?" "Yes," said the king, "I believe they do." "Well," said the queen, "It's too good for them!"

Steel Pulse, a reggae band, were in a world of their own. The members of the group came from Birmingham and they were true Rastafarians. Working with them was quite an education, as well as a pleasure, and I knew I'd never be the same again. Chris Blackwell at Island Records asked me to produce a single for the band. It was called 'Reggae Fever', and the experience was as informative as it could possibly be.

The boys lived in Handsworth, which was not the most prestigious area of Birmingham, and you got the feeling that your life was on the line at all times. The studio we used was located in a small alley and the equipment had seen better days, but sometimes this kind of facility helped to create a raw sound that was almost impossible to achieve in an up-to-date palace. I do know that restrictions often made the imagination more active, and the challenges presented sometimes gave me extra energy that allowed me to achieve a better result.

The band consisted of leader David Hinds on lead guitar and harmonies; Basil Gabbidon on lead guitar; Selwyn Brown on keyboards and vocals; Ronald 'Stepper' McQueen on bass; Steve 'Grizzly' Nisbett on drums and percussion; and Phonso Martin on percussion and vocals. David had a definite vision of what he wanted the band to sound like, and I guessed that he was influenced by his idol, Bob Marley. They were a very good band, and the song for the 'A' side of the single was certainly up to Marley's standard.

David was a bundle of energy, and he was particularly concerned with the technical aspect of the group. He was forever arguing with Steve about placing his drumbeats in the right place, and I must say that I thought Steve was one of the steadiest drummers I had ever heard. David guided everyone in the band, and from morning until night he relentlessly explained his vision of what a reggae band should sound like. He was like a stern schoolmaster presiding over his children. None of the band seemed to mind his dictatorial approach to them, for they carried out his wishes to the letter and never once complained. David was the smallest member of the band, and to see these large, heavy band members taking orders like well-disciplined children was often quite comical.

The boys had been in school together and had known each other for a long time. There was a family atmosphere about them. They would laugh, cry and argue together, but whatever happened their friendship was eternal. I remember on one occasion their wives came to the studio and had brought with them some special Rastafarian food. I entered the control room to find the wives rolling the biggest joints (marijuana) I had ever seen. They must have been six inches long and an inch and a half in diameter. The room was filled with smoke from earlier joints and the boys were floating 12 feet off the ground. David came up to me and peered into my face. He had obviously noticed my natural laid-back manner during the first few days of recording, and he said to me: "What are you on, Del?" I tried to explain to him that music was my 'high', but I don't think he believed me.

I wondered how they were going to perform that day, considering their condition. I need not have worried, however, as they worked marvellously, and I realised that this was a normal, everyday occurrence for them. To be 'straight' wasn't part of their vision, and smoking pot was part of their philosophical beliefs. They actually functioned very well musically, and so who was I to argue with that? Our aim was the same. We wanted to complete the best single we could at that time, and I believe we achieved our goal.

In 1980 'Reggae Fever' turned up on a Steel Pulse album called Caught You. It was produced by Geoffrey Chung for Penetrate Productions and was released on Island Records. It was interesting to compare Geoffrey's mixes with mine, especially because the band were at both mixing sessions and so they'd had the same opportunity to state their preferences. Chung's mixes had more echo on the voices and they were further forward in the overall picture. This meant that the band were sometimes less effective. My voices and instruments were drier, which gave the effect of being closer to the audience.

I know that these details may seem irrelevant to the reader, but musicians were always conscious of these matters. Perhaps, sub-consciously, the fans were aware of these things too, for how a disc sounded may have affected the way they reacted. If you think of the disco period, when the young danced the night away until the early hours, often the only thing they could hear in a club was the bass and drums. Dancing was the priority, so these two instruments were the most prominent sounds on the disc. Different mixes could completely alter the feeling of a track, just as different editing by a director of a film could change the final emotional result. These comments are not criticisms, they are simply observations, and the point is that the feel of the band was different. The band sanctioned both sessions and so we can surmise that they were happy with both results.

The boys had not been given a particularly good start in life, and I got the impression that they had been through some really hard times. On the 1980 record they even acknowledged The Handsworth Law Centre. I think the very mention of that place spoke for itself. To be black in Britain had its difficulties, but to be Rastafarian, and to have long dreadlocks as a hairstyle, certainly stretched the gulf between the indigenous population and those with roots from a different culture. Unfortunately, people generally reacted in the first instance to what they saw. First impressions seemed to be very important. I was always told that you should never judge a book by its cover. Perhaps I should have been told that I should never judge ... at least until I had read the book!

The band were quite active in spreading good race relations. Much of David's lyrics were concerned with the plight of the underdog, and the problems for black people in particular. The irony was that many of the Caribbean clubs in the Midlands refused to give the band live engagements. They thought that their Rastafarian beliefs were too extreme. The band told me about horrific situations that occurred when they were touring with punk bands such as The Stranglers and XTC.

Their recording career moved through many labels. The problem stemmed from the fact they were not interested in becoming more mainstream in their approach to their material. They changed to the Elektra label in 1982, with the album True Democracy; the MCA label in 1988 with State of Emergency; and then to Bluemoon in 1997 with Rage and Fury. Most companies paid out a great deal of money for the recordings to be made, and if an act wasn't a mainstream attraction that sold their work in large quantities the company waved goodbye to the band.

Steel Pulse had a growing following in Britain and America and, had a company stood by them long enough, they could have become world class. They did a great deal of touring and their live gigs were something to be seen. Wherever they were in the world, for the first couple of years, I would get a telephone call from them telling me how they were getting on. It was probably a way of saying thanks for the past. They taught me that life should be taken in slow strides and that worrying about anything never changed the outcome of events. They were good people, and wherever they are and whatever they're doing I wish them well and hope their wives keep on rolling that funny stuff, which allows them to take their journey at such a steady pace.

Around the same time as my association with Steel Pulse I was approached to produce an album for The 'O' Band called The Knife. They came from either The Isle of Wight or The Isle of Man. I'm not quite sure because it was only mentioned once and it is more than 30 years since I last saw them. The band consisted of Pix (J. Pickford) on guitar and lead vocals; Craig Anders on guitar, slide guitar and vocals; Jeff Bannister on keyboard and vocals; Mark Anders on bass; and Derek Ballard on drums and percussion. The recording took place at the Scorpio and Marquee Studios, and out of the nine tracks I produced seven and Doug Bennett produced two. The reason for this was complicated, and it made me re-evaluate my role as a producer.

During the mixing of the album, Pix, the leader, was adamant that he knew how he wanted the band to sound. He said that he wanted as natural a sound as possible. For him this meant hardly any echo on the instruments or the voices, which he said would bring the band into the rooms of the fans. He also wanted the vocals set far back in the tracks so that the instruments could be heard at their most powerful dynamic. Pix always seemed sure of himself and he was used to being in charge of the group. He was strict with the other band members and he achieved excellent musical results. But this didn't mean that he knew what was the best way to promote his album. He knew nothing about the nature of the commercial world, and this was evident by the way he wanted the album mixed.

Pix and I had long conversations about this approach to the band's work, and I wasn't happy about the idea. My past experience had taught me that whatever else producers might do they should never bury vocals so that they are difficult to hear. After all, a song is a story set to music, and if the story is inaudible the whole point of the work is lost. Do you think he listened? He was the leader of the band, and I had to comply with his wishes or walk out of the studio. The other members of the band never voiced an opinion about how the sound of the finished product should be, and that made me realise the degree of power that Pix had over his colleagues. The dynamics of all relationships in bands were different. Whatever made the band work successfully depended on the personalities in the group, and at times these dynamics caused bands to break up.

United Artists thought that extra material of a lighter nature would give the album a better chance of selling, so Doug Bennett was brought in to save the day. The two tracks he produced were short and more commercial than mine, and he remixed the album with the vocals brought forward and more echo than before. I say 'more commercial' because the added songs had a rock and roll and country feel about them, which made them more acceptable to the company. The essence of the band was more than that, and the tracks I was privileged to produce were epic tales with imaginative instrumentation behind the stories.

The band comprised a group of excellent musicians. Their arrangements were quite hypnotic and the various effects that they used on the guitars were spellbinding. The lyrics on many of the songs were about violence, drugs and the seedier side of life. Since the boys came from the shelter of an island I wondered where these influences had originated. Pix's voice could have a high, angelic sound, as on 'Venus Avenue' or 'Time Seems to Fly'. He could draw you into his web of mystery so well that you might not be aware of the significance of what he was saying. On the other hand, he could put a grit into his delivery that reminded me of a male

Janis Joplin. Tracks like 'Got to Run' and the title track 'The Knife' were excellent tales. They were evil stories about self-destruction and impotence, and Pix delivered them with absolute conviction, carrying us along on his magic carpet to his underworld.

Even the cover of the album was black, and the information on it was printed in red. Did this signify blood? On the front cover Pix was standing in front of a castle (not unlike Dracula's), with an enormous knife in his hands. The back cover showed the steps of the castle and on them lay the knife covered in blood. I thought at the time that Alice Cooper might have been a great influence on the band, but this was never discussed. I have never been able to find any material about them in popular music literature, so I am not really certain what happened to their career after making The Knife. Musicians of their calibre were probably offered other deals, or perhaps they split up and found work playing in different bands. Whatever happened to them was a mystery to me, but their effect upon me was everlasting. If there was any justice in the world, their excellence would have prospered. But life wasn't always fair, and time and place were important factors in determining the direction our lives eventually took.

Anyone who saw the film Woodstock will remember a band called Ten Years After. I knew the drummer of the group, Rick Lee. He said to me rather casually one day, "We have a track we don't know what to do with because it's a kind of a ballad, and you know our stuff is generally on the heavy side." He then suggested that I might be able to help. I suddenly got a call from Rick telling me to come to the studio, where they were mixing some tracks, to see the leader Alvin Lee, as he wanted to see if he liked me.

I arrived at the studio at the appointed time and was shown into the mixing room where the band were working. As I opened the door, smoke came billowing out and I thought there was a fire. However, it was only the band. You could hardly see across the room. They were all, except Rick, as high as kites on whatever they were smoking. I never knew how people could work under those conditions, but in the seventies it was quite common to see young people smoking dope, and especially rock musicians.

Rick offered me a chair and I was completely ignored for at least 20 minutes. Having had enough of what I considered to be rudeness, I got up from my chair and began walking towards the door. Rick stopped me and told Alvin that I was the person he had mentioned in regard to doing an arrangement. Alvin was high, and he came very close to me and peered into my face. He then said, "So you are the violin head are you?" I must say it did amuse me, for I had never heard the expression before.

Eventually we did the work and everything turned out fine. Rick told me that Alvin had recently bought a house in the country. Some months later, Alvin was told a road was going to be built and it would have to cross his land. He was offered a fortune for his property, which Rick thought was three times more than Alvin had paid for it. I guess it was a good example of the phrase, "time and place," but why the relevant council didn't buy the house before Alvin, knowing that a road was to be built, begs a question or two.

* * *

A patient was talking to his therapist, lying on a couch in a sumptuous office. "I'm having so many problems, doctor," he began. "I don't know where to start." The psychiatrist sat down behind his desk and said, "I suggest that you start at the beginning because that is always the best place to start." "Okay," said the patient in an agitated state. "In the beginning, I created Earth."

CHAPTER 17

It was always a pleasure for me to work with musical theatre people, and my favourite star was Marti Caine. She was the leading lady in Jule Styne's Funny Girl at the Crucible Theatre in Sheffield, and she was an absolute gem. Marti had a special kind of presence that was completely captivating. Not only was she a beautiful woman physically, for she had been a successful model long before I knew her, but there was a light shining brightly inside her that shone like a lighthouse beacon for all to see. She always wore fantastic clothes that were not necessarily expensive but had a flair that made her look elegant. She had a smile for everyone, which put the whole company at ease.

The show rehearsed for two weeks and ran for three, and from the very first day of rehearsal the whole cast loved her. Her attitude to everyone was so natural, without airs and graces, and she constantly worked in a way that would help others. She spent most of the coffee breaks with the dancers, as she obviously admired their expertise. At all times she was ready to discuss any point regarding the show with anyone. This was important because it helped to create a good working atmosphere for the complete cast. I have known instances where the 'star' of a show was so difficult that everyone in the cast dreaded going to work. One man even insisted that he had a star placed on the door of his dressing room.

It wasn't always easy for Marti because the lead role had a tremendous amount of dialogue and she was on stage in nearly every scene. She admitted that the number of lines she had to remember was more than she had ever tackled before. But, being a determined young lady, she said that she would stay at home, forego any socialising and give it everything she had until the job was completed. She kept her word, and every evening she performed without making a single error. Sometimes she would look at me while I was conducting in the pit and give me a quick wink. She had a wonderful sense of humour and could be quite naughty.

We began rehearsals in a large room about five minutes' walk from the theatre. Getting the cast to learn the chorus parts for the ensemble numbers was my first task. A musical director's role was exactly that. Their job was to create enthusiasm, and like any good schoolmaster they needed to make the work fun, to encourage all the time and to praise the group as much as possible so that they went home after a long day's work feeling good about themselves. The leading actors learnt their solo songs, which might include duets, trios and quartets, separately from the chorus, who were the remainder of the cast. This often included the dancers, who in my opinion had the hardest job in the company. Their days were long, very long, and their normal rehearsing day extended to 12 hours, beginning at ten in the morning and lasting until ten at night. All they wanted to do when they left the theatre was sleep. I believe that they received the least amount of money of all the cast members, which was an absolute disgrace.

Marti came to all the chorus rehearsals in order to make sense of the overall plan. On one occasion, when I was being rather strict about the rhythm of a particular song, she came up to me in a morning break and said, "You're a bit of a schoolteacher, aren't you?" She gave me a great smile, and it was obvious that my ability to shout occasionally had really surprised her. I explained that I was shouting at myself in frustration, and she understood. I felt that she liked the idea of someone being in control that she could rely on.

On many occasions we would invite each other to lunch. The company only got an hour for lunch, so I relied on Marti to know where the nearest reasonable restaurants were. It was rather fun because Marti was always dressed in fashionable clothes, and when we entered these places everyone would stare, puzzling over whether it was Marti or not. She was stunning, and yet she took everything as a matter of course. I never saw her look in a mirror, and where there were actors and dancers there were mirrors everywhere. Most of them couldn't resist glancing in them as they passed, but I thought the dancers were excused because movement needs to be observed to be improved. Marti never once referred to her professional past, and in her company it was more like being with your sister than with a well-known star.

Marti had an apartment in a small, select, modern block in the suburbs of Sheffield and she knew the city well. A couple of times I was invited there for dinner after the show. There were other guests too, including Clare Venables, the director of the show, and a couple of leading actors from the company. Clare and I had worked together before in London, on Sweet Charity, another great stage musical. I was sad to hear, many years later, that she became very ill, as did Marti. In many ways the entertainment business was really stressful for many people. Sometimes too much work, or not enough, can cause havoc with the mind and create depression.

Marti's children had grown up and left home, and I got the impression that she didn't have a partner. Once I met her son, who was in the Army and it was obvious that she adored him. He had just popped into the apartment to say hello and she held his hand the whole time he was there. It was clear that his profession meant that they didn't see each other very often. They talked about things that had happened in the past, and Marti was kind enough to include me in the conversation. She was the most considerate artist I have ever worked with, for her nature was such that she would never consider leaving a member of a group out of things.

During an invited evening the conversation around the dinner table was full of sexual innuendos, and it was possible that Marti was wide open for a relationship. For example, Clare mentioned going down to see a friend in the near future and Marti said, "Oh, that sounds wonderful. I wish someone would go down on me!" Everybody laughed, but I sensed an air of sadness in Marti's voice that suggested loneliness. She made similar innuendos throughout the evening, and I couldn't understand why somebody so attractive didn't have a partner. She later married a television producer and appeared to be blissfully happy. She told me that her previous marriage had not been too successful, and I dearly wanted her to be settled with someone who appreciated her, as she was such a generous spirit.

Marti got standing ovations every night and she deserved them. There were after-show parties on two occasions, and she never forgot to thank everyone for their support. I remember one night after the show I was invited to her dressing room to share a joint. It surprised me then, but now I believe that it was part of her extraordinary aura. Like cigarettes, it was a relaxant and a habit, and the saying that "a little of what you fancy does you good" had an element of truth in it. She appeared to have a nervous disposition, which was possibly brought on by an early marriage to someone who didn't appreciate her fine qualities. These personal matters will never be revealed, as only the people concerned knew the facts. But there was no smoke without fire, and we're all the sum total of our experience.

The show was well received by the press. The orchestra, which was in the pit under the stage, was praised by one reporter as, "a musical tape that made for a flawless performance". With criticism like this we could do no wrong. The last night for me was particularly sad. Marti had asked me to drop into her dressing room after the show to exchange numbers and addresses. After the final performance I had to collect all the scores from the stands and clear away anything that pertained to music. As this took me over an hour, I assumed that Marti had already left the theatre. However, a week later I was told by one of the backstage crew that she had waited two hours for me to arrive before she left the theatre.

We didn't meet again. I have always regretted not going backstage to see if she was still there. Her premature demise ten years later was a great shock to me. It wasn't often that you met someone that you considered a soulmate. There were many wonderful people out there, but unfortunately we couldn't meet them all. The old adage "the good die young" was certainly true in her case.

Before the days of Andrew Lloyd Webber, Hair was probably second only to West Side Story in terms of musical successes after the Second World War. The book and the lyrics were written by Gerome Ragni and James Rado, and the music was written by Galt MacDermot. Whereas Galt was a middle-class, formally trained musician, Rado and Ragni looked like two sixties hippies that had missed the boat a decade before. They wore jeans with holes in long before it became a mainstream fashion and they had a very unkempt appearance. They had long hair and looked as if they were penniless. Since they were obviously a couple of millionaires, as the musical had been performed throughout the world, it was a great shock to my system.

It was a very interesting project. In the winter of 1969 I was asked to meet Victor Spinetti, the director of the show. He was a well-known actor and had appeared in Beatles movies as well as television series. His father had been an Italian prisoner of war, and Victor said that he was subjected to a great deal of bullying from his peers at school. There were many prison camps in Wales for captured Italian soldiers, who were used as farm labourers. Some remained in Wales after the war and married Welsh ladies. Victor's mother lived in the Rhondda Valley, a coal-mining area, which was full of small villages and large slag heaps.

A very pleasant memory was that Victor decided to give the cast a treat. Halfway through the rehearsals he organised a coach trip one Sunday to go to Wales and meet his mother. The coach arrived at midday and 20 actors, singers and dancers descended on his mother's small terraced house. Luckily, the weather was fine, so most of the cast went into the little garden at the rear of the house. The whole village was overshadowed by an enormous coal slag heap, which meant that the sun only shone on its inhabitants for a short period every day.

We had a wonderful time. Villagers came to the house, bearing gifts of food they had cooked, to join in the fun. We sang Welsh hymns and songs from the show, and some of the neighbours gave renditions that were hard to believe. There was a feeling about village life that seemed to be lost in large cities. All the inhabitants of the village knew everything that was going on there and they were always ready to offer support to anyone and everyone in a crisis. It was an attitude that I'm certain has never changed.

The rehearsals continued and the two-week schedule to get the show ready for the opening night went relatively smoothly. The 20-strong cast of young, vibrant people comprised a mixed bag of nationalities: American, Canadian, Dutch, German and British. The only well-known British actor in the cast was Oliver Tobias, who had been in films and was becoming a recognisable face. The cast had no idea what they were about to experience. Victor wasn't the normal run-of-the-mill director. He had plans that would have made lesser men and women shake with fear.

Rado and Ragni came to see us at the beginning of rehearsals to give the cast some moral support. They seemed pleasant enough and were encouraging to the group. I suspected that they did this to every company that performed their show. They wanted to see what kind of cast had passed the auditions in London, as the show was being put on in Amsterdam and the conditions were that a third of the company should be Dutch, although there were no territorial restrictions for the remainder of the cast. Although none of the cast members had met before, some of them remained friends after the show had closed. Most of them, however, went in different directions.

The lyricists wanted the Dutch production to make a record that was in keeping with the other productions throughout the world. They gave me five other language versions of the show and told me to make this one different. Little did they know what was in store for the production. I assumed that they said this to every musical director of every Hair show that had ever been performed, but I was thankful for their support. It was amazing to hear the other versions of the show because they all had something unique about their approach, in addition to the obvious language differences. They had a different feel about them, which was probably due to their stemming from diverse cultures and directors.

On the very first day of rehearsal Victor told the cast that he wanted them to get to know each other so well that they thought and moved as one body. He wanted to draw any inhibitions that the cast may have to the surface so they could be discussed and hopefully dispelled. This created several problems. Two of the cast only lasted three days. They were so disturbed by some of the proceedings that they walked out of the room and never returned. Everyone, including the pianist, was surprised. Victor was as cool as a cucumber and simply said that he had expected to lose a few casualties on the journey on which we were about to embark.

The problem had arisen when Victor asked the company to sit on the floor in a large circle, with each actor taking turns to sit in the middle of the circle. Initially the surrounding members were asked to say something positive about the one in the centre. This was fine and everyone coped relatively well with the flattery. Then Victor asked the cast to say something negative about the central person. Some of the statements made were about their physical appearance, others about their behaviour patterns, and others linked to their personalities, as seen by the group.

It wasn't easy to be criticised in a negative fashion by 19 people. However, in the context of rehearsals, the fact that every member had to tread the same path gave an air of unreality about the exercise. The two members who left the room were obviously hypersensitive to this kind of criticism and it had sparked something inside that made it too uncomfortable for them to continue. Later, Victor explained that he was trying to loosen the inhibitions of the group so that they could work together without any barriers between them. This, he said, would allow for a much more interesting performance for the audience. I understood his reasoning and I actually used the technique myself on later shows. However, I only used the positive approach in the exercise. I had witnessed first-hand how easily people could be hurt and I felt that it was a dangerous path to tread.

The show opened in Amsterdam, where Victor wanted something that had not been done before by any other Hair company. He arranged for the show to open in a circus tent. He said that the audience shouldn't expect a regular theatrical experience, as they weren't going to get a stage and normal seating, and that they were going to be participants in a magical mystery event. How right he was. They certainly didn't expect to be entertained in a tent in the middle of winter. Some of the remarks I heard before the beginning of the show weren't flattering, but the audience settled down once the performance had started.

We arrived in Amsterdam during the early part of December and, believe me, it was very, very cold. Victor had arranged for four enormous hot-air-blowing machines to be placed in strategic positions to warm the inside space. If you went anywhere near them you felt as though you were in the tropics, but move ten feet away from them and your feet began to freeze. Rather than comfortable seats, the audience was accommodated on long, wooden benches. It was first come, first served; there was only one price, and one bench is as hard as another. Before the show started there were many murmurings of discontent,

There was no raised stage or proscenium arch. Instead, an enormous scaffolding structure had been built at one end of the tent, which incorporated a platform for the actors, one for the musicians, and a great deal of piping for high movement. This meant that the audience was required to look upwards, and the lighting was very effective because it gave the appearance of halos everywhere. The workmen involved in erecting the tent and supplying the air blowers were very efficient, but due to an argument over money they refused to lift a finger to do anything else unless they were paid in advance for each job undertaken. The cast called them the BUF (Bread Up Front) gang, and this procedure did slow things down sometimes, but we still opened on the first night on time, so all's well that ends well.

The musicians were the best (and the worst) we could possibly have had for the show. They were a band called Focus, a Dutch group that were selling millions of records worldwide. Two of the band members were known to be as good as you could get in their field: Thijs Van Leer on keyboards and Jan Akkerman on guitar. They could play anything, but being great soloists they soon got bored of playing the same arrangements for every performance and after a month or so they began to experiment with the music. That was anathema to the cast, as the actors needed to hear consistent sounds every night so that they could perform a fully rehearsed show. Any deviation in the sound made them uncertain of the format. The question arose: what should we do? The answer was obvious. We had a meeting with the band and they decided that they'd had enough. It was a great relief for the cast. The band understood the need for conformity, but it was against their nature to supply it. It made me sad at the time because I appreciated their expertise, but we had to part company.

We auditioned some musicians that were used to playing for musical shows and then all went well. A degree of energy may have been lost, but the security that the actors felt was well worth the replacement. To ensure that the music was being performed correctly meant flying to Amsterdam every two weeks for three months until everything had settled down. Victor and I would discuss any points that needed attention, which kept the standard of the performances at a high level. Victor was very precise in his demands and he knew exactly how to obtain what he wanted. He was very good with the actors, who liked him a great deal, and I never heard a dispute of any kind during my time with the show.

Another problem to be solved was nudity. A few of the set pieces required a couple of ladies to be naked from the waist up. It wasn't only some members of the audience that were shocked. Most of the ladies in the cast weren't particularly keen to volunteer their services and bare all. We were lucky to have European girls in the show, as they appeared to be less inhibited than the British contingent. A Dutch member, who seemed quite at ease with the prospect, and a German, who was the daughter of a German diplomat in London, both jumped at the idea. It seemed obvious to me that they both had a rebellious streak in their nature, and they thought enough of their bodies to want to expose themselves to the world at large. It was Christmas 1969 and the element of free expression was quite prevalent.

It was great fun to watch the reaction of the audience. There wasn't even a titter when these songs were being performed. Not one eyebrow was raised. I believed it to be different in Britain. In comparison to West Side Story, which opened in London only a few years earlier and only suggested the threat of violence, I thought that Hair was much more defiant. When leaving West Side Story not long after its opening, I heard a woman say as she was exiting the theatre, "How disgusting some of the language was, and how antisocial. I'm certain it will influence our young people to turn to crime." When I think of the amount of sex and violence in films today it makes me realise how much more tolerant we are in society now, and I wonder whether 'progress' is such a good thing.

The Dutch, being European, were more used to overt sexuality than the British and our neighbours across the Atlantic Ocean. Hollywood hadn't reached the level of explicit sex scenes in its movies that was the norm in the early twenty-first century. Amsterdam had its famous windows in the red light district, and city dwellers were more used to experiencing overt sex and seeing drugs taken by addicts in public places. I remember my Swedish girlfriend suggested that we go to a seedy cinema in Piccadilly Circus. She was the only woman in the place and we left as soon as the lights came on because I felt it wasn't a safe place for her to frequent. It didn't bother her at all.

During the set-up of the show I went into a disused church in Amsterdam that was painted red. It was the centre of the drug smoking culture in the late sixties. Anyone could enter and buy as much marijuana as they could afford. There were young people lying around who were out in space somewhere, and the police knew about it. It was clever of them to leave the place alone, because they had greater control over the movement of the drugs if they were openly found in one place. If you wanted to smoke the stuff for your personal use you could sit in any café and enjoy your habit in the knowledge that it was completely legal. I thought the only reason it wasn't legal in other developed countries was the fact that many 'important' people were making a great deal of money from something that was considered forbidden.

The beauty of working on the Dutch production manifested itself in its international nature. The input from different nationalities had a very positive effect on the cast, the director, me and the audience. It was the only production that had such a diverse cultural company. The blend of those differences gave the Amsterdam Hair a unique quality that was missing in the performances I saw in the USA and Britain. In that instance diversity certainly gave strength, and that was a lesson for all to contemplate.

I passed Victor in a railway station a few months ago and he didn't recognise me. Such is the nature of things. I'll always remember Victor's show as the strangest and most educational project that I was ever associated with. I have only remained a close friend of one of the cast members, and I haven't seen or heard from any of the other wonderful young actors and dancers who brought such pleasure to thousands of people. I hope they have prospered and remember those times with the warmth that nostalgia brings.

The perception of some writers towards their own work could sometimes be amusing. I was asked to arrange the music for Blood Brothers, which was written by Willy Russell, who also wrote Educating Rita and Shirley Valentine. The London version had been running for years, and the New York version needed new arrangements because the system was different in America. The number of musicians in a theatre orchestra was governed by the number of seats it contained; that is to say, its size. Because the London office were not sure which theatre the show would be in, I was asked to write new arrangements for all the orchestral instruments, but the music for the percussion instruments was not to be written until more information had been gathered.

I was invited to be interviewed by Willy, who had an office with an apartment above it in Liverpool. He was very polite and told me that he had been given my name by Jon Miller, with whom I had worked many years before. Jon had produced many records in his own studio and he was the musical right-hand man for the theatre producer Bill Kenwright, a very successful businessman, whom I had known since 1970 through the musical No Trams to Lime Street.

Willy was excited about an American opening and was concerned about the style of the arrangements. He was adamant that the sound of the music should be very basic, with no 'modern' chords, and he produced a guitar from somewhere and strummed a few chords for me as an example of his preferences. I understood his anxiety and convinced him that I completely agreed with his vision. Needless to say, I went away determined to do my best because he was such a lovely man. I wasn't sure how much Willy knew about the theory of music; he could have known as much as Lionel Bart, of Oliver fame, which was absolutely nothing. But both the writers created memorable tunes and that was the most difficult part of the musical process.

When the work was finished, with all the modern chords that were necessary to make the music palatable, the show had an opening in Liverpool with the new arrangements. There was a party after the show and Willy came up to me and thanked me for keeping the arrangements simple. "Thank God you didn't use any of those modern abominations in the music. I really enjoyed your work." He went off smiling, with yet another victory under his belt, and it felt good because I had been able to do what I wanted to do without any interference from my employer. It was just an example to show that we didn't have to know the ingredients of a meal to enjoy it.

The old saying "too many cooks spoil the broth" was a true observation, and it often occurred in the music industry. Jon Miller had not told the leader of the orchestra in Blood Brothers, who was a dear friend of mine, that the rhythm arrangements had yet to be written. This meant that the leader didn't tell the orchestra. After the first Liverpool rehearsal the drummer of the band (and they generally belonged to another planet) couldn't resist making a detrimental remark about my work. Years later I met the leader at a wedding ceremony for Jon and his partner and I informed him of the early decision that Jon had made about the arrangements. He was embarrassed and said that he knew nothing about it. He apologised for any misconception, and we both looked at Jon and shrugged our shoulders.

Another project was The Butterfly Ball and The Grasshopper's Feast. The title refers to a book of verses by William Plomer and colour plates by Alan Aldridge. By chance, Alan had discovered William Roscoe's poem 'The Butterfly Ball', which was written in 1807, in the British Museum. The year was 1971, and after intensive work the book was published in 1973. By the end of that year the publication had sold over 200,000 copies. This was followed by an LP record, a full-length cartoon film and a stage presentation.

Roger Glover, the bass guitarist with Deep Purple, wrote most of the music for the LP, which was released on the Purple Records label. He was also the producer, played piano, guitar, bass, percussion and synthesiser and sang backing vocals on the project. His vision was to create a live performance at the Royal Albert Hall in London, in aid of two wonderful charities: Action Research for The Crippled Child and the Bud Flanagan Leukaemia Fund. Roger was a seasoned musician, who had known great success with Deep Purple. He and John Lord, the keyboard player with the group and the husband of the lady who was responsible for my entry into the industry, had made a great impact on the popular music scene at the time, so they were in a position to recruit many well known celebrities for the project.

I was asked to do most of the arrangements and to conduct the show, and it was an exciting challenge for all concerned. One of the attractions for me came in the form of Vincent Price, who was to be the narrator, a great actor who I had really admired for many years, and Twiggy was to sing one of the songs. There wasn't much you could say about someone who was the face of the sixties and probably had more written about her in the world press than anyone in that decade. She lived a few doors from me in Notting Hill, and I noticed that her big, red, Italian sports car always seemed to have its bonnet up, with a workman peering into the engine, nearly every time I passed by her house.

Each visual plate in the book was a wonderful, detailed painting depicting the title of its poem. Not only were the creatures meticulously reproduced, but also the environment they were set in would have rivalled any Walt Disney full-length feature. There was humour and pathos in the work, and I think it would be fair to say that it was truly unique. The artist had obviously studied the creatures through a magnifying glass, for every hair was faithfully reproduced. I had never seen the like before, and I certainly have never seen any book since, dealing with the same subject matter, that has excited me in the same way.

Whenever money was needed for charities, people in the music industry were very generous with their time and gave their services for free. They were patrons in the true sense of the word, for there was no hidden agenda in contrast to conglomerate companies that have to advertise their products. Organisations such as the Variety Club of Great Britain had raised large sums and had given many performances for children who were disadvantaged in some way. This concert was no exception. Artists came from far and wide to participate in the venture. David Coverdale sang 'Behind the Smile'; Ian Gillan sang 'Sitting in a Dream'; Al Matthews, Tony Ashton, John Gustafson, John Lawton, Neil Lancaster, Vincent Price, Twiggy, Liza Strike, Barry St John, Earl Jordan, Judi Kuhl, Glenn Hughes, Eddie Hardin and Mickey Lee Soule all gave their best on a grand occasion for a great cause. It was interesting to see people that would haggle over minutiae in a contract give everything they've got professionally for a good cause.

Not only was the cream of the popular music world performing, but also the titles of the songs sparked the imagination to an amazing degree. Harlequin Hare, Old Blind Mole, Sir Maximus Mouse, Saffron Dormouse and Lizzy Bee were but a few of the delights that the audience savoured that night. The performers rang every ounce of nuance from their stories, and you could hear a pin drop as the atmosphere was charged with electricity.

My favourite time was always at the rehearsals. This was when there wasn't a great deal of pressure on anyone because we could stop the proceedings if need be without worrying about the audience. The performers were relaxed and everyone's sense of humour was high. I think that was how people got through a situation that required every nerve in their body to concentrate on the need to cooperate with a large body of people. Performing to an audience, where one's wits had to be as sharp as a knife, was a stressful affair, and everyone there was required to be on top form.

It was not often that creative people working together in the industry argued about anything. Of course, bands would split up for various reasons, and some people had hidden agendas, but in the recording industry most people had a common goal, and that was to create a finished product to the best of their ability. The duty of every member participating was clear. The engineers, the musicians, the producer, the arranger and the artists were there to give their expertise to the work at hand. If animosity of any kind had been present, the creative process would have been impossible to complete and the outcome would have been fruitless.

During coffee breaks we were allowed to sit around engaging in small talk and gossip, and this was when you really got to know whether you liked someone or not. Vincent Price was an absolute diamond. He was a towering six feet four inches but was one of the most gentle, softly spoken men I had ever met. This really surprised me because I expected the 'king of horror movies' to be, at the very least, frightening. I couldn't have been more wrong. Vincent had a great sense of humour and a devilish gleam in his eyes. He was wide open and very knowledgeable about many things. He spoke to nearly every member of the cast, and I noticed that a smile never left his face. He talked a great deal about his favourite works of art. It was obvious that he loved the subject because he spoke with such enthusiasm.

Vincent was a good listener. I was always taught that a good conversationalist was someone who knew how to listen to others. He gave you his full attention, and this showed what a generous nature he had. He even gave me a couple of recipes when I told him I was fed up with eating in restaurants because to cook at home was a real chore. He said he knew cooking for one was a lonely task, but there were simple meals that didn't take a great deal of effort and he wanted to share their preparation with me. What a lovely gesture!

He had a wonderful speaking voice that had the soft quality of velvet. When you consider that his stage debut in London was at the Gate Theatre in 'Victoria Regina' in 1935, and our concert was nearly 40 years later, his experience was enormous. He starred in over 100 films, was a member of the Orson Welles Mercury Theatre Company, and was a graduate of Yale University. Yet he was one of the most modest stars I have ever met. When he talked about other film people that he'd worked with I could sense a high degree of affection in his expression. In the two days I was with him I never heard him speak negatively about anyone. He was the perfect gentleman.

I remember seeing Vincent's last film, Whales in August, with Bette Davis and Lillian Gish, who were both in their eighties. It was made in 1987 and Vincent was playing a Russian nobleman called Victor who had seen better times. The ladies were unmarried sisters who lived on an island off the New England coast. Bette was blind, and when they were young they had experienced unrequited love. Victor was a visiting guest, and the underlying tension between them was very powerful to watch. The understatement of Vincent's performance was a work of art in itself. He had a quality of delicacy that is not often seen on stage or film. He was the perfect choice to narrate the story of The Butterfly Ball, and it was a pleasure and an honour to meet such a generous spirit.

Twiggy was the girl next door and was an absolute delight. She was born in Neasden, London, and was discovered by a man who took the name of Justin de Villeneuve for professional purposes. Her ambition and his know-how made her the icon of the sixties. You never knew what to expect when you were going to meet someone for the first time that was known throughout the world; someone whose every movement was captured by the press and who probably had very little privacy in their life. People like this could be quite tricky to deal with because they were often on the defensive against a barrage of intrusive questions. Although it was understandable, I often felt butterflies in the stomach just before meeting them, which was probably due to my expectations and my insecurity.

It was not so with Twiggy. She was wide open. I don't think the exposure she was subjected to had any effect on her whatsoever. She was natural, generous and quite fun to be with. She had a great sense of humour, and despite all the cameras she had posed for she seemed a little nervous about singing to 7,000 people at the Albert Hall. She joked about it just like a little schoolgirl, and I found this very endearing. Her naturalness and friendliness put you at ease at once, and her London accent hadn't changed, which belied the enormous attention she had been used to.

Twiggy had already sung and acted in the film The Boyfriend, but singing live to a massive audience rather than just a film crew was quite a different matter. During the making of a film songs could be recorded as many times as necessary to achieve the best performance, but in a live concert there was only one chance to get things right, and if you were lucky the 'muse' was with you. The old saying "the show must go on" was really true when performing live, and that was enough to make the bravest of us feel a little faint now and again. She was asked to sing the last song in the show, 'Homeward', and she made a perfect ending to a wonderful night.

Twiggy loved singing, and she told me she was about to record an album. In 1976 she recorded an album for Mercury Records. I know Twiggy was proud of the album because she telephoned me when it was finished. She sounded so excited about the project, for it wasn't often that a world-class model got the chance to become a musical celebrity. She sounded like a little girl about to receive her Christmas present. She could hardly speak because she was so elated. I had to ask her to calm down because it was difficult to understand what she was saying, but she said she would send me a signed copy, and she kept her word.

The album had a country flavour, with songs by some of the best Nashville writers. I thought she did exceptionally well in the way she interpreted the lyrics, and her harmonies were quite daring. Twiggy had a small, personal voice that was distinctly her own. I thought that more space in the arrangements would have improved the results. Someone like Paul Samwell-Smith would have made a marvellous record with her because he believed in space around the artist, which was a rare commodity. It was only seen in the records of the most discerning artists and producers, and time and place, and the people you met, were the deciding factors in the matter.

I found there were people with all sorts of agendas in the music industry during my 35 years as a back-room boy. Managers who wanted to dupe the companies that were paying for a project to be completed; managers who were borrowing from an artist's funds without informing them of their actions; musicians who needed to steal the limelight from the artist who was helping them earn a living ... and so it goes on. I suppose it was part of the human condition. There were always those who never had enough of what they craved. It has been called greed, but perhaps it was only insecurity. Whatever it was, it showed the ugly side of our existence. Most of the people I knew were generous souls, who were more giving than greedy. They were fine examples of the best side of our nature. Twiggy was such a person.

The letter she sent to me with the record suggested that she hoped I would like the album. I did like it, and listening to the disc now I still feel the same way. I thought she was great. She had the potential to make a 'Broken English' album, and perhaps in other hands she might have done. As her voice will have matured now, she should try again. Who knows what might happen with today's technology. It was a great pleasure working with her, and she will always be close to my heart.

I mentioned Paul Nicholas earlier, when reviewing the album of Andrew Lloyd Webber's songs. K-Tel Records asked me to produce an album for Paul called Just Good Friends. The title related to a television series that Paul was doing at the time, and everyone thought that the series would give the album tremendous exposure. The album consisted mainly of great hits from other artists, but the title song from the series was added to the list and it didn't stand up against the power of the other songs. It was also ironic that the best performance Paul gave was for his own co-written song called 'Don't Wanna Go Home Alone'. I think the reason for this was because most of the songs were pitched too high for Paul's best range. In his own song he pitched the key so that his middle and lower range was heard. This gave the song a warm feeling; in terms of colours, brown rather than blue.

When I was invited to Paul's home in Highgate, he and I sat in his garden and discussed the list of songs to be recorded. We then went into the music room and tried out the keys for the songs. He seemed to be in love with the idea of a high voice. This wasn't what I expected because I had heard him sing songs in much lower keys. The quality of his voice was really fantastic, and quite sexy, when he produced a sound akin to Barry White, for example, but he seemed determined to reach the heavens and I had to go along with his wishes. In the end I felt I had to compromise with him over this matter, but I could have exercised my producer's power. Had I done this, however, not only would it have created a barrier between us, but also it would have been everything that I despised in producers who worked in this way.

I often found that artists had secret desires to make albums like their own favourite artists. This was never possible because they had to be themselves, otherwise their fans would probably stop buying their records. On many of the tracks I think Paul was too influenced by the original versions, which probably caused him to pick the high keys. The keys really did affect the sound of the arrangements. The lower keys would have given the backing voices and strings a 'browner' sound, which I feel would have been more seductive to the fans. It is always easier to see these things in hindsight. At that time we were under a great deal of pressure, with deadlines to meet, budgets to control, studios to organise and the album to finish. As I mentioned before, an international artist had as much time and money as a project needed, but these luxuries were denied to lesser mortals.

Paul was always cooperative and easy to work with. He had a great sense of humour, and I can remember chuckling on many occasions on my way home from the studio, thinking about the day's progress. I believe that K-Tel had the option to do other albums with Paul, and Paul would have been happy to do another album sometime, but it never transpired. I think that, given the chance, I could have persuaded Paul to sing in the deeper regions of his range and, who knows, we might still be working together today.

It seems to be fashionable these days for actors to try their hand at singing. It wasn't so in the seventies. Brian Protheroe was a rare example, for his first love and main occupation was acting, and music was really his hobby. He had reasonable success in the theatre, and on occasion he would appear in cameo parts in film and television. He reminded me of the typical leading man. He was tall, dark and handsome and had a really good speaking voice. But, more importantly for me, he was an excellent singer, who could perform perfect nuances on any syllable he wrote.

Brian would have made a great James Bond. I'm not certain why he wasn't better known, but perhaps his love of music had some bearing on his career. Maybe the answer lies in what he once told me when we first met. His attitude to the music industry was quite unusual. He said he wasn't interested in sales, or live performances, and his real joy was to be in the studio, recording his songs. Harry Nilsson had the same attitude to studio work. Someone with that attitude to the industry might well have felt the same about his work in the theatre. I do know that he was great fun to work with, as he was a professional performer and his training gave him complete control over his ability to achieve whatever effects he desired.

Brian was an excellent pianist and guitar player. He said that music was a hobby and he just loved being in the studio and watching his tracks grow as a metamorphosis was taking place. He played and sang nearly everything that was on the tracks and was aided only by a bass guitar and drums, as well as the occasional input by yours truly. He was a pleasure to work with because he was wide open to suggestions that could improve his work. He would listen carefully to anyone who had something to say that was constructive, and he was open to experiment, which could often have very pleasant surprises. Perhaps being multi-talented wasn't always a positive thing, as the energy could diffuse in different directions and some of it could get lost on the way.

The first album we made was called Pinball and it was recorded in 1974. Brian wrote six of the twelve songs and the remainder were co-written with Martin Duncan. It was interesting to observe the difference between Brian's songs and those that were the result of the collaboration he had with Martin. Brian's lyrics were clever and they were delivered at great speed. Their construction necessitated a strong rhythmic pulse that made you want to move to the beat. The structure of his phrases was the harbinger of the rap style, and in listening to his music today I really feel he was the first rap artist. Of course, he was able to create memorable melodies that stayed with you for days, but the delivery of those melodies, in rhythmical terms, was definitely ahead of his time.

The collaboration with Martin was another thing altogether. I only met Martin once, when he came to the Crucible Theatre in Sheffield to meet the director of Funny Girl, starring Marti Caine. His personality seemed to match the input he made to the album. He reminded me of a 1930s star you would meet on Sunset Boulevard, and their joint efforts had the slow, romantic style of that period. They had a Hollywood gloss about them that didn't seem to be in touch with reality. I didn't know which of the two writers created what part of the collaboration, but the finished product sometimes seemed like a different artist was performing on a different record.

'Moon over Mali' and 'Changing my Tune' were examples of this style. The former came from a work called 'Lotte's Elektrik Opera Film'. The title of this work at least showed the theatrical nature of their joint approach to writing songs. The one exception in the collaboration was 'Mickey Dollar Dreams', which had a great deal of energy, with the voice and the bass using the same melodic line. But I sometimes wondered whether combining different genres on the same album gave the best results.

A year later Brian recorded his second album called Pickup. Like the director Alfred Hitchcock, Martin Duncan is in the background on the front cover picture. I felt that it was not only a theatrical gesture, but also seemed to me to be a little arrogant. When you consider the amount of talent that the British film director displayed, and the amount of pleasure he gave to millions of people, I felt the gesture was so obvious that it would be like me comparing myself to Beethoven.

Pinball must have sold reasonably well for a first album because the album sleeve of Pickup was considerably more expensive. Of the eleven songs, six were co-written with Martin Duncan. I thought the continued flavour of the theatrical nature of the collaboration did much to confuse the listeners with regard to the direction Brian was taking. We were not only getting the beautifully constructed songs of

Brian Protheroe, but an amalgam of theatrical material that Brian and Martin had written earlier for two works called Kino Tata and Lotte's Elektrik Opera Film.

The value of each is not in question, but whether it was prudent to put them together on Brian's solo albums was another matter. Brian's solo work was direct and sincere, and its construction was beautifully expressed in the simplest manner. The collaboration, on the other hand, was on a different plane. There was an overt 'cleverness' about it that I found uncomfortable. Even if a work was created with a tongue-in-cheek attitude, its effect on the stage could be quite different from someone sitting at home with only their aural imagination working, and without the visual reality to help their belief. Perhaps if Brian had recorded his own material for the first two albums, we might have seen a major artist emerge who could have had international acclaim. I sincerely believed he deserved no less.

A year later, Brian recorded his third album called I/You at Nova Sound and Marque Studios. Richard was the engineer, and there were as many as five assistant engineers between the two studios. There were four collaborations, three with Martin and one with singer William Shakespeare. The sleeve states that Martin wrote the lyrics in the collaboration and Brian set them to music. This shed some light on the material for me because it confirmed the reason for the differences in content between Brian's solo work and the work that came from the duo.

Martin's work seemed to have many coded sexual references in the lyric, and I can only guess at the sexual preference of the writer. Such lines as, "You are under thirty, I am thirty-one. Thirty's dirty, one is fun," leaves little doubt in the mind as to the subject matter. Much of the remote 'cleverness' of the lyrics may have created a wall between Brian and his audience. I thought that what most people enjoyed was a direct simplicity that went straight to the heart. When we think of worldwide hits like 'Once, Twice, Three Times a Lady' or all the nursery rhymes that have been with us for hundreds of years, the common aspect they shared was their simplicity; there was no complication about the work. The words and music were direct and simple and this made them memorable. Generations have felt empathy with such writers and their creations.

For decades, the music of The Beatles had been a fine example of that kind of communication. Each new generation appreciates what they have said, and only a handful of rock artists have had the power to influence people to the same degree. I don't mean that all valuable work by all artists must necessarily be simple or easy to create. I knew by my own study that work of the highest quality and of the greatest significance could require complicated structures and ideas. The point I'm making is that in order to communicate successfully with others, even the complicated structures should appear inevitable, so that they go directly to the heart, and mind, which gives the receiver emotional satisfaction. I was always told by my music teachers never to make my work sound too complicated for the audience to understand, because if I did, I would be working in a vacuum and my ideas would fall on stony ground.

The song 'Battling Annie' was a miniature epic about a circus boxer, and its construction was a visual feast for the imagination. It included cameos of carousel music, and you could almost sense being there as the story unfolded. It would have made a great foundation for film scripts. The part of Annie was sung by Stephanie de Sykes, who was a promising artist in her own right. It was interesting how many artists sensed a promising album and wanted to be a part of it by giving their talents to enhance the project. They would often discover embryonic work through the grapevine and seek it out. There wasn't much going on in the industry that well-known singers and musicians didn't know about.

With such an array of talent on Brian's albums, the playing was always first class. The session musicians were always helpful and generally in good spirits. I always had the feeling that they gave more of themselves than their fee dictated. I thought that the very best musicians were generous spirits and anything less was beneath them. I do know that Brian really appreciated their talent and generosity, for he mentioned it to me on several occasions. He asked them many questions about their instruments, which helped him to hear the possibilities he could use on his tracks. The players welcomed his inquisitiveness, and it created a tighter bond between them and him. His fascination with the studio wasn't only because he could see his work grow. He loved to work with other musicians. In this way, he himself grew, and like the other musicians, he developed his own talent.

* * *

A very flash young man from the city was taking his girlfriend for a drive in his new Porsche. As they approached the countryside the young man realised that he wasn't certain where he was, so he thought he should ask someone for directions. Sitting on a fence by the side of a field, another young man was chewing a blade of grass. "I say," said the driver, "can you tell me how we can find the right road to Leatherbridge?" The local man thought for a moment and said that he was sorry but he couldn't. "Ah," said the driver, in an agitated state. "Well, can you direct us to Rummage?" "I'm sorry," said the local, "but I don't know Rummage." Becoming quite red in the face, and trying to impress his young passenger, the driver shouted to the local, "You don't know very much, do you?" "No," said the local, with a slight smile on his face, "but I'm not lost."

CHAPTER 18

The theatre has a magic of its own, where music can be combined with great acting and dancing. An old friend once asked me if I liked Randy Newman (no relation) and I replied that he was one of my favourite people. He, and many others like Bob Dylan, were poets who observed the realities of their countries and weren't afraid to express what they saw. It was said that if you sweetened a pill, it was easier to take. The fact that many political statements were made in rock and roll, and the powers that be had either ignored them or failed to observe them, said much to substantiate that theory. Many political people made similar observations and were silenced.

My friend was Susan Cox. She was born in Liverpool and studied at Manchester University. She was an exceptional actress and played the lead in the musical Sweet Charity, directed by Clare Venables, in a beautiful little theatre near London University. Susan emigrated to Canada soon after the show and became a successful actress and director on both television and the stage. Much of her work was seen at the Vancouver Playhouse in Canada, where she was Artistic Director for many years. We kept in touch over the years and the chance to work with her again was very exciting for me.

Sue, as I call her, had developed a wonderful project she called Trouble In Paradise, a celebration of the songs of Randy Newman. I don't think anything like it had been done before, as it dramatised on the stage the songs that Randy had recorded on his albums. It was a great idea and we approached Randy in Los Angeles to see how he felt about it. He listened carefully to Sue's ideas and visualised them in his mind. I heard him laughing at the end of the telephone line, as it seemed to amuse him, and then there was silence. He then gave us his blessing, as he could see the potential and all publicity is good publicity.

There were two versions of the show. It played off

Broadway as, Maybe I'm Doing It Wrong, and then a revised version for London was developed called Trouble In Paradise. Sue suggested that we start rehearsals as soon as possible, as she had already secured the famous Theatre Royal in Stratford, East London, where a great deal of experimental work had been performed. The work was for four actors, two women and two men. It had a five-piece band on the stage, consisting of keyboards, bass, guitar, drums and woodwinds/synthesiser. It was a hard task for the actors because they had to learn 26 songs, stage directions and Sue's idea of emotional input in a rehearsal period of two weeks.

The emotional input was the essence of the show. There was to be no flamboyance in the vocal delivery. The cast were to sing like Randy, in a stark, direct way, more like a conversational than singing style. There were four acts, each one highlighting the political, social and ethical attitudes found in America. The overall feel of the work had to have the raw energy of a rock concert. It had to reflect the elements of America that were outrageously broad, vulgar and opinionated, but essentially big-hearted and honest. It needed to be a show that was optimistic, funny, rambunctious and real, but never ingratiating, and the players portrayed these sentiments to perfection.

One of the prospective ladies, who didn't get a part, subsequently did well in films and moved to California. Another, the famous Helen Mirren, who was a well-respected actress, might have been a contender. I had seen her previously as the singer in a band in a theatrical production and she was excellent. There was a last night party after her production and a friend of mine, who worked the lights, invited me to join in the fun. She and I spent most of the time under a table, as that was the most peaceful place backstage. Helen came to see if we were all right and then joined us for a while as if we were all friends.

She talked about the show and her future projects and I could see she was a nice person and unpretentious, She offered to bring us drinks and it was obvious that she had a giving nature, plus oodles of talent. We thought that she would be perfect for one of the parts in the new show. When we rang her agent to enquire whether she would be available he said, "Miss Mirren doesn't do auditions," and that was that. Everyone needed to be auditioned because the nature of the songs demanded more than just a voice. The actors needed to be able to project their renditions unlike any other musical I had seen. The sad thing was, I was certain she would have enjoyed being in the show. Beware of agents who have the power of the telephone.

We were lucky to secure Belinda Lang (who starred in the fun television series 2point4 Children), who was always full of fun and was tremendous in her role; George Costigan (who had a distinguished television career and was in the great film Calendar Girls), who had fair hair, an impish smile and the most searching eyes I had ever seen; Fiona Hendley, the wife of Paul Jones (of Starlight Express fame), who was such a surprise because she looked as if she belonged in Sloane Square, but she handled the stark reality of the script with ease and was a tremendous social asset; and Peter Straker, a handsome, tall, brown-skinned actor, with long black hair and an amazing voice, who wore very expensive clothes, was terribly sophisticated and was perfect for his role. They all gave exceptional performances, and for three weeks curtain calls were taken before standing ovations.

The cast got to know each other very well. Because of the short time we had to prepare the show they worked very long hours, sometimes ten or twelve a day. We ate together in various restaurants, and they told stories about their experiences in the industry, which kept their energy high. They laughed a great deal, which was the best tonic I knew. Many of the anecdotes in this book were related in times like these. Eating was always a social occasion for theatre people and not something you did as quickly as possible twixt rushing from here to there. Fast foods were unheard of when I directed the music in theatricals, and people can't sing well when they have hurriedly pushed mounds of stodgy food down their throats.

Sue and I were hoping to take the show to the West End of London but we needed funding. We managed to get a few people to see the show who had the power to bring it to the centre of the city, but problems arose that couldn't be surpassed. They were excited about the show when they saw the reaction of the audience, but they wanted internationally famous actors to play the parts. Sue would not agree to that idea. She told them that the reason for the show's success was purely because it had these actors performing the parts, so if they didn't go to the West End, neither did the show. I thought that she was right to be loyal in that instance, as our actors were perfect for the show. It was because they were not internationally known that the story of each song unfolded without the presence of previous typecasting. Potentially, actors' other associations could have diverted or weakened the audience's concentration. Sue placed great importance on the essence of a scene, with the actors approaching the songs like American method actors, which made the scenes appear more realistic.

We were all sad that we couldn't find anyone that saw our point of view. I have always believed that if the show had gone to the West End back then it would still be there now. Willy Russell's shows, such as Blood Brothers, and other shows with archetypal stories to tell, survived for years. A good show, well done, could tell its story to millions of people. That is why the old shows of the thirties and forties were continually revived. They had a timeless message to tell their audiences, who kept coming back for more. It was unfortunate that the people who had the power to fund the show didn't see the essence of our vision. We were powerless to do anything about it and a great show was prevented from having a very long life.

Another project that didn't reach the West End of London was the musical Guys and Dolls, based on a story and characters by Damon Runyon. It was performed at the Northcott Theatre, which was situated on the campus of Exeter University. Among the cast were Robert Lindsay (who has played many serious Shakespearean parts as well as great TV roles, such as Fagin in Oliver Twist). He had an affinity with D.H. Lawrence, who was born in Eastwood, only five miles from Robert's home. In fact Lawrence taught English at Robert's old school and was a great influence on him. The same situation happened to Richard Burton, who took the name of his English teacher because of his great influence.

Roy Marsden (who has recently been seen as Adam Dalgleish in the P.D. James' crime series) was another member of the cast. I was always amazed at how many actors had really good singing voices. It didn't necessarily follow that a good actor would be a good singer, and it was always a pleasant surprise when working with multi-talented people.

The music was a joy to perform, for it had humour and pathos and several characters that were quite difficult to bring to life. An American show was always difficult for British actors when it came to language, as the American accent is not easy to imitate. I have seen many British productions of American shows where the spoken accent has been a disappointing factor. The cast in Trouble were exceptionally good and delivered their lines in their own dialect, which made their expression completely believable. Robert and Roy, the lead players, helped the remainder of the cast whenever they could, and the atmosphere was full of fun most of the time. There were occasions when we reached a logistical problem and tempers began to boil to the surface, but that was more out of frustration than anger. With very believable American accents for the dialogue and an excellent wardrobe, we could have been in Chicago.

Robert played the part of Nathan Detroit, a small-time card-game operator, and Roy played Sky Masterson, a big-time gambler. Roy looked so menacing in his character, for he was very tall, that at times he scared me. He was actually a gentle giant, but large people can sometimes appear overpowering. There was never any difficulty with either of them in regard to personality. They wanted the show to be as good as it could be, and they gave everything they had to make that happen. The most difficult parts of musicals were the ensemble scenes. Sometimes we had more than 20 people moving and singing different melodies, and to organise these scenes to ensure that there wasn't an accident took a considerable amount of time. It was a pleasure working with the whole cast, for musicals and light opera were favourite activities of mine.

When working with young talent, I often wondered what would happen to them in their future careers. It was very pleasing to see someone become a national or even international star. I saw tremendous potential in many actors because they exhibited an aura that was unique. They stood out among the talented because they had a special gift. It was similar when considering film stars. Some actors had tremendous presence on the screen, whether in film or television, a good example being Marlon Brando. Others seemed to have hardly any at all. Whether 'The Touch' was pure luck or ordained, I usually found that their degree of talent was equal to their degree of humility.

The Elephant Man was the show that got away. Joseph Merrick was called The Elephant Man because he was grossly disfigured by masses of flesh that began growing on his face and body when he was a child. He was exhibited as a freak until Frederick Treves, a surgeon at London's Whitechapel Hospital, befriended him and gave him accommodation at the hospital, where he died at the age of 27. Treves called him John, which led to confusion about his true name, and although Merrick stated that he was born in 1860, it was believed that 1862 was the true year of his birth.

Like other great stories that have fired the imagination, Joseph's story was perfect to bring to life as a musical. Jon Barker, a very likeable young man, had written a very good script and wonderful songs based on Joseph's story. A Canadian named Stephen McKernan had taken Jon under his wing and I believe had procured the rights for the musical's performance. The show was to be performed at a theatre in Spitalfields Market, and I was asked to arrange and conduct the music for a special performance for a group of Canadians, who had put money into the show and had come to London to see its progress.

I didn't know the audience was expecting a run-through of the songs by the cast with the accompaniment of a piano. Stephen, unfortunately, had hired a respected New York director, and I arranged 25 songs for a rhythm section and choral group for the whole company. We spent a week rehearsing everyone at a rehearsal studio, and the run-through finished up as a complete performance, with acting, singing, lighting and scaffolding, which cost a great deal of money. It was obvious that the audience liked the show because its response at the end was very encouraging, but I think that they were surprised with the finished product, and even more surprised with the total expense.

The cast, who were excellent considering the short time we spent rehearsing, was made up of all shapes and sizes. They were young hopefuls who longed for a secure place in a West End show. They worked hard and acquired a high standard of proficiency, but they knew little about the expertise of Mr McKernan. After a gruelling week of work, and a period full of expectation, McKernan's entrepreneurial skills and their dreams of stardom were dashed to the ground. They dispersed, hoping that the show would get a theatre in the West End of London, but, alas, their wish was not to be.

It seemed that Stephen had a great deal of explaining to do to the Canadians. It was obvious from the attitude of the chairman of the group that not only were they surprised about the development of the show, but also they had not authorised McKernan to spend as much as he had. The chairman thanked me for my efforts and said that we would meet again, but that meeting never materialised. I got the distinct feeling that the visitors were about to pull the plug on their financial commitment, and I believe that McKernan knew it too. I saw a problem because he had the rights to the performance of the show, for he'd done a deal with Jon, which included giving him a retainer.

After the show I was invited to dinner by Stephen and Jon to discuss the future and the possibilities that lay before us. Stephen suggested that one of the songs would make a great single for radio exposure. He asked me to go ahead and record a demonstration disc in a studio, and I chose Snakeranch Studios in London. Having assembled a keyboard player, bass and guitar players, a lead singer who also did the backing vocals, and an engineer, the project was finished in one day. The cost was £2,500 for the musicians and my services and a considerable amount for the engineer and the studio.

When Stephen received the tape he said that he was delighted and he would send the money to the studio immediately. Remember that term: "The cheque is in the post"? Well, you've guessed it, the cheque never arrived. For years we have been told that the money is on its way. The studio decided to add interest to the money owed, and I decided to pay my musicians myself in order to maintain my credibility. The amount has probably tripled by now, and Stephen even had the nerve to ask me to post him the arrangements because they were going to perform the show in some American college. Luckily, I had collected them after the show and had kept them safe at home for many years. I have been conned by people I've liked, but Mr McKernan wasn't one of them. There were lots of sharks out there, but it was difficult to sense this until you'd been bitten.

The first professional work I did was copying music for the musical Robert and Elizabeth. The story was about two poets, Robert Browning and Elizabeth Barrett, and their whirlwind courtship and secret elopement to Italy. It was based on The Barretts of Wimpole Street, a play by Rudolph Besier. Elizabeth was ill and physically very frail. At first she was bedridden, but Robert brought sunshine and a feeling of hope into her life, and through his strength she became well. They knew each other's work before they met and appreciated each other's talent. Although her father was a family tyrant, who ruled with a rod of iron, they defied him and escaped to happiness.

It was one of those real-life tales from which great legends were made, and at every performance I could see that there wasn't a dry eye in the theatre. In theatrical stories such as Oliver, Sweet Charity and many others, the premise is that 'good' will prevail. Walt Disney's work is probably the best example of purporting this ideology, but unfortunately life wasn't like that. Disney even changed the Brothers Grimm's efforts into wonderful fantasies, but they were originally horror stories. Perhaps this was the reason why many young people looked for 'Prince Charming', or a Fairy Tale Princess', believing that all that was necessary was a chance meeting and everyone would live happily ever after, instead of realising that they had to work hard on relationships every day to make them work.

The musical director for Robert and Elizabeth was Alexander Faris and the producer was Wendy Toye. The music was composed by Ron Grainer, an Australian, who also wrote the theme music to the TV series Doctor Who. The lead actors playing Robert and Elizabeth were Keith Michell and June Bronhill, but the father was played by John Clements, a well-known film actor, who was responsible for the 'star on the door' incident I mentioned earlier. He was an exception to my earlier rule, as he was an excellent actor but had no humility whatsoever. Captain Cook was played by Jeremy Lloyd, who was the army officer in the Agatha Christie film Murder on the Orient Express, and has subsequently written many successful TV comedy scripts for various series, such as 'Allo 'Allo, that have become known throughout the world.

The show had a large cast, who went on tour throughout England for some weeks before coming to London. Touring was hard and exhausting but great fun. The singers and dancers usually socialised in their free time, so I joined them on several occasions. It was in Manchester that I had my first experience of Asian food. I was told that Manchester had more Asian restaurants than any other city in England. This was probably true in the sixties, but it's quite possible that this is not the case now. It was also my first experience in 'digs', which was quite wonderful. The landladies of houses for theatre people were unique. They would have made great housekeepers for the landed gentry a century earlier. They were efficient, always positive, and they could talk the best of us under the table, but they were marvellous.

The weeks of touring prior to arriving in London gave the writers and arrangers time to change things to make it run smoother. Once in the West End it ran for ages. A recording was made of the show with the original cast, which I still have to this day although I haven't played it for 40 years. Relationship camps remained the same. The musicians, dancers, actors and backstage people usually kept company with their own groups. This was natural because they felt they had much in common. They perceived their role in the theatre from different perspectives, but they were all friendly and respectful. Only one person was a nightmare.

Romance often reared its head in theatricals because the actors and dancers were usually under 25 years old and they were away from home for considerable periods of time. The close proximity and tactile nature of their work seemed to spark their emotions, and it wasn't uncommon to find people pairing off during a long run of a production. I got used to dropping in on people and finding them in embarrassing situations. Their favourite places were dressing rooms, especially after a performance when most people had left the theatre. I often had to retrieve music that someone had borrowed in order to refresh their singing part. More often than not they would forget to return it to me, as they had other things on their minds.

Some of the cast weren't particular where they exercised their lust. On one occasion a piece of clothing fell from the wings backstage, and as I looked up I noticed tremendous movement near one of the light pillars. I was probably the only other person in the theatre, but I'm sure the couple involved didn't care whether that was true or not. Another time one of the toilets was bursting at the seams, and the noise was deafening during an ecstatic moment. I even heard noises coming from the orchestra pit late one night, and the sound was certainly as invigorating as any music I had heard before or since.

When you consider the atmosphere in a theatre during a long run of a play or a musical, where as a norm people are scantily dressed most of the time, whether changing from their normal attire into a theatrical costume or vice versa at the end of a show, it isn't difficult to see why liaisons occurred. It could be quite lonely on tour with a production, and some tours went on for months. There were some instances when an actor or dancer had to be replaced on tour because they weren't lucky enough to pair up with anyone and didn't feel as though they could cope alone and away from home for such a long period.

I knew how they felt because once the touring show was under way there was a great deal of time away from the theatre. There were only the evening and matinée performances, and perhaps one rehearsal a week for the dancers. People had the whole of the daytime to themselves, and if you had nobody to share a strange city with it could be unbearable. Directors and musical directors didn't have this problem. They were working on some aspect of the show every day that it was open. Choreography and musical arrangements were always being updated, which meant that there wasn't enough time for these participants to get bored.

I always thought that musical theatre, including opera, was the most satisfying medium in the entertainment industry. It involved all aspects of the performing arts. Singing, acting and dancing were combined to tell magnificent stories, and the appreciation and delight of thousands of people has been manifest in the fact that their telling has been with us for centuries.

* * *

Q: What is the definition of an optimist?
A: A musician who has taken out a mortgage.

CHAPTER 19

I was invited to arrange and conduct a song for Italy for the Eurovision Song Contest, which was the only time I was associated with that august body. The contest was held in Holland and the song was to be sung by a young American of Italian extraction who reminded me of a young Frank Sinatra. He came to Europe with his young wife, also of Italian descent, but they didn't seem very compatible to me. They were always arguing, but perhaps that's the Italian way.

Italy came seventh in the contest, but I had expected a better result. We could have made the top three, as the rehearsal in the afternoon had gone very well. It was our misfortune that the artist had a terrible argument with his wife just before going on stage, which affected his performance. It was the first time that Italy had reached the top ten, however, and this result led the managing director of RCA in Rome to invite me to produce an album for one of his artists. The strange thing was that in the contest the musicians were London session men and the backing singers were American, who were absolutely gorgeous. One was black and the other was white, and it seemed to be a hobby for them because the black girl was a top New York model and the other singer owned an inherited factory in Los Angeles.

The hotel we stayed at probably accommodated half the performers singing in the song contest. You could hear several languages being spoken in the bars and restaurants, but everyone was on a high and they were friendly and courteous. When I considered the state of everybody's nerves, it's a wonder there wasn't an incident caused by someone losing their temper. In the three days we spent preparing for the show I didn't see or hear of one single argument. It made me wonder, much later, whether the problems we saw in football matches were accidental or predetermined.

Rome was the perfect place to record. RCA had a complex just half an hour from the city centre and it was amazing. They had an art department, a record production plant, three studios (including the largest studio in Europe, where the great operatic recordings of the fifties and sixties took place), a restaurant that could seat over a hundred employees, and a suite of offices to die for. Ennio Morricone, who wrote the music for the now famous Italian westerns that brought fame to Clint Eastwood, recorded in the largest studio many times during my three years in Italy. He appeared to be a very quiet, gentle person, who knew his craft completely. He had a masterly way of getting what he wanted from his orchestral players. I never heard him raise his voice once, and I watched him for hours. He wrote over four hundred film scores as well as many serious, extended works. He was probably the most successful film composer in Europe, and he certainly produced a body of work equal to film composers in the USA like Jerry Goldsmith and Alan Menken. Ennio should have got an Oscar for his movie score for The Mission, in which he combined a classical, choral style with South American chanting, but it was not his year.

I thought that an album would take six weeks to produce, but the Italians and I worked so well together that I stayed three years in that wonderful city. The managing director of RCA had been there 25 years, and before that he had been a secretary to one of the cardinals in The Vatican. He was a wise businessman who, in order to keep up with current practices, invited people from around the world to input fresh ideas. There were Americans, Europeans, Australians and British people giving their knowledge to the company, and it felt like one big, happy family.

The managing director's association with The Vatican allowed us to make a record with Pope John Paul II. An associate of the director had the idea to put the Pope's voice over a serene piece of ancient music. The melody of the music had already been chosen and I was asked to arrange it for a string orchestra. When the recording was finished the Pope was asked to give a sermon over the music. The company released the finished product as a single, and it was in the number one spot throughout the Catholic domain for several weeks. I hoped that the royalties would go to various charities, and I thought it was a unique experience that would probably never happen again.

Looking at the positive side of my Roman engagement, the first artist I produced was a man named Apollo Morello, who was managed by his brother. They took me to their home in the countryside to meet their mother. She was a sweet, fragile, old-fashioned lady of days gone by, and the atmosphere had a feeling of elegance about it. Their home reminded me of many of Dickens's novels. Memorabilia were everywhere and went back decades, and it was as if we had stepped back in time for a few moments. Apollo's mother wore lace dresses, and the tea set placed on a lace-covered table was made of old silver. Her sons had the same aura around them, as if they belonged to another century, and there was a gentleness about them that was very appealing. They thought that I should buy a cottage and live near Rome permanently. What a fool I was not to take their advice. When I think of how peaceful it was and the perfect climate I realised, "he who hesitates is lost". His album was called Carezze. It was full of love songs and pathos, and Apollo had the perfect voice for his material. It was sensitive and fragile, which created a feeling of sadness in nearly everything he sang.

Rome, like any other city, had an underworld that wore a respectable face. The Hilton Hotel was meant to be my initial watering hole for the first two days, but I liked it so much that I stayed there for nine weeks. In the evenings there was dancing in the upper ballroom, which was frequented by beautiful prostitutes. I was told that the management had made a deal with them and took a percentage of their earnings. I must say that they did very well. I was offered a short stay of an hour by one of them at a cost of £400, which in 1981 was a considerable amount. It would have been £1,000 for the whole night. The high prices were aimed at the many wealthy Arab businessmen, involved in oil production, who stayed there on a permanent basis. I was told that some of them would order three or four ladies for the whole night quite regularly.

Wealth is relative, and I remember my minder going ape

and reminding me that I could have bought a small car in Italy for the cost of my nine weeks in the hotel with full board. I then thought of the Arab businessmen who thought nothing of spending enormous amounts every evening on pleasure. Then there was my minder, a university graduate of 35 and fluent in four languages, who was still living at home with his mother because he couldn't afford an apartment anywhere near the centre of the city. His Irish partner worked for the United Nations in Rome. She told me that lots of Irish girls went to Italy to find husbands, as many of them are tall, dark and handsome. She also said that people wouldn't believe the amount of money that was spent on wages, lunches and other perks. The same would also be true of Paris and New York. Perhaps the real issue was that nothing really changes, and there will always be a huge gap, materially, between the rich and the poor.

Looking at the negative side of my experiences in Rome, the third artist I worked with was a good example of a nightmare. His name was Renato Zero. When he was a young man he was quite beautiful to look at, and he told me that the people in the industry gave him a bad time because he was gay. As he became older and more successful, he had become more difficult with the people at the company. Success gave an artist a great deal of power and independence, and Renato wasn't slow to exercise that power. He was an excellent performer, with a tremendous following of fans, but I think the past attitudes of some of his colleagues had made him very bitter.

He had a summer home on the coast of north-west Italy, which had beautiful surroundings and views of the sea. There were always two or three pretty young men around the house and Renato's behaviour towards them was atrocious. He was sarcastic and dictatorial with them and he would denigrate them whenever he had the opportunity. I noticed that my suede coat had been taken by one of his guests, but he didn't appear to be bothered about the matter at all. He showed the same attitude towards his guests in his house in Rome. With his wealth and comfort one would have thought he had everything he could desire, but life obviously requires something more. His actions weren't protective, they were venomous.

One evening I was invited to his house for dinner. As I was leaving he invited me to stay. We were only halfway through completing the album, which was one of a pair called Arctic and Antarctic. I had to explain my reasons for not staying, which was embarrassing for us both. Our working relationship changed as a result of this rejection and my views about the way he treated his entourage. It was obvious that this was going to be my only project with him, and I felt lucky to end our relationship without visible scars. I last saw him in the company bar, and as he greeted me I made some ludicrous remark as a joke, but he never forgave me. I have always been sorry about the remark, and I pitied him for his bitterness, but what has been done cannot be undone. He returned to his previous producer, who was an excellent pianist and arranger named Pintucchi, and I probably lost some royalties.

Of all the artists I heard while I was in Rome, the most enjoyable for me was Lucio Dalla. He was a little man who sported a beard and John Lennon-style glasses. He was never without his woolly hat, which he wore at all times, wherever he was. His clothes looked as though they had been purchased from a second-hand store, but somehow it made him appear endearing. I was told that he was gay, but he kept himself to himself, and maybe that is how rumours begin. He had a voice that could cut steel and the phrasing of his words when he performed was mesmerising. Unfortunately for me, his producer was an old friend named Alessandro Colombini, who was a lucky man to have been able to produce all of Lucio's records. The artist asked me to arrange a string orchestra for one of his songs and I was delighted to oblige.

The surprise came when months later he asked me to go to see one of his concerts in Düsseldorf, Germany. I wondered why he was touring in Germany, but I soon found out: the theatre was completely sold out to Italians. I was told that there were over a million Italians working in Germany at that time. This was long before the EU, so it really did come as unexpected news. Many parts of Italy had little work for their men and they were highly sought after in Germany because in financial terms it was better for the German economy. The audience adored him and on many occasions they stood up and cheered their hero. Northern Europeans seemed to be more reserved in their behaviour in regard to entertainment than Mediterranean people. Perhaps the climate dictated the amount of passion they expressed but, whatever the case, the Italians were certainly very demonstrative.

While I was in Rome I did some television work with an orchestra, and it was so successful that RCA asked me to make a record comprising the most well known Italian songs. The back-room boy became a front-room boy for a while. I engaged some backing singers, including Vicki Brown and her daughter, Sam. They were, of course, the wife and daughter of rock and roll star Joe Brown. Sam was just 17 but old enough to perform as a professional in Italy. They were really the stars of the show and Vicki sang all the solo parts of the arrangements. She was, in fact, the breadwinner in the family for many years, as Joe's career had died a long time before our Italian adventure. Joe came out to see the girls on a couple of occasions, and although it was one of the best times of my professional life I felt that Joe was jealous of Vicki's success as a session singer. She could have been a star in her own right, but she put family before stardom.

Unfortunately, language barriers often limited the number of people who might have derived great pleasure from wonderful creative works, including popular song. Even literary works that were translated lost their original fire. A great deal of language couldn't be translated word for word because there were no exact counterparts. The spirit of the work, however well constructed, was never the work itself. I once knew a man who learnt the Greek language in order to appreciate Homer, and another who learnt Chinese to understand Confucius.

I felt the same about Italian and French works, whether they are popular song or opera, literature or the dubbing of film. Having lived in France for some time, I was well aware that dubbed dialogue bore no real relation to the original language, and often not even the same meaning. It was hopeful to think that with so much travelling about the world these days, there might be a possibility that various languages would be acquired by people in the future, so we might understand each other better. The idea of a universal English, or a universal Chinese, seemed preposterous to me. Perhaps 'Worldspeak' will be the only possible future language for communication. Ridley Scott's Blade Runner had the right idea.

The entertainment industry has certainly suffered because of the universal use of the Internet. The fact that many products were available to be downloaded free suddenly changed the goalposts. The rules of copyright reared their ugly heads on every possible piece of visual and audio equipment. It was an area created by publishers in the literary and musical world, for it didn't exist before them, and it now included every possible product we could imagine. Living in a world of 'do it yourself', a great threat engulfed many industries. The various corporations had great power over their markets and the prices established in the marketplace. Now, certain websites were allowing people to download material at no cost, or technology was enabling people to make copies of material without the need of retail establishments. This was why practically everything you bought had a copyright warning stamped on it. The excuse that the copyright owners made was that, in the case of music, the artists were being denied their income through the lack of royalties. However, it was the decline of their own royalties that worried them.

There were double standards involved here. A perfect example of these standards was shown with regard to the arrangements of artists' music. An arranger had the copyright of his own work, but he signed a contract stating that he or she would not use the same work for anyone else for a period of ten or fifteen years. What the contract didn't state was that the company would use that work many times, whenever it felt like it and over as many years as it wanted, without consulting the arranger. Remember that the arranger was only paid once for a particular project and that each new release, especially in a different language, was another project and that it was actually stealing from the arranger.

I entered my name on the Internet one day and found that

an American company was selling over a hundred different discs with my work on them. The re-releases were dated in the 1980s, 1990s and early 2000s, and not one word was offered to me by the respective companies who released the discs. A session musician was paid for his work on the session. An arranger was paid for the use of his work, for a period of time, on a particular project. The work was not owned by the company. Surely there was something drastically wrong, and this greed on the part of the companies was what was threatened by the free use of the Internet.

These inequalities will probably continue while the law and the Monopolies Commission are heavily weighted on the side of the wealthy. Even the committee for deciding who got money from the National Lottery consisted of people from the wealthy end of the spectrum. I remember the case of the Royal Opera House in Covent Garden, London, when they were given £4 million to sort out bad management; an institution that lost money nearly every year. I tried to get £1,000 from the Lottery to buy wind instruments for a group of young players in West Wales, and it took nearly a year to process, after filling in a multitude of forms. The balance seemed wrong to me, for more people in the local Welsh community would have seen our group perform for charity had we had more resources. £4 million was an enormous amount of money to be given to a relatively small group of people who, because of bad management, couldn't sustain enough income in spite of the ridiculous entry prices for the ROH's lavish productions.

I'm making the point that mud sticks to mud, and money sticks to money. Many people in the music industry, and probably in the entertainment industry in general, have not received the money that was due to them because the structure in place was not user friendly to the people who actually create the material. It appeared that the non-creative element in the entertainment industry was rather wanting, with regard to atonement, when it came to its obligations.

France, too, had different ways of working. Catherine Lara, who was contracted to CBS in France, was an excellent musician who played the viola and the guitar, the same instruments as John Cale, and I went to Paris to arrange for her. She was asked to write the music for a French film about a mother and doctor, who had just discovered that she had terminal cancer. It was a superb film starring Annie Girardot. At the same time Catherine made an album called The Nile, which was superb. It had excellent musicians playing on the sessions, who had such sensitivity that when we were listening to playbacks of some of the tracks, two of the players were weeping with emotion. Everything went well until Catherine asked me to stay and mix the record with her. It was the most important part of the process, and in the USA and Britain the one who got to mix a product was the producer.

The point was that producers got royalties, and that recognised the important part they played. I suggested this fact to Catherine, who asked me what I would charge her instead of a royalty. When I told her she went ape. I think she thought I would do it for nothing. It would have meant staying in the studio all day for at least a week. She explained that all French arrangers did that, and as she was labelling me I gently told her that only producers mixed albums. The pity of the situation was that I really liked and respected her. Since her uncle was a publisher, I thought that money was probably not the issue. She said that she thought my efforts were good, but she obviously didn't want to pay for them.

Françoise Hardy was just beautiful, and there were no problems in regard to her recording company or any other aspect of our association. Only one track needed my attention, which was a beautiful ballad that was written in a way that was unique to French chanson. Many of the songs on the disc were sad, with lyrics that were full of despair, and I felt that this was part of Françoise's character. It was said that the French character was a cerebral one. They loved to play mind games, and they placed great importance on their school system. Education was not used as a political tool, as in some countries I could mention, where the people who made the decisions about the structure of their system had never taught and had no real idea what goes on in schools. The truth may be that they didn't care. Dressing children in smart uniforms to make them conform didn't increase their capacity to learn. There were no uniforms in French state education.

I found that the people in Sweden and Denmark had a very liberal attitude towards music, love and life in general. They were not inclined to label people, things and different styles in music in an elitist fashion. I remember that when working in Stockholm with a successful duo called Amazing Blondel we were asked to perform on a very popular radio programme. There was a live audience in the studio and the atmosphere was really electric. To my great surprise it was to be a British evening, for each night of the week the station chose a different country's music to play to the audience. The other participant was a symphony orchestra playing music by Elgar.

The audience seemed to enjoy both styles of music and gave both groups resounding applause. The next day we were interviewed on the station, and a dear friend of mine heard it and telephoned me from Uppsala. She travelled to Stockholm and we spent the weekend together. I asked her how she had found the hotel we were staying in and she told me that she had rung the station and they were very obliging. The whole experience was very rewarding. Amazing Blondel were happy, my friend was happy, and if I could have conducted the Elgar I would have been in seventh heaven, but beggars can't be choosers.

Iceland was quite an experience. It was like being on the moon. I never saw a tree anywhere, and I was told that this was because the Vikings had cut them down to make longships. I arrived in Reykjavik, which was a one-street town, and the first thing I was greeted with was an incredible smell. I just couldn't place it. However, as I walked to the end of main street I found my answer. Iceland is a fishing nation, and at the end of the high street was a whaling station. People were cutting up a whale, which was still steaming because it had recently been killed. It was enormous and was hanging from a large crane while several men hacked it to pieces with large, curved knives. You don't see a sight like that every day, and it became ingrained in my memory.

It was so expensive to live in Iceland that many people had to have two or even three jobs to survive. A sandwich was £5 and a bottle of Scotch was £20. Remember, too, that this was in the seventies. I was told that the inflation rate was 45 per cent at that time. The American Navy had a nuclear submarine base on the island and they gave the Icelandic people money in order to keep their base there. The age for legal drinking was 21, but I went to a disco where the kids, who were underage, were drinking coke laced with alcohol. There were three liquor stores in the city that only opened at certain hours during the day and there were always long queues waiting for opening time. Perhaps it was the balm that kept them sane in such insular conditions.

All the houses I saw around the dock were wooden and each was painted a different colour. The colours were bright and the houses were spotlessly clean. It looked like a wonderland film set, but this was real, and it was obvious that the people were a bright nation. When we were there we saw the Northern Lights (the Aurora Borealis). Words fail me, as it was cosmic. We were taken to the top of a mountain near the city, and the sparse landscape resembled the Moon, with craters and hot springs everywhere. I tried to imagine what it would be like to live there permanently. In a disco I asked a young girl, who was already a mother, why she stayed in such a hostile environment. She told me that although the young who went to university had the choice of studying in Europe or the USA they always returned because Iceland was their home. What she said made me feel such a fool because her reply suddenly seemed obvious. Of course family and friends are the most important people in one's life, and wherever they are is where we want to be. I should have known better.

During the seventies I met a man called Junior Telfer. He told me that he was responsible for starting the Notting Hill Carnival in London. He was indeed a strange individual. He was Trinidadian, very intelligent, and had been educated in New York. He was tall, well spoken, and considered himself to be something of an entrepreneur. But he was a poser. To hide the fact that his ancestors were African, he used to paint long hair sideburns on his face, which came to a curled point, and wear a turban, which he hoped would make people believe he was Asian.

Junior said that he would be going to Trinidad for three week, during the time of the Shrove Tuesday Mardi Gras

Festival, to record background sounds for a record he was producing. The sounds would be introduced into the grooves between the songs and would make a collage of atmospheric music of the island. I thought it was a great idea, and he mentioned that not only would there be payment but also that all expenses would be taken care of. He told me that he had a wealthy benefactor who was prepared to pay for himself and his partner, my wife and me, my engineer and his wife, and Junior, and it seemed like a very attractive offer that shouldn't be refused.

We arrived in Port-of-Spain safely and were taken to a small hotel. The place was clean, but there were rather large insects crawling around the accommodation, so Hilary and I transferred to a private house that was built on stilts. When I asked the owner about the stilts she told me there were snakes on the island and that it was safer to have a raised house and it also made it easier for the snake catcher to retrieve any snakes that ventured under the property. Apparently snakes enjoyed the shade under buildings and often made their nests there. On one occasion a snake catcher, armed with only a sack and a bamboo stick with a wire ring attached to it, came to the house, crawled under it and within two minutes re-emerged having caught a large snake that had been bothering the neighbourhood.

On our first working day my engineer Richard and I did three hours' work recording a drum band that was rehearsing for the carnival. It was the only work we did during our three-week stay on the island. Junior's dreams of musical stardom went quietly down the drain. His cousin, whom we never saw and who supposedly had a studio, never seemed to be able to get anything together. The backer and his partner had a wonderful holiday, Junior posed all over the town as if he was the 'Godfather', and Richard, his wife, Hilary and I relaxed, waiting with great anticipation for the festival to begin. The weather was gorgeous, and there were many delights to see around the island.

It seemed that the last thing people had on their minds was work. Junior was unbelievable. Part of the island culture included individual status. If an appointment was made with anyone, the last person to arrive was always considered to have the highest kudos. I remember Junior asking Richard and me to meet him at a well-known restaurant at two in the afternoon. We arrived on time, but to make certain that we weren't the last people to arrive Junior turned up well after four o' clock. He breezed in as if nothing was wrong, with a slight smile of victory on his face, but nothing was mentioned. I realised from that moment that the project wasn't the reason for our visit but rather that Junior wanted to show us how important he was on his home ground, and I saw that the whole thing was a childish whim.

Junior was always polite and acted the perfect gentleman, but at the backer's expense. The group took a trip to Tobago, a small island to the north-east of Trinidad. Junior told us that one of his cousins had a weekend retreat there, where we could relax away from the bustle of the impending carnival. We flew in a plane that had only eight seats and was held together with chewing gum and string. I had never been so scared in my life. We flew about a hundred feet above the water, and the wings were flapping in the wind. The pilot kept turning round to talk to us, and I kept crossing myself, convinced that this was my last journey. How silly I was. The pilot had probably flown the plane hundreds of times, and West Indians were probably the most laid-back people in existence. The best was yet to come, however.

The weekend retreat was in reality a corrugated shack and the perfect place for a recluse. There were three rooms with holes for windows, no doors or lighting, and iron single beds with old mattresses but no linen. The only saving grace on the excursion was the wonderful distant view of Venezuela. Junior's cousin was a handsome 30-year-old man, with a beautiful young wife and an eight-year-old daughter, and they were very generous people. On the first night Hilary and I had a bed each, and around three in the morning I was awakened by a strange hissing noise. Making its way across the room was a 12 feet long iguana, its tail wagging and its tongue popping in and out, creating the hissing sound. My heart nearly stopped. When I mentioned it the next morning Hilary said she had heard nothing, and Junior's cousin told me not to worry as there were hundreds on the island and they were vegetarians and completely harmless.

The carnival was the most liberating experience I had ever had. The weekend before the final Tuesday, bands were practising their movements and their music in the hope of winning the coveted prizes. A band consisted of more than a truckful of musicians, who played a variety of instruments: percussion, upright bass, trumpet, trombone and tuba. In a way it was very similar to football, in that each suburb of Port-of-Spain had a band, which included not only the musicians but also scores of dancers, who would dress in the most exotic and elaborate clothes, and followers (fans), who could number as many as a hundred. On the last day, Tuesday, they would congregate at their appointed station at three or four in the morning in preparation for their journey, which ended in the centre of the city. All the followers had canisters tied around their necks containing their favourite iced drink, and at the allotted time everyone would begin dancing behind the musicians as they made their way to the centre for nine o'clock.

The atmosphere was electric. A warm climate, rural views, intoxicating rhythms, and a general feeling of goodwill made it an unforgettable occasion. I never saw Junior on the trip, which was significant. I believe that he was only a catalyst in any human activity and he was like a cardboard shadow of a person; he was there, and yet he wasn't there. It was as if he was unable to be his essential self because he might expose something that he was really ashamed of being. I felt sorry for him. He wanted to be someone else and, as we know, you can't change the spots of a leopard.

The native islanders were an amazing physical group. History had played its part in producing an enormous variety of specimens. The island had been part of the trade routes for centuries, and the Caribbeans had mixed with the British, French, Spanish, Chinese, Portuguese and who knows who else. There were Europeans (who probably had African blood in their veins if they went back far enough), and different degrees of hair colour from black to blond. They grouped their skin colour into seven different categories - I belonged to the 'reds', as when the sun darkened my skin it gave off a red hue – and there were black, brown, hazel, grey, blue and green eyes, regardless of the skin colour. There were European, African, Chinese and Arabic influences in their features, and I couldn't stop marvelling at their variety.

The day after the carnival we all met at the restaurant to discuss our plans for travelling back to London. I asked Junior why we didn't see him during the festivities, but he was vague and noncommittal. The others all said that they'd had a great time as far as they could remember, for copious quantities of alcohol had been consumed during the event. The backer didn't seem to mind about the small amount of work done, as he thought the holiday had been a great success and the experience had been worth every penny. He and his partner decided to stay on the island for another two weeks, so he wished us all a pleasant journey home and they disappeared, never to be seen again. On arriving at Heathrow Richard and Pat said their goodbyes, Junior was nowhere to be seen, and Hilary and I returned to the Brompton Road completely exhausted. We never saw Junior again, but I will never forget him.

* * *

Cecil B. DeMille, the great director of Hollywood biblical epics, passed away and went to Heaven. On arriving at the Pearly Gates he was greeted by an angel. "Yes," said the angel, "can I help you?" DeMille replied, puffing on a very large cigar, "I'm Cecil B. DeMille, and I wish to come in." The angel went to an enormous book and thumbed through it until he came to the appropriate page. "I'm sorry," he said apologetically, "your name is not on my list and I am afraid that you cannot enter." "Not enter?" DeMille roared, beginning to perspire with rage. "I wish to see the Boss."

The angel rang through to Jesus Christ and explained the situation. The Gate slowly opened and a smile grew on DeMille's face. "Jesus will see you now," the angel said in a quiet but authoritative manner. DeMille walked along a beautiful red velvet carpet and eventually reached some very, very large doors, which opened automatically. When he entered, DeMille found himself in a gigantic room, with an enormous desk at the farthest end.

Jesus beckoned DeMille, who was still puffing on his cigar, to approach. He sat down on a small seat, which was situated in front of the desk, and looked around the room in amazement. "I understand that there is a problem," Jesus uttered in beautiful dulcet tones. "Yes," said DeMille, in a more tolerant vein. "I've been told that I cannot enter Heaven."

Jesus went to his enormous book and carried out the same procedure that the angel had followed. "Well," said Jesus, "the angel was correct, for your name has not been entered, so you will have to go to the other place."

Outraged, DeMille got up from his chair, pulled Jesus to him by the collar of his robe, and shouted, "Listen, you! I made you, I can break you!"

CHAPTER 20

During the mid-seventies there was a strong Union problem relating to musicians from America playing in Britain; in fact there was no reciprocity in either direction. Stan Kenton's band had to play in Ireland for that very reason. It was possible, however, for American artists to come to London and perform on television, providing they had a British MD (musical director) to conduct the orchestra. There were two occasions when I was asked to fill the position. This meant that I received the music only hours before the performance.

The BBC Theatre in Shepherds Bush, London, was chosen both times, and there was always a live audience. The artists were Johnny Mathis and Charlie Rich. They were as different as chalk and cheese, not only in their appearance, but also in the style of music they sang and the way they performed it. Mathis was very tall and sleek and wore expensive, fashionable clothes. Rich wore denims, top and bottom, and was round and cuddly, with a mop of white hair that many younger men would have envied.

The theatre was full both times and there was an atmosphere of eager anticipation, for the people were real fans who had travelled great distances to see and hear their idols. The orchestra was small, which gave the evening a feeling of intimacy, and the low lighting made the studio feel more like a nightclub than a concert. Each artist sang six songs, which was probably suggested by the management because it was the perfect number for a 30-minute show. Americans liked to travel to Europe because their live television performances helped to keep the sales high on this side of the Atlantic.

The problem for me related to the speed of the music. As I had never performed or even heard the material before, I was worried that I might not get the tempos right. Luckily for me, Mathis had brought his American drummer with him. I wasn't certain how the Union got around that point, but I was eternally grateful. The drummer gave me the necessary clue to the tempo of each song just before it began. The last song, however, was stopped by the artist within the first 30 seconds because the tempo was wrong. We were able to begin again because we were in a studio, and such things are quite common in television. It was possible that the drummer was showing me that he was in control of the situation, but I never spoke to him, and if that was the case I hope he got a great deal of pleasure from it.

The control and expertise that Johnny Mathis showed in the way he delivered the songs that evening were remarkable. He had the audience sitting on the edge of their seats. It was an absolute joy to see him work, and it reminded me of the way Scott Walker worked. To get a phrase exactly how he wanted it he would contort his face at times, and sometimes he looked as if he was in pain, but the end result was perfection. He was taller than I had imagined, for I had to look up to him whenever we had a point to discuss. He must have been six feet four inches tall, yet when I saw him in films he didn't strike me as being that tall. He was one of the best singers I ever worked with and he certainly deserved his popularity. He wasn't a social animal and I didn't see him smile or converse with anyone about anything other than the task at hand. He may have been shy, but I didn't think so at the time. I would say he was a very cool character.

Charlie Rich, on the other hand, was as laid back as it was possible to be and he was very friendly to everyone. He was a good pianist and sat at the piano as if it was an armchair. His delivery was typical of the southern country speech. His songs were all about the girls who got away and his voice was like treacle, dark and smooth. His face always seemed to be smiling and he projected the personality of a man who had seen it all and was quite content with his existence.

There was something really endearing about the musicians from Nashville. They projected a warmth that was not always felt in other parts of America. They all seemed laid back, as if they took the whole of existence in their stride. Perhaps it manifests itself in the slow way they talk. Whatever it was, it was charming, and Charlie had a great deal of it to give to everyone. He spoke to the audience in between songs and they loved him. Their enthusiastic applause said it all, for it was a memorable evening.

There were many wonderful singers, and songs, that were dedicated to religious worship. In 1975 I worked with a group from Switzerland, under the umbrella of Gospel Films Incorporated. They were young and vibrant, and the enthusiasm they displayed when recording their music was a joy to behold. Their professionalism was a surprise for me because I hadn't expected the group to be so good, and their technical know-how about microphone technique was equal to the best professionals I knew. They were exceedingly positive about everything they expressed.

Whenever I thought about church music I imagined a typical local group of amateurs; the sort of situation you might find in your town or village, involving singers who would never aspire to the professional level of session musicians. However, my preconceived ideas were proved completely wrong and to my surprise they were first-class performers. They had their own rhythm section and two male and two female singers, and any of them could have worked in a professional capacity had they wanted that kind of life. They approached their songs with tremendous ardour, which would have been a lesson for many young hopefuls waiting to be discovered.

We spent a day together, and during the recordings we conversed frequently about all sorts of subjects, including our beliefs and desires, and their intelligence and common sense shone through every topic. I envied them their faith, for it was obviously a great strength for them to be able to identify with others who believed in the things they thought were important. They knew how to listen and weren't just waiting to get their point of view across irrespective of what had been said before, as was the case with so many conversationalists. They seemed so certain about their direction and purpose in life for people so young, and I felt a tremendous respect for them.

On another occasion, in 1977, I worked with an American group from Baton Rouge, in Louisiana. The company was called the Record Company of the South and their label was Pyramid Records. It reminded me of my time in Nashville.

Like all southerners, they were very laid back, but their dedication was no less than the Swiss group. They, too, were young, and they sang about the love they had for Jesus, just as a secular song told about the love we had for our partner. If the lyrics had not been religious I think that their songs could easily have been in the top ten of the record charts.

The ladies sang ballads that referred to love, and sometimes it was difficult not to think of the lyrics as belonging to the secular world, but the difference was that all the feeling and intensity was directed towards Christ. The men, too, showed the same enthusiasm when delivering a lyric. Their relationship to one another was a giving one, and they supported each other without there being a feeling of hierarchy. I couldn't get over the fact that the melodies were so beautiful and the structure of the songs was so well constructed. I shouldn't have been surprised because people generally learn music at a very early age, and it was probable that their dedication to their religion came when they were already quite proficient in their craft.

They were very open and welcoming to everyone they spoke to and it seemed that, like the Swiss, they felt very secure in their beliefs. I questioned both groups from a secular perspective and they didn't mind in the least. Their beliefs seemed to deny any need to rationalise the founding tenets of Christianity. Obviously, our beliefs are more important to us than any facts might illuminate, and perhaps we need the spiritual aspect of life to make any sense out of existence. The important thing was that both these groups were completely at peace with themselves, and how many of us can truly say that?

Gordon Giltrap was more than a client; he became a soulmate. We have been friends for more than 30 years, but it seems like only yesterday that we first met. Our initial encounter was in 1971, when I was asked to contribute to his Testament of Time album. Gordon was writing songs at that time and I had no idea what a tremendous guitar player he was. He told me about his early days when he played in Les Cousin's club in London's Soho. He had associated with such well-known artists as John Martyn, Bert Jansch, John Renbourn and Al Stewart, and he was always ready to learn from the playing of his contemporaries. Getting to know him as an open, flowing person, I could see that it was inevitable that he would become a great talent.

Gordon made many references to the Bible in his songs. He was very conscious of religion at that time, and probably nothing has changed, but we never discussed the subject. Songs about Christ's betrayal by Judas, his crucifixion and his resurrection were central to much of Gordon's lyric writing. He was open about his youth and posed many philosophical questions. Some of his themes had a medieval flavour about them, and it seemed as if he was on some kind of quest. He was searching for answers, in the same way that the Knights of the Round Table went out to find the Holy Grail. There was a great deal of sadness in his lyrics, and some time later I assumed that he had found some of the answers to his questions because he stopped writing words and became an instrumentalist.

Gordon was able to develop a style that merged early folk roots with the medieval and classical elements of music. He assimilated these genres and made them his own. The amazing thing was that he was successful in creating a distinct style that was totally unique. I had heard many strange attempts to marry classical styles with popular styles and had always been disappointed. I believed that the problem lay in the training that was on offer in these two distinctly different worlds. Formally trained musicians could play any music that was placed before them, but the feel of jazz syncopation (playing slightly behind the pulse) was not a natural habit. Popular music training in jazz, dance bands and rock allowed a greater degree of elasticity. It was Mozart that said, "True music is between the notes." Formally trained musicians played with an exactitude that didn't quite 'swing' and in both styles the aim was different.

A good example of this is found in Leonard Bernstein's West Side Story. Bernstein, a formally trained musician, knew that he wasn't familiar with popular styles of writing and engaged popular music arrangers to create the sound of much of the orchestral landscape. Bernstein wrote the songs, but the presentation, the arrangements, were created by others. The works that I have heard by 'classical' composers who have entered into the realms of jazz have been pathetic. When they were played by symphony orchestras the 'swing' element was absent. I also felt that formally trained singers should stay in their own area of expertise, for their efforts in performing popular songs were generally diabolical.

I thought that Gordon's instrumental work was a tremendous step forward in his career. He began to develop his playing in a way that encompassed many styles, and after many years his playing became quite unique and could be recognised by all who heard it. In 1976 he created an album called Visionary, which was based on a work by William Blake. The eighteenth-century poet was one of my favourites and I knew that it would be an interesting project. Gordon sent me a tape of the concept and asked me if I would help by orchestrating the work. I was very impressed by the tape, but to my everlasting regret I declined Gordon's offer. It would have meant spending a great deal of time on the project and I was very busy writing my own work at the time. Gordon understood my reason for not being available and it didn't interfere with our relationship.

I was asked again in 1998 to help Gordon with an album for K-Tel Records. He wanted me to produce and arrange his latest efforts, which I thought were absolutely superb. The album was to be called Troubadour and I made sure that I didn't decline the offer this time. It was like a 'déjà vu' for me. Gordon had performed in the stage musical Heathcliff in 1995, and Cliff Richard, who was the star of the show, was kind enough to offer his services to Gordon at any time in the future. So when he was asked to help he spent many hours in the studio singing backing harmonies on a song from the show.

I was surprised how tall Cliff was, as I'm six feet one but I had to look up into his face whenever I was conversing with him. I noticed that his hair was black, with not a grey hair to be seen, which also surprised me because he must have been close to 60 years of age. It must have been the result of good living, or a hair spray, I suppose. He was quite distant in his social behaviour, but he was always obliging in respect to the work that we were doing. I wasn't certain what to call him because he had been knighted, and so I asked him how he would like to be addressed. He said, "You can call me Cliff, or you can call me Sir, but don't call me Mister." He was very serious when he replied, and I thought that it was a strange thing to say. I made sure that I didn't call him anything during the recording because I had already made one mistake that morning. I had tried to be polite and engage in some small talk, and had said, "I believe you are interested in golf." Everyone, except him, gave a small titter in response to my remark. "No," he barked, "it's tennis that I'm fond of." Thank heaven that there was only one fool in the studio.

Cliff was in the studio for almost two hours and he only took a small break. He was courteous and showed a great interest in the project. He was quick to react to suggestions made by me, and it was obvious that a man with so many years' experience knew exactly how to get the best out of his performance. Cliff sang different melodic lines many times to create a wall of sound that was more like a choir than an individual voice. He had come to the studio with another man and when the session was over he thanked us for our hospitality and departed like a wisp of smoke.

The album was recorded at Snakeranch Studios in Lots Road, London. Jack Rothstein led a fantastic string orchestra that was comprised of only nine players, but their sound was wonderful. Unfortunately Jack died unexpectedly, and the musical world lost a shining star of incredible influence. He was a gentle, softly spoken man, with tremendous sensitivity and a wry sense of humour. I thought that he was the most accomplished musician that I had ever met and he was well respected by other orchestral players. He was always my first choice as orchestral leader, and he not only played 'classical' works but was also a great exponent of middle European gipsy music. On occasion he would honour us with a few tunes played in the gipsy style, and when he finished his performance he would laugh furiously and his eyes would gleam. He is sorely missed.

The Troubadour project was particularly interesting for me because Gordon had completed all his guitar recordings at home. The tapes that he brought to the studio were the finished product as far as the guitar was concerned. This meant that the orchestra had to be very flexible in order to match the varying speeds of Gordon's performance. The musicians enjoyed this kind of task because it gave an extra dimension to the challenge. I had worked with them for 30 years and their generosity was shown in the fact that if they were asked to do something that was beyond their commitment they would always agree to the request. I don't think that K-Tel knew what to do with the album, as they hadn't had anything similar to Gordon's disc before. They sold the product mainly through television advertising, which was limited as it was an expensive undertaking and probably the company didn't think that an instrumental disc would appeal to the masses. As a result it only sold a few thousand copies. All worthwhile art has a minority audience. The majority of the population enjoys light entertainment, and perhaps that's how it should be.

* * *

Having no luck training his pet, a dog owner asked an evangelist to help him get his hound sorted out. A week later the evangelist returned the dog and demonstrated his success. He threw a stick and ordered the dog to retrieve it by shouting, "Fetch!" The dog returned with the stick and, on the command "Drop", placed it at his feet. Next the evangelist said, "Roll over," which the dog immediately did. Excited, the owner told the dog, "Heel." The animal placed his paw on him and said solemnly, "May this sickness leave you within 24 hours."

CHAPTER 21

Working in the medium of television advertising was more like being in a Walt Disney world than anything experienced in real life. A dear friend, Kate Hawthorne, had an agency called Mothers and Masters. She introduced me to that world and I'm not sure that I've recovered yet. I've never seen such indecision, or large amounts of money spent on trivia. The agencies that wrote the scripts and had the films made will never go to heaven. The whole truth got lost among a myriad of ideas and what we were left with was pure fantasy.

Whenever I went to a supermarket and bought a packet of something, such as soap powder or cereal, and found an enormous box that was only half full, my blood curdled. I knew that the consumer was the one who always paid, but the fact that we allowed such profits to be made has always astounded me. I'm old enough to remember when packets were full, long before the fantasy began.

During a period of three years Kate introduced me to several clients. They obviously wanted to sell their product to as many people as possible, and the modern way to do that was through television. Before television, the media used were billboards and newspapers, but it was soon recognised that it was possible to reach millions of people at once through television. Some corporations spent millions of pounds on advertising to sell their products, yet there were people telling us that television didn't influence people at all. I never thought that the business fraternities were stupid. Lever Brothers did an experiment and stopped advertising one of their products for three months. The sales figures showed that the product sold less than was usual. After advertising the product again the sales increased to their normal level. Yet people still said that television didn't influence us.

My work involved creating music for visual images already filmed. The format was 13, 28, 43 and 58 seconds of sound because two seconds were needed for technical reasons. The clients were British Airways, McDonald's, Ladbrokes, Kellogg's, Braun, Sun Alliance, Sunsilk, Ladybird clothes, Barkers, Colman's Mustard and Nescafé. It was certain that the really large corporations that sold a great deal of product knew that the power of suggestion needed to be continuous in order not to be forgotten.

The people I met in their various offices seemed to belong to a club. They all wore expensive designer clothes; they all spoke advertising jargon that I didn't understand; and they all agreed with other colleagues' suggestions without a moment's thought. You may think I'm being rather hard on them, but for what they were earning I would have thought a little more individual creativity would be expected. Remember, I'm only speaking of the offices I entered.

One of my friends who lived in south-east London, near Blackheath, was in advertising. He invited me to his home one Saturday evening, and told me that it was his turn to give a party. When I arrived there were already six couples in the living room dancing to popular music with the lights turned low. As the evening progressed I noticed the couples constantly changing partners and yet they seemed to be acting in an amorous fashion with whomever they had paired up with. The host took me into the kitchen, where we began to talk about a project he had in mind. Then out of the blue he told me that the get-together was a wife-swapping party and all the guests lived on his estate. He explained that everyone would eventually pair off and go to the home of the male partner. At first I thought he was joking, but I soon realised that he was deadly serious. The evening event even included his wife.

He seemed proud of the fact that he was in the forefront of the wife-swapping craze. He said that each week a party was held at a different couple's house and the same thing happened. The only rule was that you couldn't take the same person home on consecutive weeks; in fact there was a six-week rota. I couldn't believe my ears. I always thought that that sort of thing only happened in swinging inner cities, but I soon found out that the suburbs and rural areas were just as adventurous. Life was certainly a learning curve.

Kate got me a job with the Japanese branch of one of the biggest agencies in the world, J. Walter Thompson. The product was Nescafé, and a gentleman and his wife arrived from Tokyo with a suitcase full of money. I met them in their London hotel and the representative told me that this was an important assignment and whatever I needed would be forthcoming. His words were music to my ears, for it wasn't often that such a remark was made.

He wanted a large orchestra, and the music was to be written for all the possible time structures - 15, 30, 45 and 60 seconds - for pictures in spring, summer, autumn and winter. I was delighted because it meant 16 different versions, and the time to complete the project was generous because he and his wife wanted to see as much of Europe as possible. He was adamant that I should not rush things because they wanted to take a photographic history of their time in Europe. When the work was completed he paid everyone in cash, told us how happy he was, and took the first available flight back to Tokyo.

It may have been a great desire to want to be involved with and be part of a group, but it was certainly true that too many cooks spoilt the broth. I recall an instance of disappointment when working with Roger Chapman. His manager, Tony Gurvish, asked me to produce a single, using a catchy Rolling Stones song, which was used in an advertising commercial. In his office he told me that I needn't do a great deal as far as input was concerned because the band knew what they wanted to do. He assured me that the band always worked out their arrangements before entering the studio. I agreed, and three days later I went into the studio to meet the boys. We greeted each other and everything seemed fine.

When we began rehearsals I waited to see what they had in mind, and after a while Roger seemed to get upset because I didn't contribute to the rehearsal. He said, "You're the producer, so why don't you start producing?" I didn't tell him about my meeting with the manager and began helping with the various possibilities that would make the recording an attractive product. The point I'm making is that the band were as cold as ice because I didn't tell them about the manager's suggestions, and the manager's information was quite wrong.

The advertising world reminded me of a meeting with Christopher Gunning, who wrote music for the detective television series Poirot. He had great success with the advert for Asti Spumante sparkling wine. The advert was a worldwide success and brought him a great deal of money. I was living in a village in Gloucestershire at the time, and he had bought a house that was situated next to my local pub in a nearby village. When Kate Hawthorne spent a weekend at my cottage she suggested that we go and visit him, since he lived so near and we did the same kind of work. On arriving at the pub Kate invited Chris and his wife to join us. I believe she was an astute businesswoman, for she owned the publishing copyright to Chris's work.

I had not prepared myself for meeting such an obnoxious couple. On complimenting him on the success of the advert he sneered and shouted, "Christ," implying that it was the least of his accomplishments and that my judgement was trite. He obviously missed the point. I was referring to the financial success, which, by the way, allowed them to live in the house next to my local alehouse. I could deal with anything but rudeness, and without another word I made it obvious that I was in the wrong company. When Kate and I left the pub I glanced at Chris's house and almost had a heart attack. On the wall, next to the front door, he had erected a blue plaque that read, "Christopher Gunning lived here". I couldn't believe my eyes. Mozart yes, Beethoven yes, Einstein yes, but CG was too much to bear. It was amazing what the ego would allow some people to do, but in the end we had to live with ourselves, and that could be a heaven or a hell. Needless to say I never, thankfully, met them again.

Always remember that the media, the magazines, the television and the newspapers were creating information, whether it was true or not, for that was their job - to fill their pages with information. The more sensational the information, the more information they sold, and the more money they made. It was one of our failings that we were addicted to gossip, which among other things could be tragic or sexual. Any kind of privacy that belonged to someone else sparked great interest in us, as if we needed to fill ourselves with that information because we were curious or our own lives seemed empty. It appeared that positive situations were less interesting for the majority of the population than negative ones.

The nature of television in general had changed over the years. On the one hand technology had broadened its scope, and colour had made a great difference to perception and enjoyment. On the other hand it was also true that the rising cost of productions had a drastic influence on what was on offer. I thought that the influence of television had taken its toll, and had, perhaps, changed the level of expectation of a great number of people.

Many years ago, a friend of mine worked for London Weekend and he told me that the 'game show', another American import, would be introduced as much as possible. Having worked on the wonderful drama, An Englishman Abroad, which took weeks to make and had a large cast and film crew, he made the comparison between the interactive game show and intelligent drama. For many years the BBC Theatre in Shepherds Bush had been used for programmes that needed audience participation. Such a place could be used all day, he said, and three game shows could be filmed there for relatively little cost. The same audience could remain, with no cost to the BBC, and once the set was built only the presenter would be given a fee. Later, many programmes were given to private companies to produce, so that less responsibility became the norm. Once again the bottom line reared its ugly head.

The advent of independent television, and sponsorship, changed the very nature of what was on offer on the BBC channels. The arrival of the newspaper magnate Murdoch and the development of digital Sky satellite television gave rise not only to a sports channel, which was wonderful for the fans, but also to the various film channels. I was a film buff myself, but the amount of violence and overt sex, which was seen in a great deal of contemporary film-making, certainly had a profound influence on British culture, and probably Continental culture too.

I was always amazed at the way censorship was so stringent about sex in the early days, and yet allowed violence to rampage on the screen with little concern about its effect on the young, or the not so young. If people weren't influenced by what they watched on television, how did we account for our present gun culture and gangs of young children carrying knives, not to mention the incessant advertising campaigns? Even cartoons were exercises in violence under the guise of comedy. If you think I'm being prudish, pick up some of the popular newspapers and see to what degree sex and violence are being displayed today, and then go to a library and look at some typical newspapers of 50 years ago.

Young hopefuls who wished to enter the industry should have taken as much advice from seasoned entertainers as possible. There certainly were sharks in the deep water. I remember working with Ralph McTell. He was a lovely person, but his brother was his manager, and managers were a unique species. I was producing one of Ralph's songs for a singles release on the Warner label, and his friend was playing the string bass. I got the feeling that they were old friends and had played together for years. I had agreed with the manager to accept a 2% royalty, which was normal practice, when the disc was released.

Having finished the recording, I received a phone call from the manager a week or so later asking me to share half my royalty payment with the bass player. I explained to him that, as nothing was mentioned about this before we had begun working on the project, I thought it was dishonourable of him to ask this of me. He then proceeded to tell me how mean I was to take this stance and promptly put the phone down. To my knowledge the recording was never released, and this was not an isolated case. The ocean of the music industry was full of predators, and the bigger they were the more subtle were their devouring ways of manifesting their power. I was very lucky in my career to avoid their clutches most of the time. On odd occasions relationships got tricky and verbal misunderstandings happened, but these were soon rectified by my ability to keep calm. Young hopefuls beware.

It was not always easy to judge the wishes of others correctly, and the following is a good example of this. I was working in a studio with Greg Lake, of Emerson, Lake and

Palmer, and we didn't finish until the early hours of the morning. He gave me a ride home in his chauffeur-driven limousine and as we got to the Earl's Court Road, which was full of Victorian mansions, he said that he had just bought a house close by. The area was one of the busiest and noisiest in London. I told him that he could have bought a mansion with a hundred acres in the country for the same money. "Don't tell me about the country," he said. "I was born and brought up in a country village and know all about country living." I immediately saw what he meant. He was referring to the lack of amenities and privacy in rural areas. We often seemed to think the grass was greener somewhere else.

Quite often the backing singers had more talent than the artists. Many of them made discs and had contracts from the large recording companies, but they seldom achieved long-term success. Bridget St John was signed to Chrysalis Music Ltd, and Madeline Bell, another talented performer, never seemed to have the same luck as many household names. Perhaps they didn't have the right connections, or maybe their material was at fault, or it was just a simple case of being in the wrong place at the wrong time. The only thing I knew for certain was that without memorable song material the yellow brick road was a hard path to follow.

Hazel Dean (Decca), Half Brother (Hansa) and Catherine Howe (RCA) all bit the dust because success never came their way. I was particularly impressed with Catherine. I produced an album for her called Harry, and the single of that name got a great deal of radio play, but alas she got lost in the crowd. She was a lovely, vulnerable lady, and years later someone told me that they'd seen her driving a bus. It was much easier for singer-songwriters to be successful in the seventies because many companies were run by people who knew something about music, or at least liked it. As time went on, the business was gradually taken over by lawyers and accountants, and the bottom line was the only important issue. There was no time for nurturing potential winners.

I suppose I was lucky not to know what the future had in store for me. I sometimes reflected on the story of The Picture of Dorian Gray, written by Oscar Wilde. It was based on the universal legend of someone who sold their soul to the devil to attain what they desired most in the world. In Gray's case it was eternal youth. Even the thought was frightening. Imagine everyone you loved growing old and dying while you remained the same as when you made the pact. We had to be very careful about what we wished for because life had a strange way of surprising us, and it wasn't always in a positive way.

Most of the folk/rock singer-songwriters of the sixties and seventies earned a living playing in the folk club circuit. Britain and Europe had hundreds of small venues where folk enthusiasts could go to enjoy an evening of fine music for very little cost. The Troubadour, near Earls Court, was such a place. Many famous people began their careers in these clubs, and I saw Bob Dylan and Paul Simon play in the above-mentioned club some 40 years ago. These venues were small and intimate, rather like the musical salons of centuries ago.

Mike Silver, a talented singer-songwriter, and I made an album for Elton John's label, Rocket Records. Unfortunately, it never saw the light of day. Mike told me recently that he went to Island Records and was offered a deal. Soon after, Rocket offered him more money and he accepted Elton's offer. It was obvious that both companies liked the songs on the demo tape and the performance that Mike gave. However, when the album was finished Elton said that he didn't like the songs, which meant that he didn't like the album. Consequently it didn't get any promotion and it drowned amongst hundreds of other discs that got made that year.

The tragedy was that if Mike had taken Island's offer he would have received better treatment. Chris Blackwell, Island's owner, really looked after his artists. He nurtured them and gave them tremendous exposure until they became well known. It is said that money isn't everything, and in Mike's case never was a truer word spoken. Undaunted, Mike has made many discs at his own expense, and in the 30 years that I've known him he has delighted everyone who has heard him play. It was the old story of time and place, and the little bit of luck we all needed to be given the opportunity to display our talents to a wider public.

Mike suffered from periods of depression, but he was basically an optimistic, jolly person. His disappointments were caused by just missing the boat of commercial success, and I thought that anyone in the same circumstances would have felt occasionally low. For me, he did for music what Lowry did for painting. His songs were about ordinary people and ordinary events, but he could craft a song that would make you cry. That was a gift. He had acute perception when it came to observations of everyday life, and this was the mark of a great storyteller. I don't know why Elton changed his mind - perhaps there was a hint of jealousy involved - but whatever the reason, it was certain that Mike's life would have been different had he not done so.

Many really talented people had bad luck with regard to their careers. Paul Millns was another example of missed opportunity in the industry. He was a pianist with a voice like rich chocolate, dark and sharp. He sounded like a deep Joe Cocker at times, yet on other occasions his voice was as smooth as silk, which reminded me of Nina Simone. His manager was Tony Hall, who occasionally was the master of ceremonies at Ronnie Scott's London jazz club. Paul, like Mike, was a true observer of the human condition. He was too good to be a 'pop' artist, for his songs had great depth and weren't good for dancing, but listening to his music would have brought its own reward.

His house was full of music, as he had two daughters who were musical. He was a great performer and when I saw him at the Troubadour the atmosphere was electric. He, too, toured the clubs and made his own discs, but a major record company would have given him much more exposure. His song, 'When Love Comes Calling', brought a lump to my throat and a tear to my eye, yet nobody would give him a deal that would allow him to write without touring. When I saw what was being performed on television by punk groups, The Spice Girls and various boy bands, who were manufactured groups with very little talent, I then realised that 'mass media' had arrived, for what they looked like was more important than musical ability.

I knew we didn't always get what we deserved, whether it was good or bad, and perhaps that was the tragedy in life.

Some writers had the gift to express a universal truth with a simple melody that could be remembered easily. By this I mean the ability to say something in such a way that it touched the essence of everyone's being. Both Mike and Paul had that gift, and had there been luckier circumstances they would both be household names today. I still listen to Mike's Troubadour album, as I do Paul's first three albums, and I'm certain that if the public were to hear them today the guys would be commercially successful.

Artists had different ways of creating their song material. Some would write a complete tune that they were satisfied with, such as 'The Long and Winding Road' by Paul McCartney. Others would complete a poem (for that's what words are without the musical element), an example being Leonard Cohen's 'Suzanne'. The latter method was probably more common. If we saw telling stories as the primary object, the words would be the most natural starting point. In the wider field of 'serious' music, operas, masses and literary poems were all set to words that already existed. Some would create a phrase of music to a phrase of words, and some would do the opposite, like growing twins. I knew writers, however, such as Nick Drake, who would always consider the melody, and a melodic idea, as their primary concern. Many roads lead to the same place and, whatever the processes involved on the journey, the only important thing was the end result.

Like all of us, the degree to which artists protected their work during the recording process depended on their security or insecurity. Some of the artists were overprotective, which manifested itself in a lack of trust towards their studio colleagues. Others were more inviting when it came to the quest for fresh ideas. The more open and relaxed the artists were, the greater was the respect they showed their colleagues, manifested in a higher degree of mutual collaboration. There were times when some artists would leave the studio for days and let the staff carry on doing whatever was required. Others would be looking over the shoulders of everyone, afraid of leaving any task to the staff in case of human error. Because many studio technicians, producers and arrangers were freelance participants in the recording process, they had the wonderful choice of being able to walk away from difficult clients, or continue to serve the artists they liked and with whom they were socially compatible. Luckily, the ones they couldn't tolerate were rare, and the long periods of time spent achieving their goals were very enjoyable.

Some artists only asked me to work with them once, and others I knew and helped for years. I enjoyed doing an arrangement for Kiki Dee, who was on the Rocket Records label. The song was 'Nothing Gonna Stop Us Now', and it was used for the end credits of the film Stir Crazy. Gene Wilder and Richard Pryor were the stars in the film, and the catalyst was Michael Masser. Michael had a finger in many pies. He played me a tape of some work he was doing with Diana Ross, and I envied him his connections. He wrote good songs, and was connected with Columbia Pictures. He lived in a lovely place, high in the hills outside Los Angeles with a view to die for, but I felt that to be near him too long would drive me mad.

Michael seemed to me to be a rather nervous man. I remember he changed his mind a great deal. He loved to work under stress and we had ridiculous deadlines to keep. It got so bad that I had to work all through one night in order to get the arrangement finished in time for the recording session. The Musicians' Union laid down certain rules about payment for night work and I put in an invoice that he didn't expect. I eventually got paid, but Michael and I never saw each other again. Nervous people were not good to work with, for their insecurities could be contagious and a potentially pleasurable experience could turn into a nightmare.

Happier memories came with artists like Roy Harper, Donovan and Clifford T. Ward at the Royal Festival Hall. Dave Clark lived in a penthouse apartment in Curzon Street, just off Park Lane in the centre of London. He wanted me to arrange a new musical that he was putting on at the Dominion Theatre called Time, and he never forgave me for putting my trip to Rome first. I believe that Mike Moran stepped into the breach, and there wasn't a better choice. Dave was very generous and was very protective towards his mother, so I always thought very highly of him.

I had a brief association with Shirley Bassey (United Artists), who nearly had a heart attack because, during the first run-through of an arrangement I did for her, the drums were not being beaten loud enough at a climax in her song. She acted like a neurotic bitch, and I heard that she was often very difficult to work with. She certainly had a bad day when I met her.

I haven't forgotten Tim Hollier, who was mad about a famous racehorse called Mill Reef, a fantastic Derby winner, who lived to a ripe old age in comfort because of the tremendous services he rendered. Tim made an album that was dedicated to the beast and all the material used related to the horse. They are, of course, wonderful creatures, but it was the only time in 35 years that I was involved in revering an animal.

Many unexpected things happened when I worked as a freelance person in the entertainment industry. There were so many different areas involved, and when the telephone rang I had to be prepared for anything to occur. There was also the personality question to be considered. I must admit that the majority of the people in the industry were exactly the same as the majority of the people you see in the street. They were average men and women who happened to have the opportunity to exercise their unique talents. Whether in front of a microphone, or at a desk in an office, they tried to do the best that they could at something they enjoyed.

* * *

The e-mail of the species is more dangerous than the mail.

EPILOGUE

The catalyst for all relationships was, of course, oneself. We only got out of the cupboard of life what we put in it. When I held out my hand to someone they either took it or rejected it. This was true in every communal experience, and in the music industry the direction of one's career depended not only on one's talent, but also on good social skills. There were many hidden agendas, for people carried their own emotional baggage, but generally a relaxed, open disposition worked very well.

There were managers and companies who were nothing less than ruthless when dealing with any matter that concerned their artists, for money was the only motive for their actions. Some were even greedy enough to steal large amounts of money from their artists, in spite of the fact that they already got a significant percentage of their charge's income. There were entrepreneurs who had no intention of paying for the work that people did for them, and yet they slept soundly in their beds. There were artists who were so insecure that they needed sycophants around them, constantly telling them how wonderful they were so that they could get through another day without falling apart. When things didn't go well they poured their venom on their closest associates, who were the crutches for their sick egos.

I read recently in the Musicians' Union magazine that prior to the introduction of CDs an artist received a certain royalty figure while the record company made another. The article stated that during the 1980s and the 1990s record companies grew rich by selling back to the public, in CD form, all the albums they had previously bought on vinyl. The record company profit margin on a CD album more than doubled, whereas the artist's share remained the same. Various clauses in company contracts made them even richer because certain royalties were withheld from television-advertised CDs. For many years the British public had paid between £13 and £16 for CDs that are now selling for less than £7 in supermarkets. Because we knew that the cost of living had continually increased, it became obvious that the greed of the record companies, finally exposed, was unforgivable. They were now in trouble, at last, because the Internet had a profound effect on them. Illegal sites allowed the sharing of music without cost and, since the legal copyright of music was introduced by publishers in the first place, the wheel had turned full circle. The powerful were dying, and those that wished could determine for themselves what music they listened to, at no expense.

But that wasn't the only scenario, for the other side of the coin was quite different. There were performers who gave their expertise without payment because they were such generous spirits. The string orchestra that played on Gordon Giltrap's album were such people. Those who couldn't pass a beggar without dropping some coins in his or her hat were such people. Mike Silver was such a person. Those who laughed all day while working 16 hours in a studio full of recycled air were such people. They were all generous spirits who gave themselves, in a positive way, to any task that was asked of them.

I didn't keep a diary, and there are people I haven't mentioned. Perhaps this is because whatever happened between us wasn't impressive enough for me to remember. When looking through the Milarus Mansion Discography of 2005 I noticed that I had worked with Donovan, Family, Earl Jordan, Duffy Power and a host of different people on compilation albums called Various Artists discs. Keyboard players were numerous, but I would like to name Gordon Beck, Steve Grey and Mike Moran for being outstanding; Barry de Sousa on drums; Paul Keough, Daryl Runswick, Pat Donaldson and Paul Hart who were great guitar players; and Frank Riccotti, Tristram Fry and Chris Karan who were exceptional performers on percussion instruments.

Last but not least, the backing singers were essential for creating colours to a song that would have been less attractive had those colours been missing. Sue and Sunny, who were gracious enough to invite me to their home to meet their mother, Stevie Lange and Kay Garner were all indispensable.

No task was attempted by them without enthusiasm and the desire to please the producer and the artist, for their reputation was as fragile as mine, and the social aspect was always present. An unwilling participant, or a miserable one, would not have lasted very long in the industry because the claustrophobic nature of the studios would have made such relationships intolerable.

A freelance musician's reputation was as important as his or her talent. The gossip grapevine was as accessible then as the Internet is today. Every time a confrontation between an artist, a producer or musicians occurred with a company, everyone in the industry heard about it, for there was nothing as interesting as negative gossip. These occurrences affected livelihoods because companies wanted to take as little risk as possible. They believed that negative relationships created an unacceptable quality of product, and they were probably right. I knew a few people who received very little work because of their involvement in negative incidents, whether they were at fault or not. Andrew Lloyd Webber's employee was a good example of mistreatment, even though he was blameless.

My journey was an interesting and fulfilling experience. A few opportunities arose, which I gladly embraced with both hands, and the course of my life changed dramatically, for my entry into the popular music industry happened by accident and not by design. The book relates a personal view of the popular music industry and is, therefore, subjective. I regard the statements I have made as observations rather than criticisms, and others may disagree with my findings. It has been a journey down memory lane, and I sincerely hope that the reader has found reading the book worth their time. The most important thing that I have learnt from the journey is that none of us knows whom we are going to meet, or what is going to happen to us, tomorrow. I believe that the not knowing is the exciting element in our lives, and I hope that the reader shares the same excitement.

I was speaking to a very old lady about the American Civil War, and at one point she said, "Don't forget that all people are cremated equal."